BONEYARD

VOLUME ONE
RICHARD MOORE

NANTIER · BEALL · MINOUSTCHINE
Publishing inc.
new york

Also by Richard Moore:
Boneyard Vol.2, $9.95
Far West, $13.95
Horny Tails (adults only), $12.95
Other books of interest:
Wake, vols. 1: $9.95, 2: $8.95, 3: $9.95, 4/5: $14.95

P&H: $3 1st item, $1 each addt'l.

BONEYARD
VOLUME TWO
RICHARD MOORE

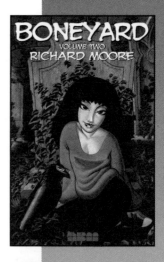

We have over 200 titles,
write for our color catalog:
NBM
555 8th Ave., Suite 1202
New York, NY 10018
www.nbmpublishing.com

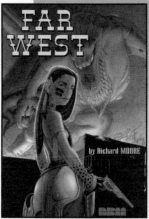

FAR
WEST
by Richard MOORE

WAKE

ISBN 1-56163-316-X

Printed in Hong Kong

5 4 3 2

BONEYARD

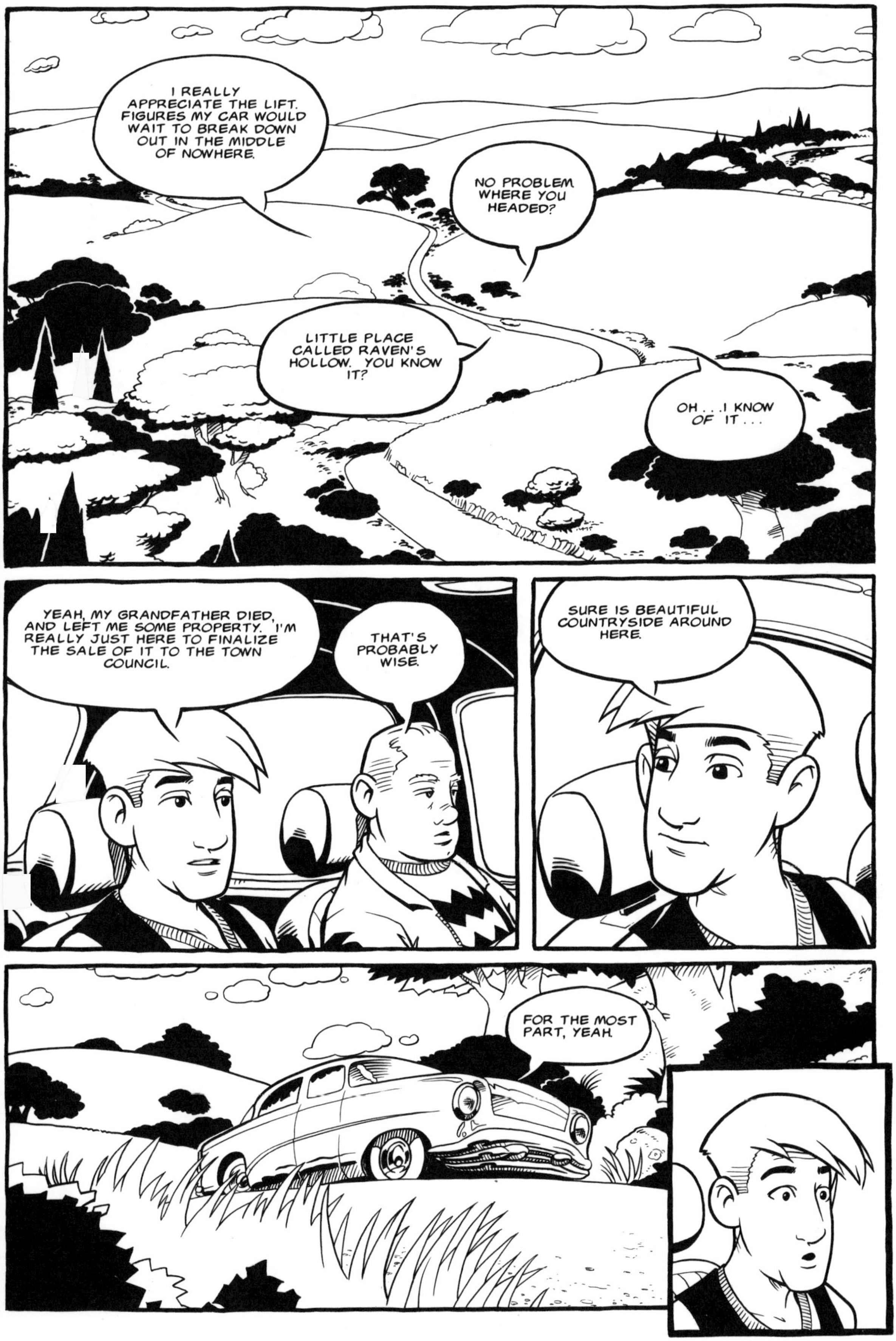
I REALLY APPRECIATE THE LIFT. FIGURES MY CAR WOULD WAIT TO BREAK DOWN OUT IN THE MIDDLE OF NOWHERE.
NO PROBLEM. WHERE YOU HEADED?
LITTLE PLACE CALLED RAVEN'S HOLLOW. YOU KNOW IT?
OH . . . I KNOW OF IT . . .
YEAH, MY GRANDFATHER DIED, AND LEFT ME SOME PROPERTY. I'M REALLY JUST HERE TO FINALIZE THE SALE OF IT TO THE TOWN COUNCIL.
THAT'S PROBABLY WISE.
SURE IS BEAUTIFUL COUNTRYSIDE AROUND HERE.
FOR THE MOST PART, YEAH.

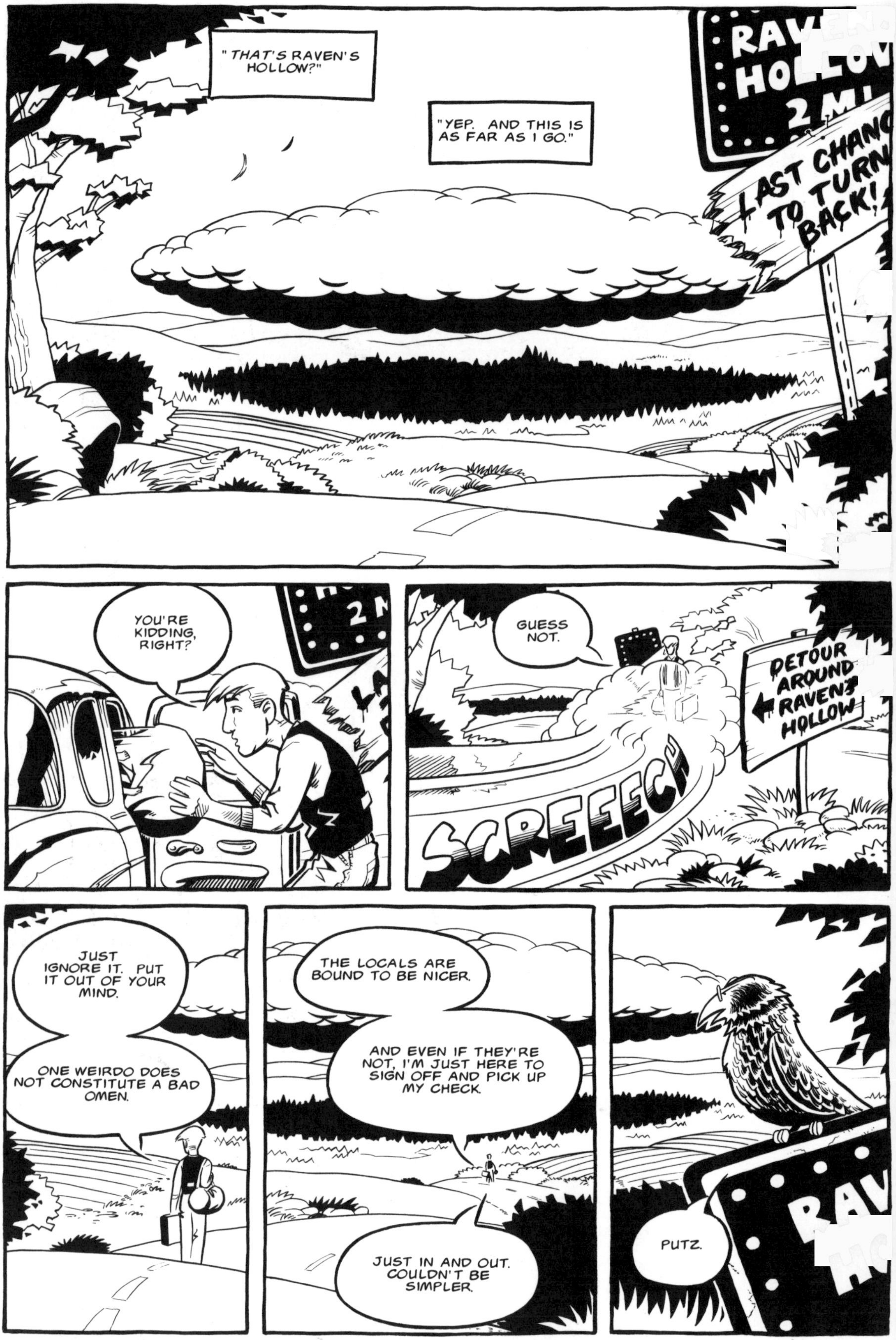
"THAT'S RAVEN'S HOLLOW?"
"YEP. AND THIS IS AS FAR AS I GO."
LAST CHANCE TO TURN BACK!
YOU'RE KIDDING, RIGHT?
GUESS NOT.
DETOUR AROUND RAVEN'S HOLLOW
SCREEECH
JUST IGNORE IT. PUT IT OUT OF YOUR MIND.
ONE WEIRDO DOES NOT CONSTITUTE A BAD OMEN.
THE LOCALS ARE BOUND TO BE NICER.
AND EVEN IF THEY'RE NOT, I'M JUST HERE TO SIGN OFF AND PICK UP MY CHECK.
JUST IN AND OUT. COULDN'T BE SIMPLER.
PUTZ.

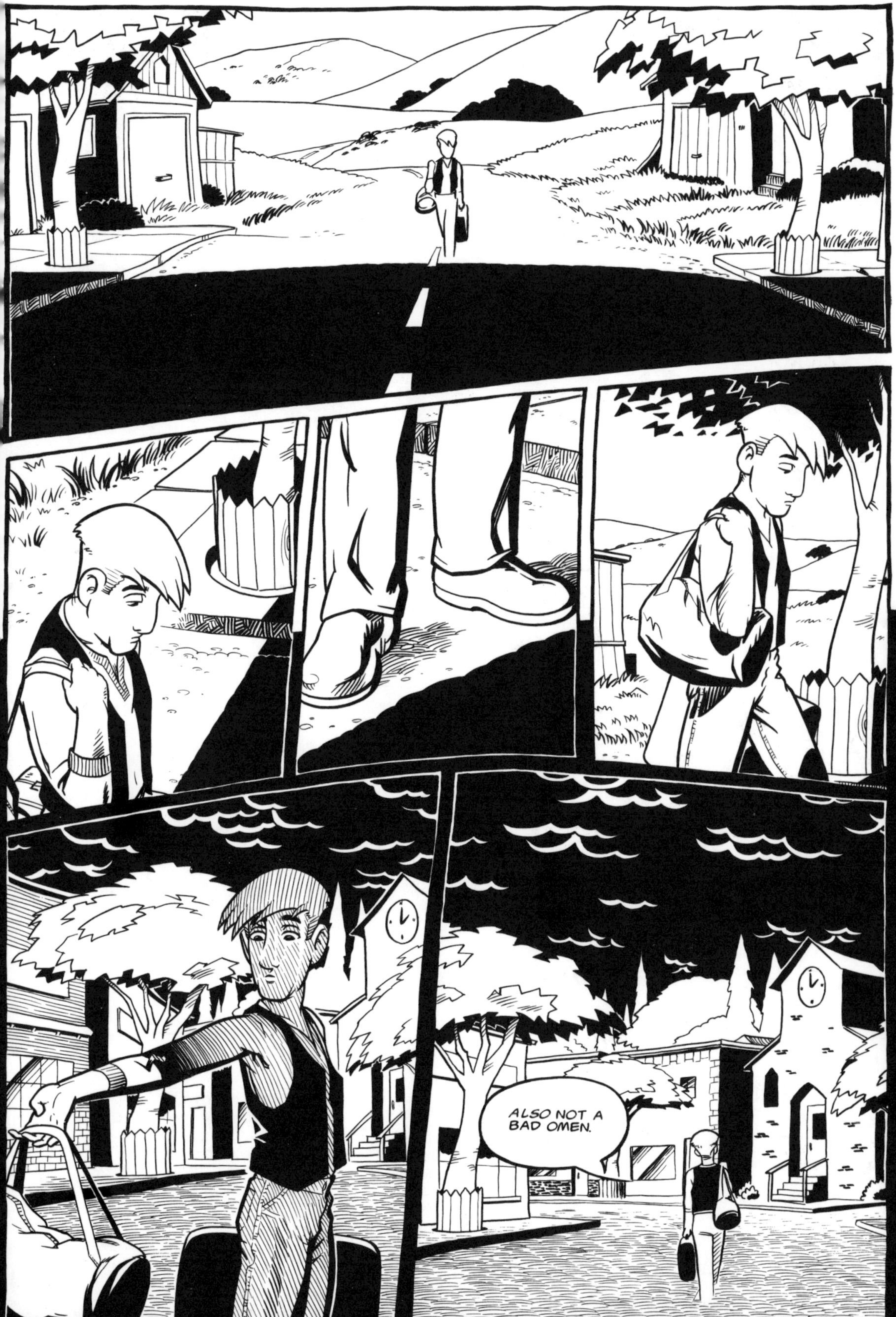
ALSO NOT A BAD OMEN.

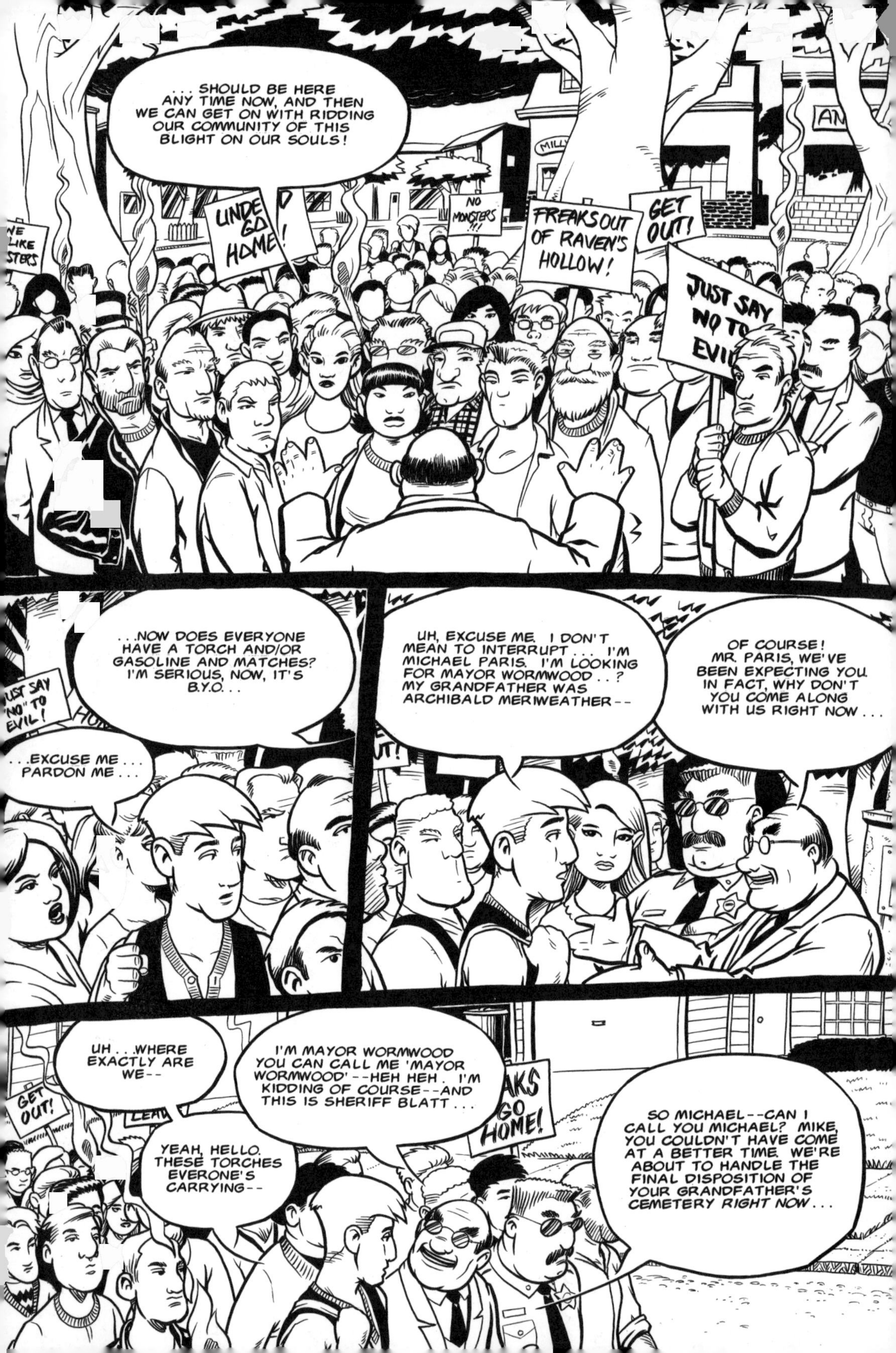

... SHOULD BE HERE ANY TIME NOW, AND THEN WE CAN GET ON WITH RIDDING OUR COMMUNITY OF THIS BLIGHT ON OUR SOULS!
NO MONSTERS ?!!
FREAKS OUT OF RAVEN'S HOLLOW!
GET OUT!
...NOW DOES EVERYONE HAVE A TORCH AND/OR GASOLINE AND MATCHES? I'M SERIOUS, NOW, IT'S B.Y.O...
...EXCUSE ME... PARDON ME...
UH, EXCUSE ME. I DON'T MEAN TO INTERRUPT... I'M MICHAEL PARIS. I'M LOOKING FOR MAYOR WORMWOOD..? MY GRANDFATHER WAS ARCHIBALD MERIWEATHER--
OF COURSE! MR. PARIS, WE'VE BEEN EXPECTING YOU. IN FACT, WHY DON'T YOU COME ALONG WITH US RIGHT NOW...
UH...WHERE EXACTLY ARE WE--
I'M MAYOR WORMWOOD. YOU CAN CALL ME 'MAYOR WORMWOOD'--HEH HEH. I'M KIDDING OF COURSE--AND THIS IS SHERIFF BLATT...
YEAH, HELLO. THESE TORCHES EVERONE'S CARRYING--
GET OUT!
SO MICHAEL--CAN I CALL YOU MICHAEL? MIKE. YOU COULDN'T HAVE COME AT A BETTER TIME. WE'RE ABOUT TO HANDLE THE FINAL DISPOSITION OF YOUR GRANDFATHER'S CEMETERY RIGHT NOW...

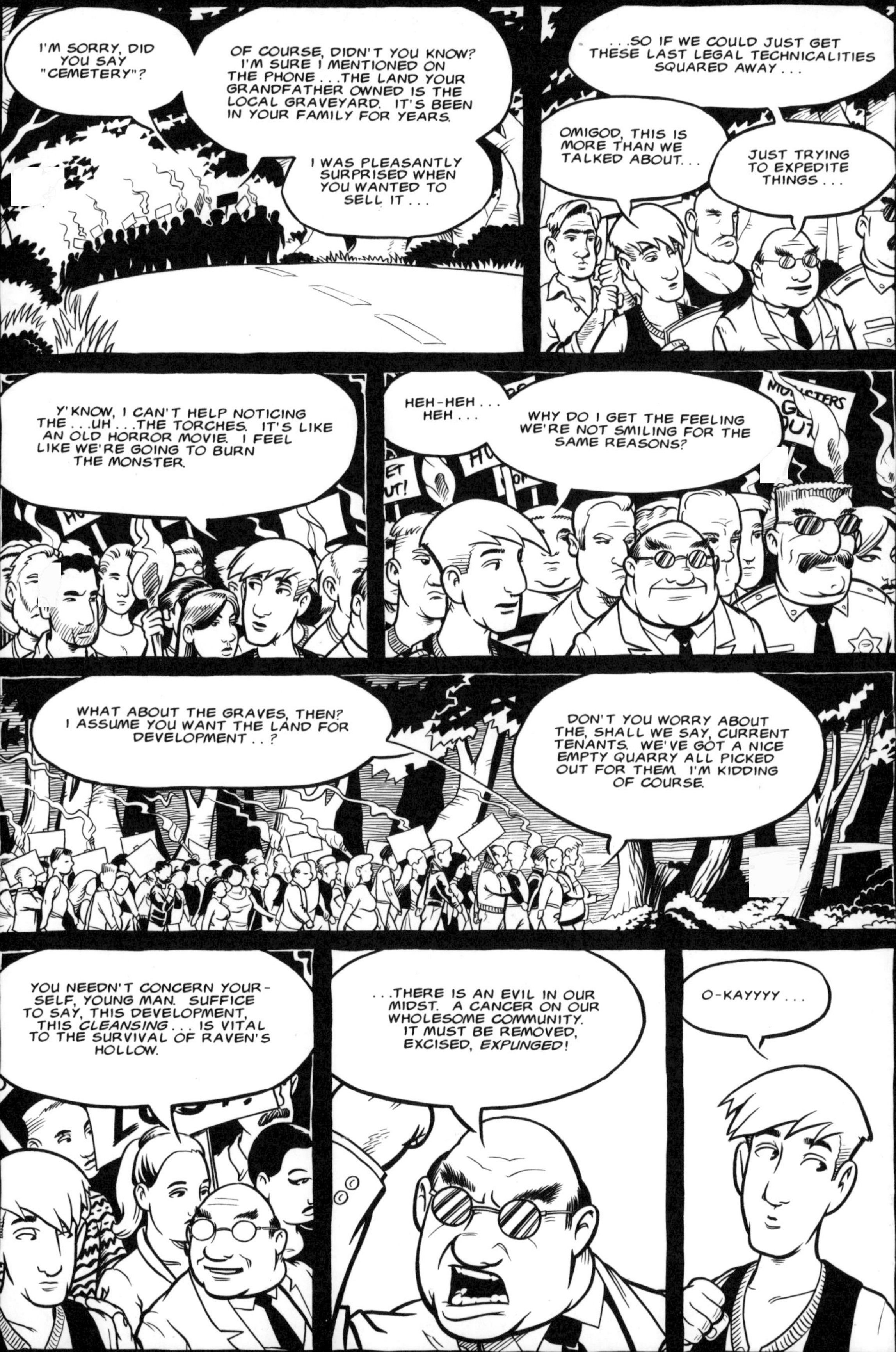
I'M SORRY, DID YOU SAY "CEMETERY"?
OF COURSE, DIDN'T YOU KNOW? I'M SURE I MENTIONED ON THE PHONE . . .THE LAND YOUR GRANDFATHER OWNED IS THE LOCAL GRAVEYARD. IT'S BEEN IN YOUR FAMILY FOR YEARS.
I WAS PLEASANTLY SURPRISED WHEN YOU WANTED TO SELL IT . . .
. . .SO IF WE COULD JUST GET THESE LAST LEGAL TECHNICALITIES SQUARED AWAY . . .
OMIGOD, THIS IS MORE THAN WE TALKED ABOUT. . .
JUST TRYING TO EXPEDITE THINGS . . .
Y'KNOW, I CAN'T HELP NOTICING THE . . .UH . . .THE TORCHES. IT'S LIKE AN OLD HORROR MOVIE. I FEEL LIKE WE'RE GOING TO BURN THE MONSTER.
HEH-HEH . . . HEH . . .
WHY DO I GET THE FEELING WE'RE NOT SMILING FOR THE SAME REASONS?
WHAT ABOUT THE GRAVES, THEN? I ASSUME YOU WANT THE LAND FOR DEVELOPMENT . . ?
DON'T YOU WORRY ABOUT THE, SHALL WE SAY, CURRENT TENANTS. WE'VE GOT A NICE EMPTY QUARRY ALL PICKED OUT FOR THEM. I'M KIDDING OF COURSE.
YOU NEEDN'T CONCERN YOURSELF, YOUNG MAN. SUFFICE TO SAY, THIS DEVELOPMENT, THIS CLEANSING . . . IS VITAL TO THE SURVIVAL OF RAVEN'S HOLLOW.
. . .THERE IS AN EVIL IN OUR MIDST. A CANCER ON OUR WHOLESOME COMMUNITY. IT MUST BE REMOVED, EXCISED, EXPUNGED!
O-KAYYYY . . .

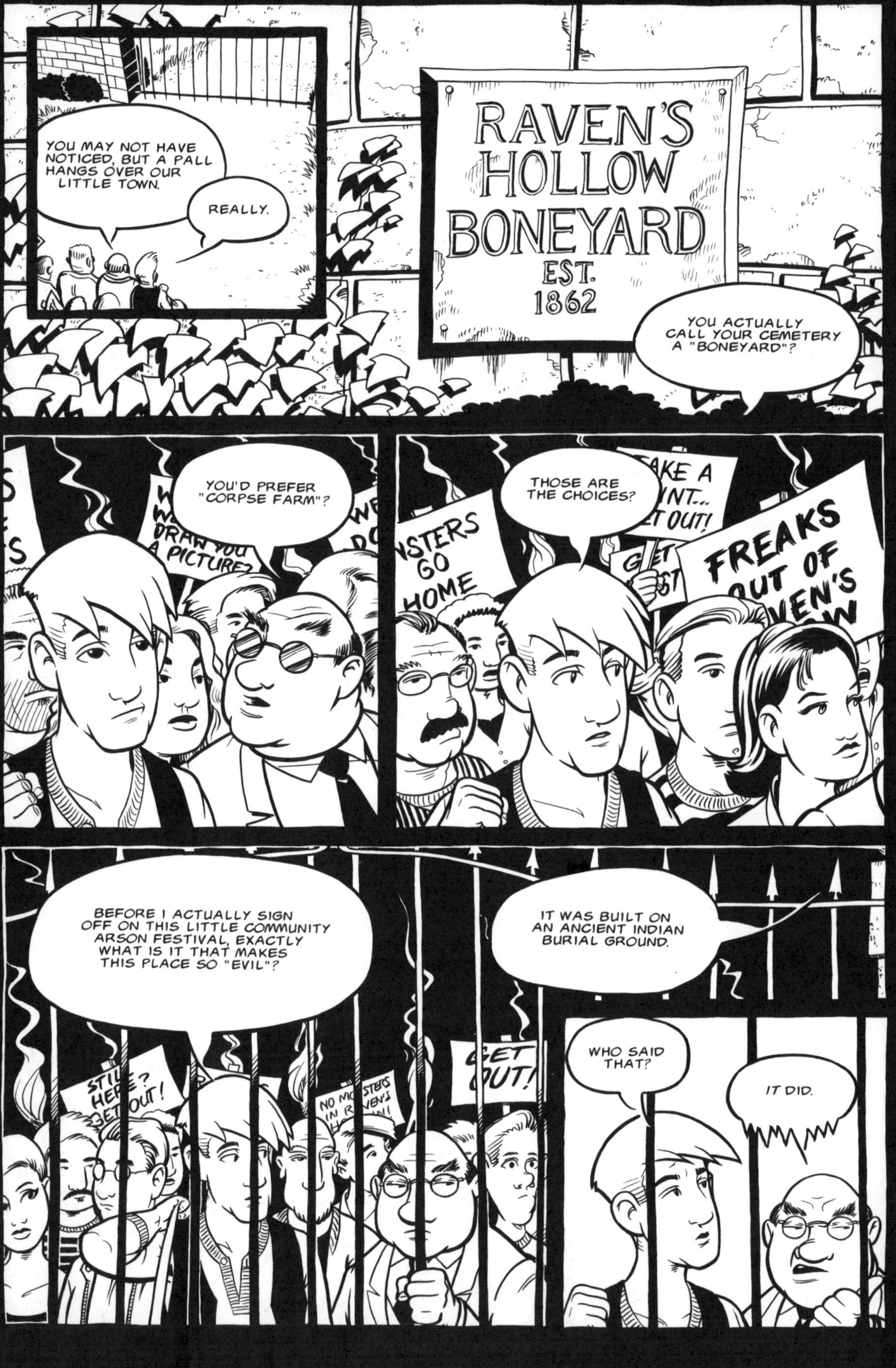

YOU MAY NOT HAVE NOTICED, BUT A PALL HANGS OVER OUR LITTLE TOWN.
REALLY.
RAVEN'S HOLLOW BONEYARD EST. 1862
YOU ACTUALLY CALL YOUR CEMETERY A "BONEYARD"?
YOU'D PREFER "CORPSE FARM"?
THOSE ARE THE CHOICES?
FREAKS
BEFORE I ACTUALLY SIGN OFF ON THIS LITTLE COMMUNITY ARSON FESTIVAL, EXACTLY WHAT IS IT THAT MAKES THIS PLACE SO "EVIL"?
IT WAS BUILT ON AN ANCIENT INDIAN BURIAL GROUND.
GET OUT!
WHO SAID THAT?
IT DID.

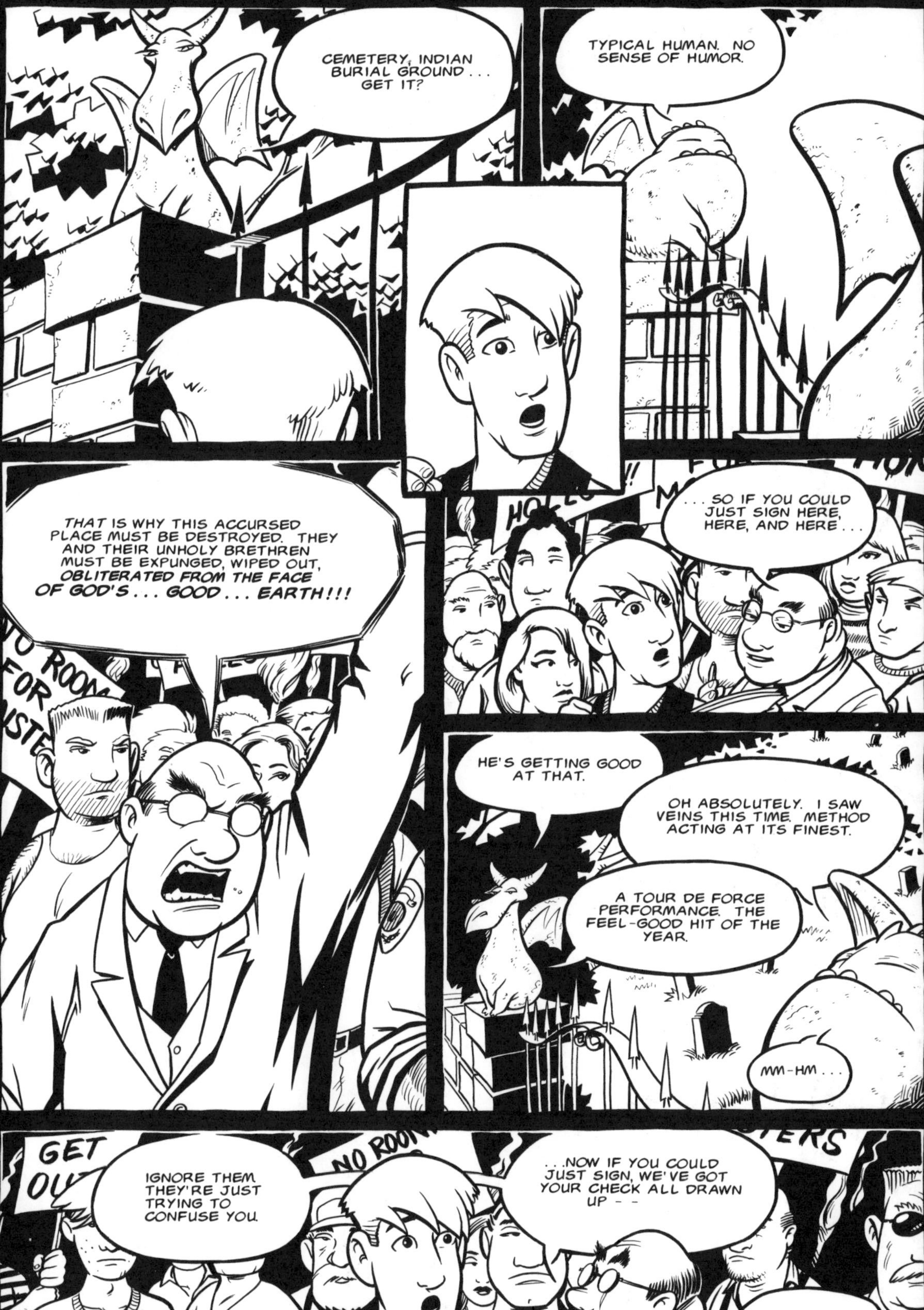
CEMETERY, INDIAN BURIAL GROUND . . . GET IT?
TYPICAL HUMAN. NO SENSE OF HUMOR.
THAT IS WHY THIS ACCURSED PLACE MUST BE DESTROYED. THEY AND THEIR UNHOLY BRETHREN MUST BE EXPUNGED, WIPED OUT, OBLITERATED FROM THE FACE OF GOD'S . . . GOOD . . . EARTH!!!
NO ROOM FOR
. . . SO IF YOU COULD JUST SIGN HERE, HERE, AND HERE . . .
HE'S GETTING GOOD AT THAT.
OH ABSOLUTELY. I SAW VEINS THIS TIME. METHOD ACTING AT ITS FINEST.
A TOUR DE FORCE PERFORMANCE. THE FEEL-GOOD HIT OF THE YEAR.
MM-HM . . .
GET
IGNORE THEM THEY'RE JUST TRYING TO CONFUSE YOU.
. . .NOW IF YOU COULD JUST SIGN, WE'VE GOT YOUR CHECK ALL DRAWN UP - -
I WISH YOU WOULDN'T.

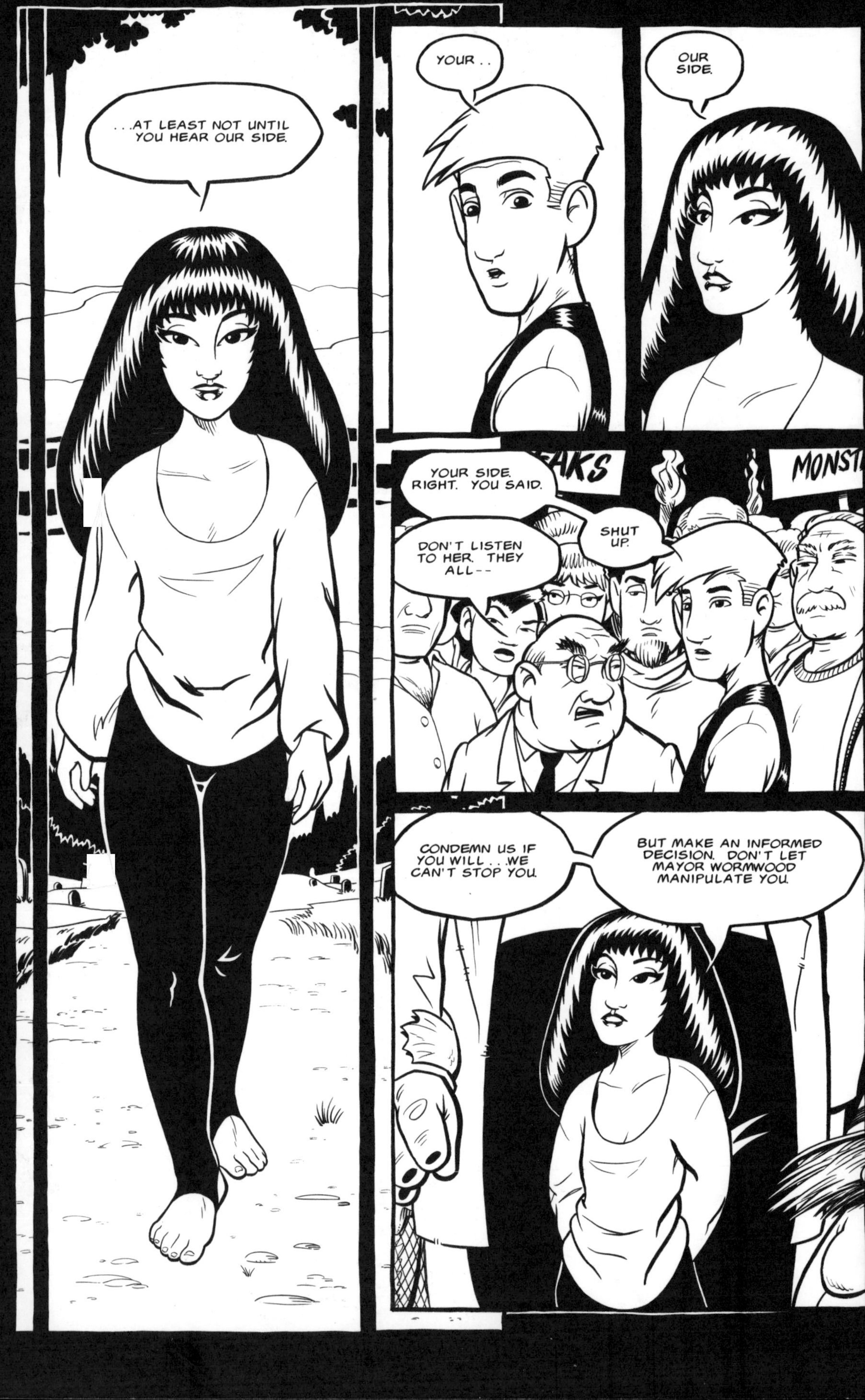
. . .AT LEAST NOT UNTIL YOU HEAR OUR SIDE.
YOUR . .
OUR SIDE.
YOUR SIDE. RIGHT. YOU SAID.
DON'T LISTEN TO HER. THEY ALL--
SHUT UP.
CONDEMN US IF YOU WILL . . WE CAN'T STOP YOU.
BUT MAKE AN INFORMED DECISION. DON'T LET MAYOR WORMWOOD MANIPULATE YOU.

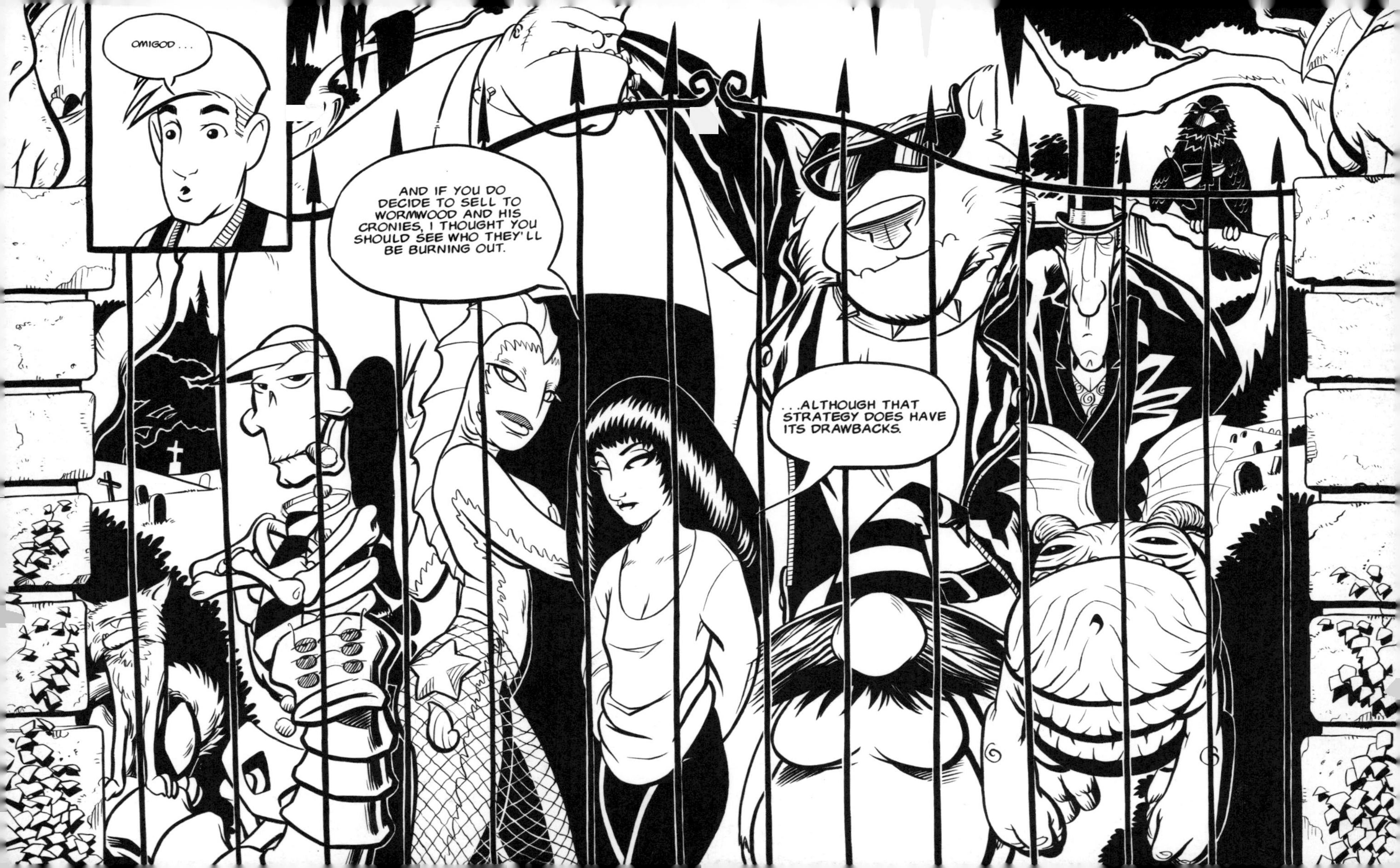
OMIGOD . . .
AND IF YOU DO DECIDE TO SELL TO WORMWOOD AND HIS CRONIES, I THOUGHT YOU SHOULD SEE WHO THEY'LL BE BURNING OUT.
. . .ALTHOUGH THAT STRATEGY DOES HAVE ITS DRAWBACKS.

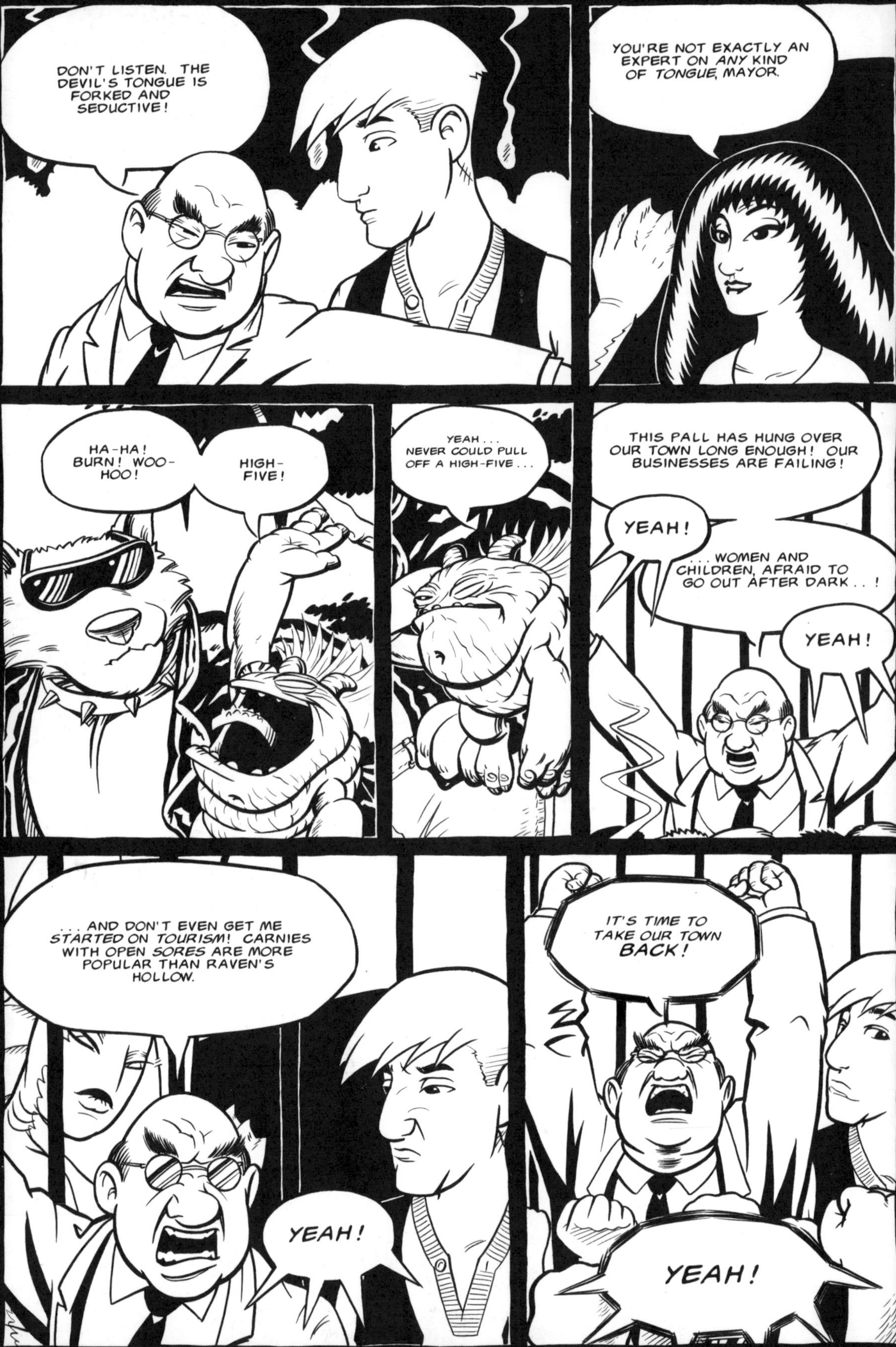
DON'T LISTEN. THE DEVIL'S TONGUE IS FORKED AND SEDUCTIVE!
YOU'RE NOT EXACTLY AN EXPERT ON *ANY KIND* OF *TONGUE*, MAYOR.
HA-HA! BURN! WOO-HOO!
HIGH-FIVE!
YEAH... NEVER COULD PULL OFF A HIGH-FIVE...
THIS PALL HAS HUNG OVER OUR TOWN LONG ENOUGH! OUR BUSINESSES ARE FAILING!
YEAH!
...WOMEN AND CHILDREN, AFRAID TO GO OUT AFTER DARK...!
YEAH!
...AND DON'T EVEN GET ME *STARTED* ON *TOURISM*! CARNIES WITH OPEN *SORES* ARE MORE POPULAR THAN RAVEN'S HOLLOW.
YEAH!
IT'S TIME TO TAKE OUR TOWN **BACK**!
YEAH!

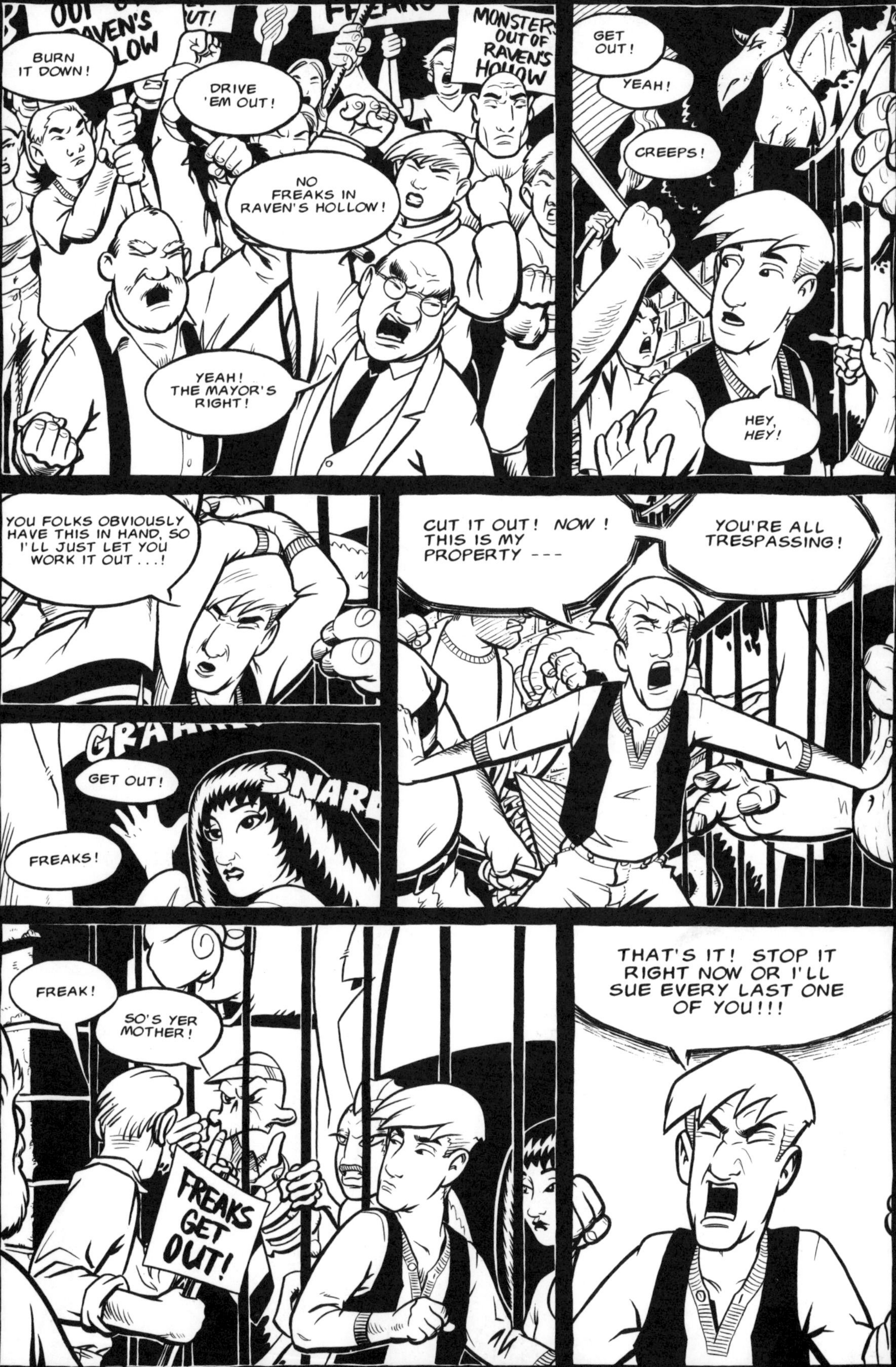
OUT OF RAVEN'S HOLLOW
BURN IT DOWN!
DRIVE 'EM OUT!
MONSTERS OUT OF RAVEN'S HOLLOW
NO FREAKS IN RAVEN'S HOLLOW!
YEAH! THE MAYOR'S RIGHT!
GET OUT!
YEAH!
CREEPS!
HEY, HEY!
YOU FOLKS OBVIOUSLY HAVE THIS IN HAND, SO I'LL JUST LET YOU WORK IT OUT . . .!
CUT IT OUT! *NOW* ! THIS IS MY PROPERTY ---
YOU'RE ALL TRESPASSING!
GET OUT!
SNARF
FREAKS!
FREAK!
SO'S YER MOTHER!
FREAKS GET OUT!
THAT'S IT! STOP IT RIGHT NOW OR I'LL SUE EVERY LAST ONE OF YOU!!!

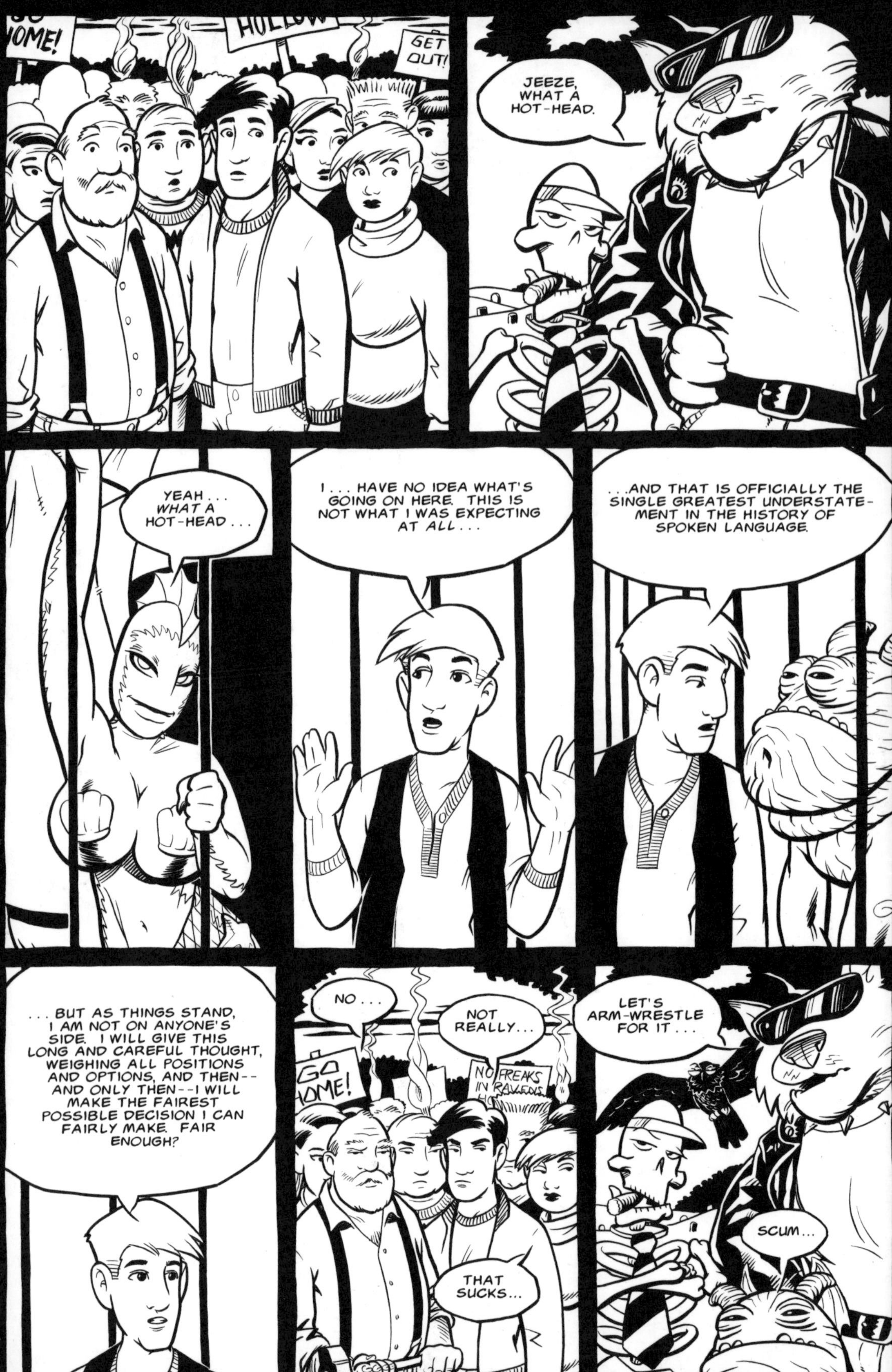
HOLLOW
GET OUT!
JEEZE, WHAT A HOT-HEAD.
YEAH... WHAT A HOT-HEAD...
I... HAVE NO IDEA WHAT'S GOING ON HERE. THIS IS NOT WHAT I WAS EXPECTING AT ALL...
...AND THAT IS OFFICIALLY THE SINGLE GREATEST UNDERSTATEMENT IN THE HISTORY OF SPOKEN LANGUAGE.
...BUT AS THINGS STAND, I AM NOT ON ANYONE'S SIDE. I WILL GIVE THIS LONG AND CAREFUL THOUGHT, WEIGHING ALL POSITIONS AND OPTIONS, AND THEN--AND ONLY THEN--I WILL MAKE THE FAIREST POSSIBLE DECISION I CAN FAIRLY MAKE. FAIR ENOUGH?
NO...
NOT REALLY...
THAT SUCKS...
LET'S ARM-WRESTLE FOR IT...
SCUM...

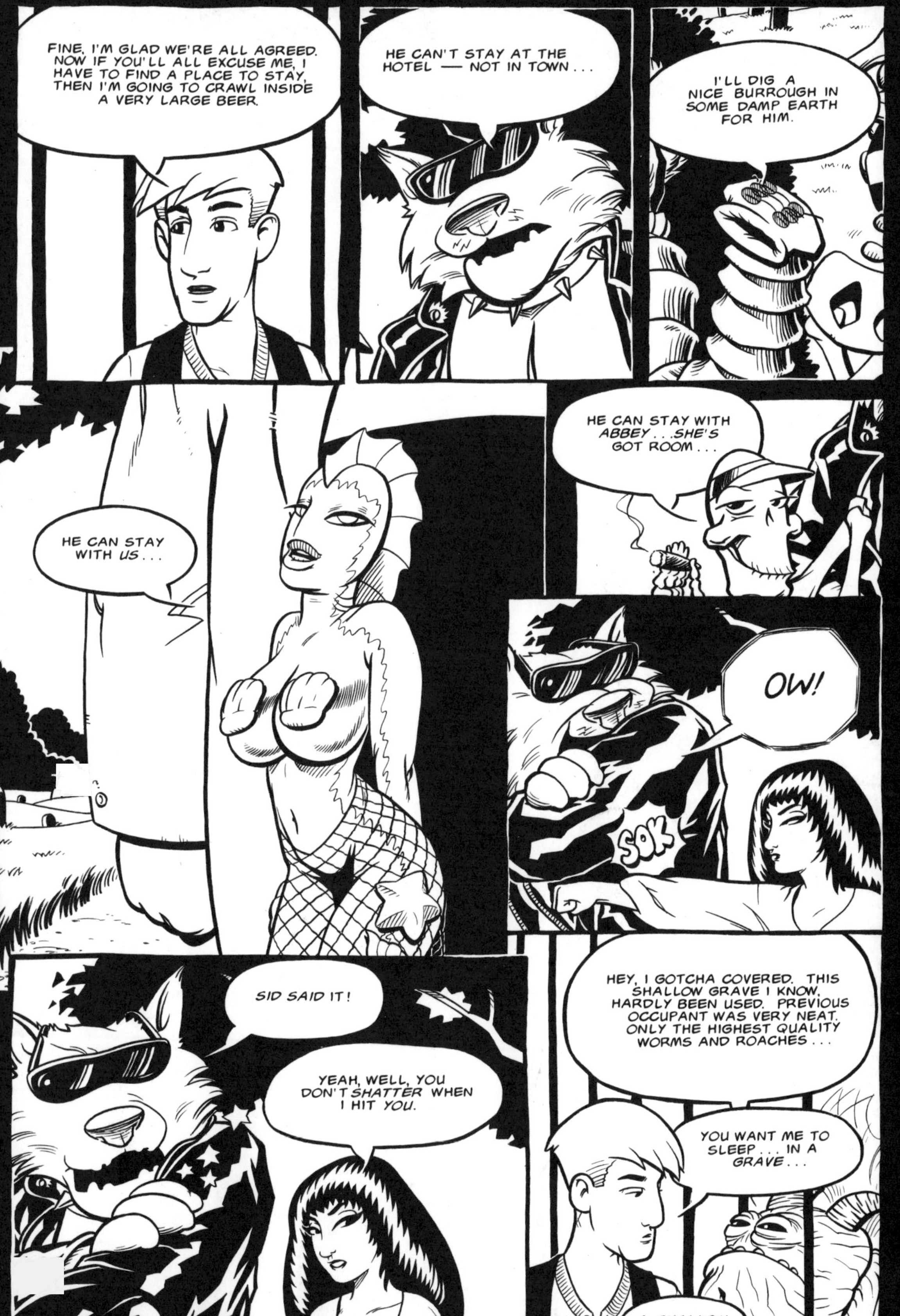
FINE, I'M GLAD WE'RE ALL AGREED. NOW IF YOU'LL ALL EXCUSE ME, I HAVE TO FIND A PLACE TO STAY, THEN I'M GOING TO CRAWL INSIDE A VERY LARGE BEER.
HE CAN'T STAY AT THE HOTEL — NOT IN TOWN . . .
I'LL DIG A NICE BURROUGH IN SOME DAMP EARTH FOR HIM.
HE CAN STAY WITH US . . .
HE CAN STAY WITH ABBEY . . . SHE'S GOT ROOM . . .
OW!
SOK
SID SAID IT!
YEAH, WELL, YOU DON'T SHATTER WHEN I HIT YOU.
HEY, I GOTCHA COVERED. THIS SHALLOW GRAVE I KNOW, HARDLY BEEN USED. PREVIOUS OCCUPANT WAS VERY NEAT. ONLY THE HIGHEST QUALITY WORMS AND ROACHES . . .
YOU WANT ME TO SLEEP . . . IN A GRAVE . . .
A SHALLOW GRAVE.

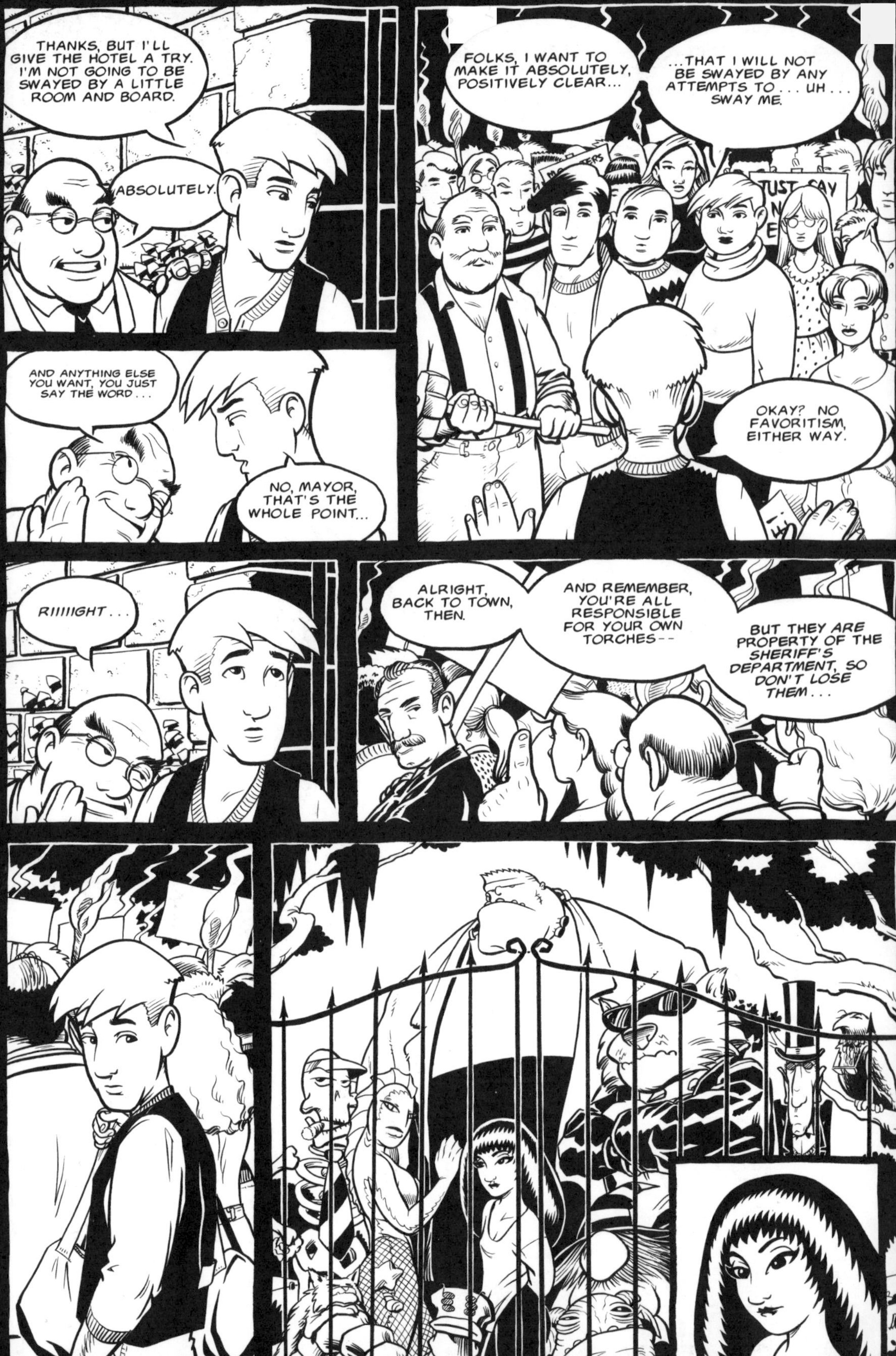

THANKS, BUT I'LL GIVE THE HOTEL A TRY. I'M NOT GOING TO BE SWAYED BY A LITTLE ROOM AND BOARD.
ABSOLUTELY.
AND ANYTHING ELSE YOU WANT, YOU JUST SAY THE WORD . . .
NO, MAYOR, THAT'S THE WHOLE POINT...
FOLKS, I WANT TO MAKE IT ABSOLUTELY, POSITIVELY CLEAR...
...THAT I WILL NOT BE SWAYED BY ANY ATTEMPTS TO . . . UH . . . SWAY ME.
OKAY? NO FAVORITISM, EITHER WAY.
RIIIIIGHT . . .
ALRIGHT, BACK TO TOWN, THEN.
AND REMEMBER, YOU'RE ALL RESPONSIBLE FOR YOUR OWN TORCHES--
BUT THEY ARE PROPERTY OF THE SHERIFF'S DEPARTMENT, SO DON'T LOSE THEM . . .

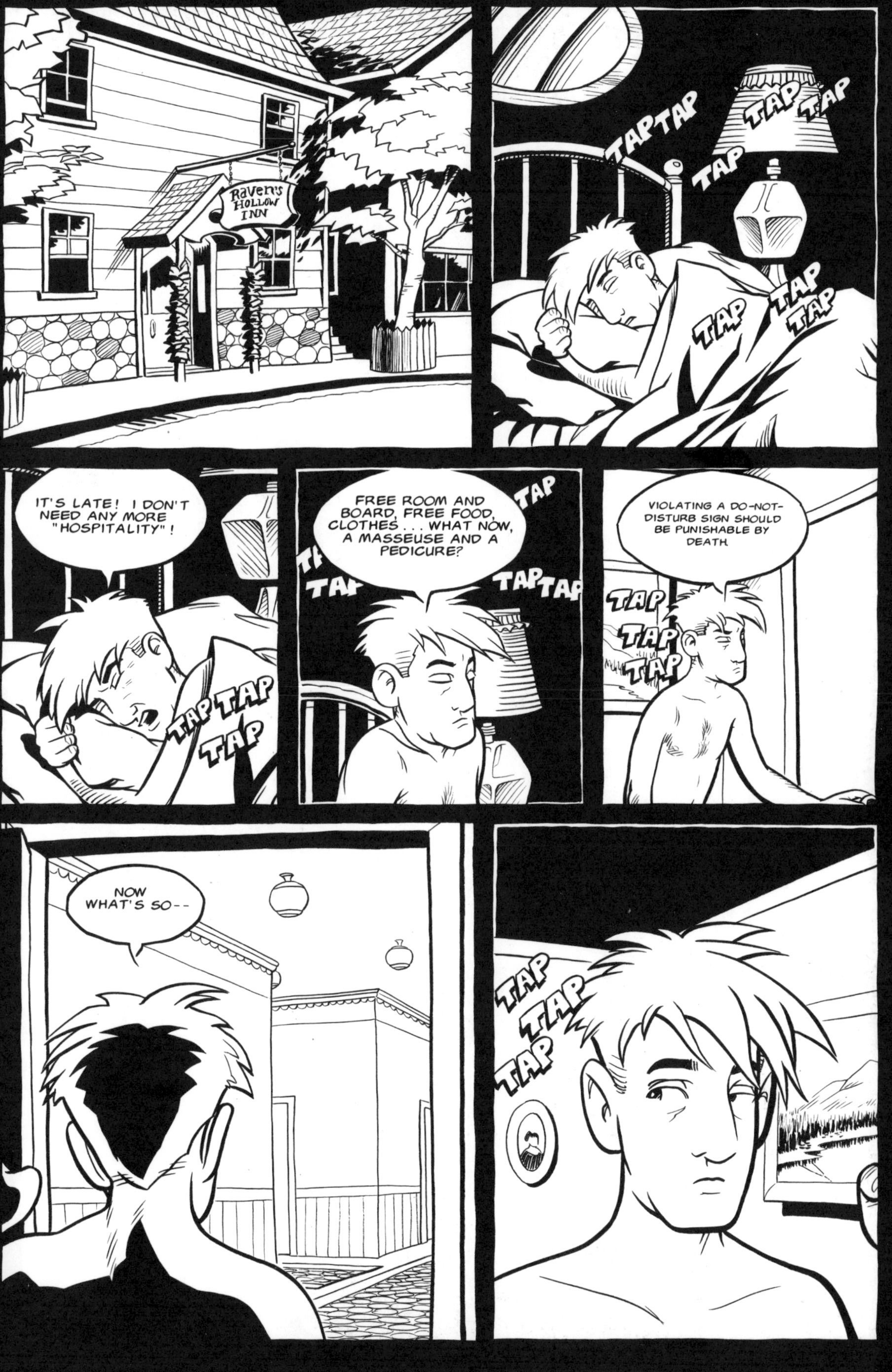

Raven's
HOLLOW
INN
TAPTAP
TAP
TAP
TAP
TAP
TAP
TAP
TAP
IT'S LATE! I DON'T NEED ANY MORE "HOSPITALITY"!
TAPTAP
TAP
FREE ROOM AND BOARD, FREE FOOD, CLOTHES . . . WHAT NOW, A MASSEUSE AND A PEDICURE?
TAP
TAP
TAPTAP
VIOLATING A DO-NOT-DISTURB SIGN SHOULD BE PUNISHABLE BY DEATH.
TAP
TAP
TAP
NOW WHAT'S SO--
TAP
TAP
TAP

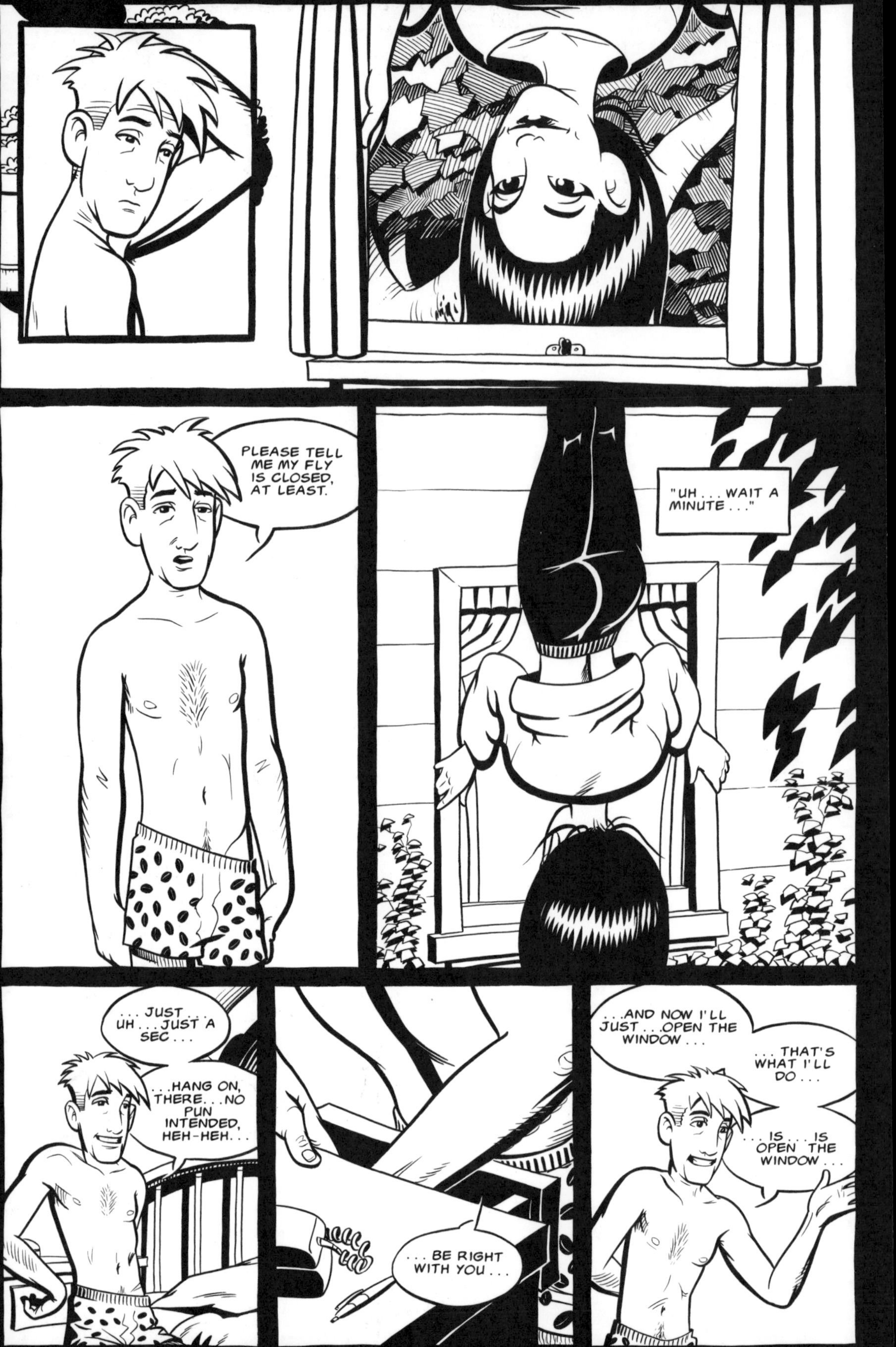
PLEASE TELL ME MY FLY IS CLOSED, AT LEAST.
"UH . . . WAIT A MINUTE . . ."
. . . JUST . . . UH . . . JUST A SEC . . .
. . .HANG ON, THERE. . . NO PUN INTENDED, HEH-HEH. . .
. . . BE RIGHT WITH YOU . . .
. . .AND NOW I'LL JUST . . . OPEN THE WINDOW . . .
. . . THAT'S WHAT I'LL DO . . .
. . . IS . . . IS OPEN THE WINDOW . . .

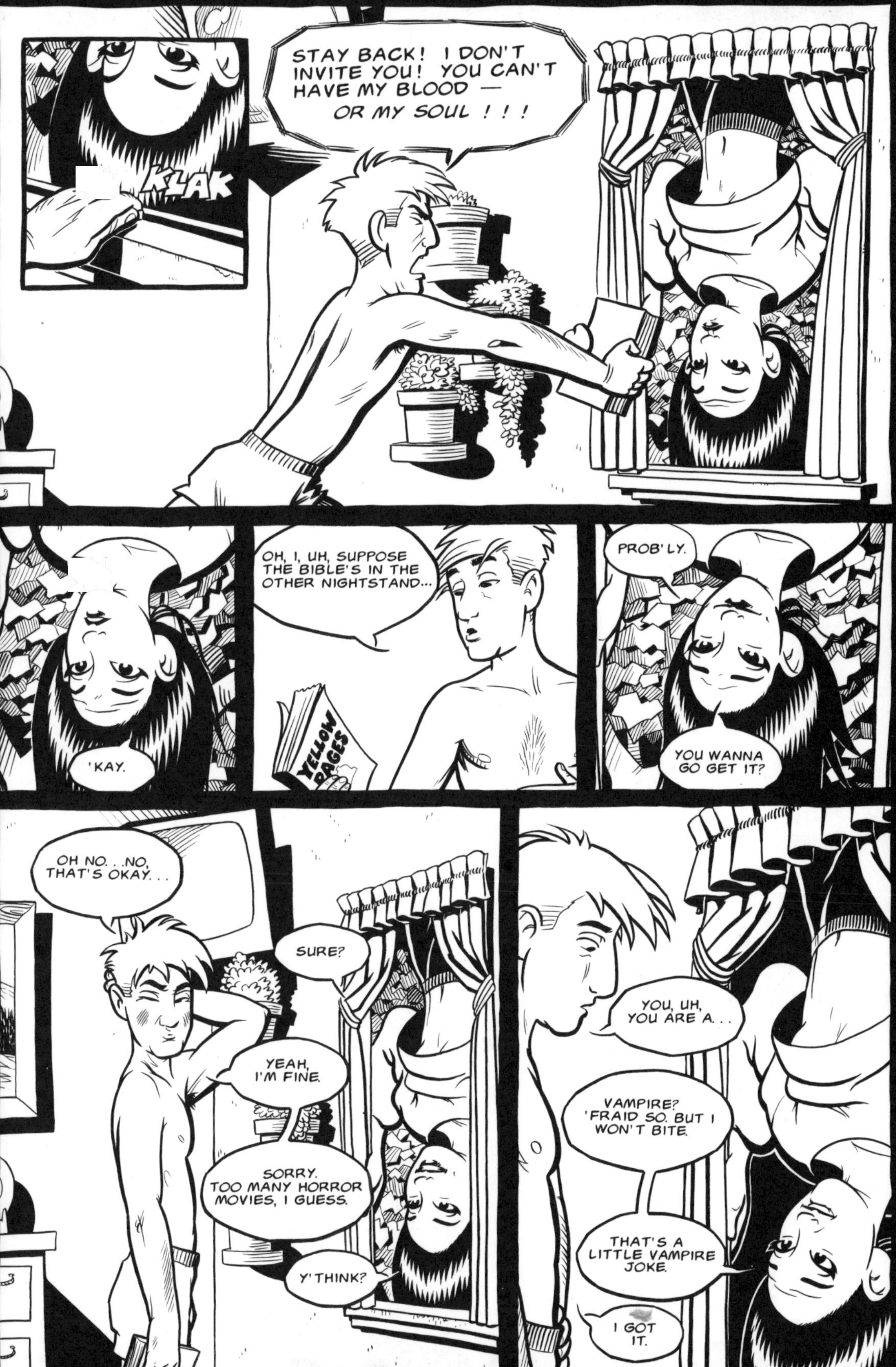
KLAK
STAY BACK! I DON'T INVITE YOU! YOU CAN'T HAVE MY BLOOD — OR MY SOUL ! ! !
'KAY.
OH, I, UH, SUPPOSE THE BIBLE'S IN THE OTHER NIGHTSTAND...
YELLOW PAGES
PROB'LY.
YOU WANNA GO GET IT?
OH NO. . .NO, THAT'S OKAY. . .
SURE?
YEAH, I'M FINE.
SORRY. TOO MANY HORROR MOVIES, I GUESS.
Y'THINK?
YOU, UH, YOU ARE A. . .
VAMPIRE? 'FRAID SO. BUT I WON'T BITE.
THAT'S A LITTLE VAMPIRE JOKE.
I GOT IT.

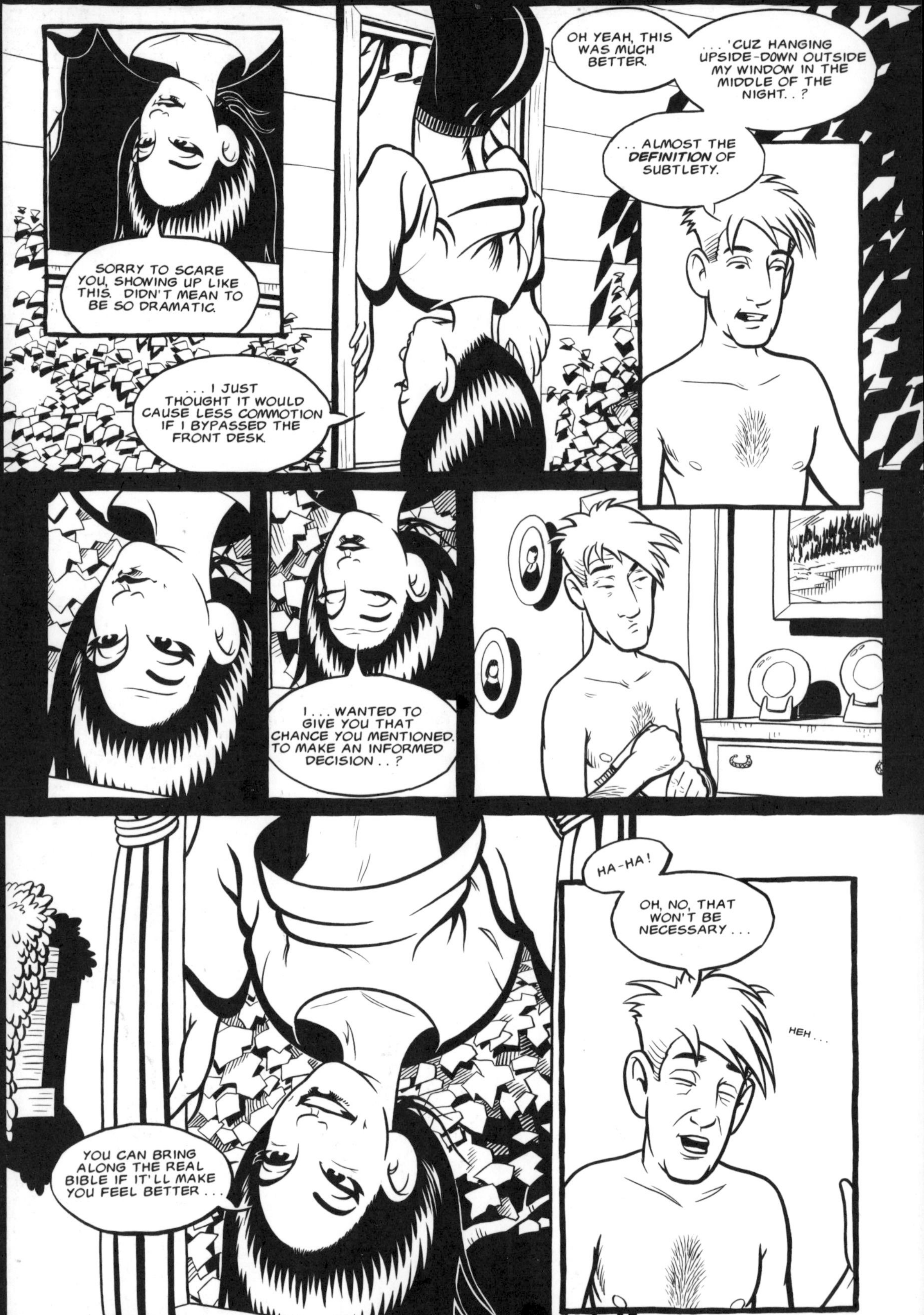
SORRY TO SCARE YOU, SHOWING UP LIKE THIS. DIDN'T MEAN TO BE SO DRAMATIC.
. . . I JUST THOUGHT IT WOULD CAUSE LESS COMMOTION IF I BYPASSED THE FRONT DESK.
OH YEAH, THIS WAS MUCH BETTER.
. . . 'CUZ HANGING UPSIDE-DOWN OUTSIDE MY WINDOW IN THE MIDDLE OF THE NIGHT. . ?
. . . ALMOST THE DEFINITION OF SUBTLETY.
I . . . WANTED TO GIVE YOU THAT CHANCE YOU MENTIONED. TO MAKE AN INFORMED DECISION . . ?
YOU CAN BRING ALONG THE REAL BIBLE IF IT'LL MAKE YOU FEEL BETTER . . .
HA-HA!
OH, NO, THAT WON'T BE NECESSARY . . .
HEH . . .

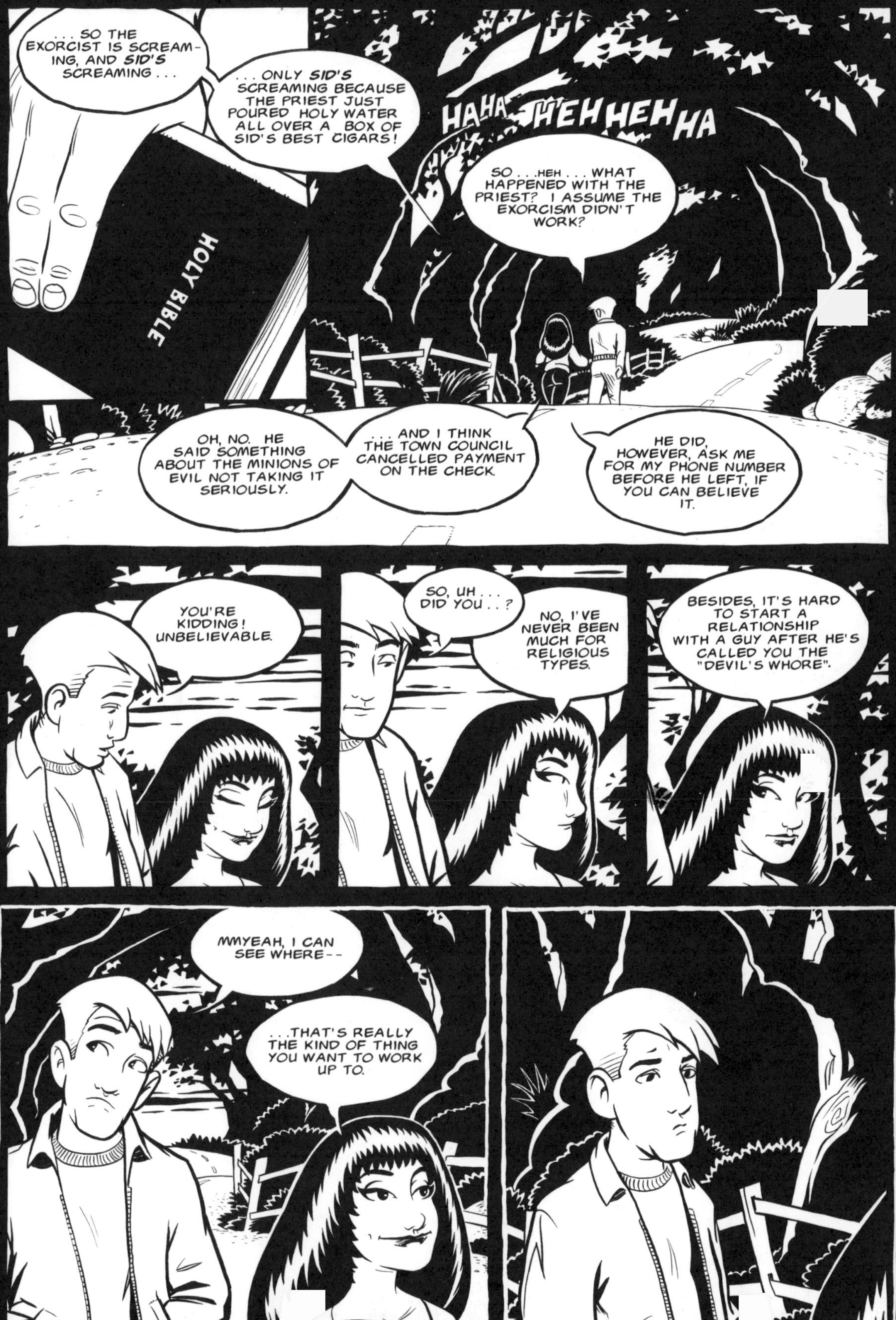

. . . SO THE EXORCIST IS SCREAMING, AND SID'S SCREAMING . . .
. . . ONLY SID'S SCREAMING BECAUSE THE PRIEST JUST POURED HOLY WATER ALL OVER A BOX OF SID'S BEST CIGARS!
HOLY BIBLE
HAHA HEHHEHHA
SO . . .HEH . . . WHAT HAPPENED WITH THE PRIEST? I ASSUME THE EXORCISM DIDN'T WORK?
OH, NO. HE SAID SOMETHING ABOUT THE MINIONS OF EVIL NOT TAKING IT SERIOUSLY.
. . . AND I THINK THE TOWN COUNCIL CANCELLED PAYMENT ON THE CHECK.
HE DID, HOWEVER, ASK ME FOR MY PHONE NUMBER BEFORE HE LEFT, IF YOU CAN BELIEVE IT.
YOU'RE KIDDING! UNBELIEVABLE.
SO, UH . . . DID YOU . . ?
NO, I'VE NEVER BEEN MUCH FOR RELIGIOUS TYPES.
BESIDES, IT'S HARD TO START A RELATIONSHIP WITH A GUY AFTER HE'S CALLED YOU THE "DEVIL'S WHORE".
MMYEAH, I CAN SEE WHERE--
. . .THAT'S REALLY THE KIND OF THING YOU WANT TO WORK UP TO.

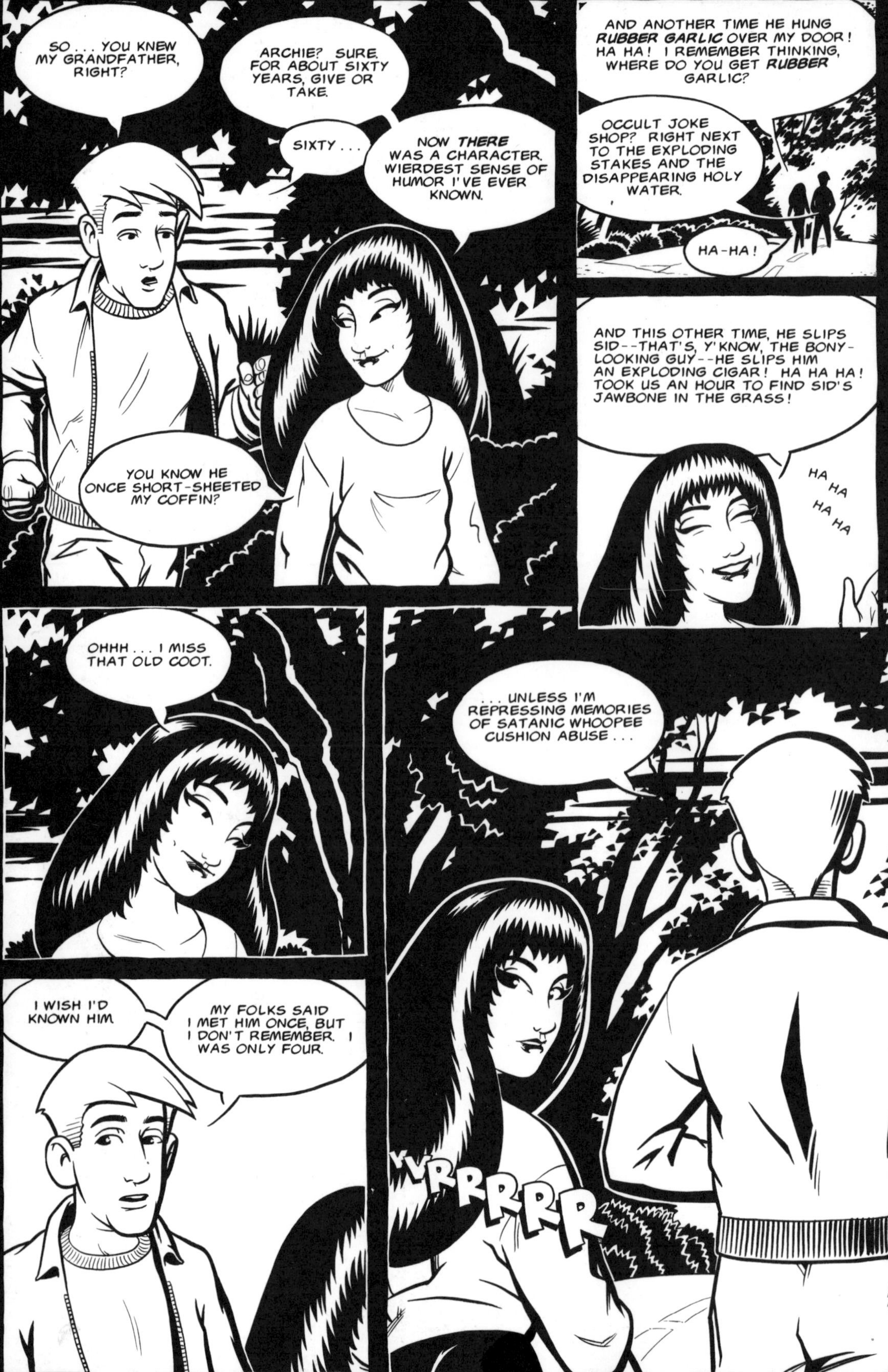

SO . . . YOU KNEW MY GRANDFATHER, RIGHT?
ARCHIE? SURE. FOR ABOUT SIXTY YEARS, GIVE OR TAKE.
SIXTY . . .
NOW THERE WAS A CHARACTER. WIERDEST SENSE OF HUMOR I'VE EVER KNOWN.
YOU KNOW HE ONCE SHORT-SHEETED MY COFFIN?
AND ANOTHER TIME HE HUNG RUBBER GARLIC OVER MY DOOR! HA HA! I REMEMBER THINKING, WHERE DO YOU GET RUBBER GARLIC?
OCCULT JOKE SHOP? RIGHT NEXT TO THE EXPLODING STAKES AND THE DISAPPEARING HOLY WATER.
HA-HA!
AND THIS OTHER TIME, HE SLIPS SID--THAT'S, Y'KNOW, THE BONY-LOOKING GUY--HE SLIPS HIM AN EXPLODING CIGAR! HA HA HA! TOOK US AN HOUR TO FIND SID'S JAWBONE IN THE GRASS!
HA HA HA HA
OHHH . . . I MISS THAT OLD COOT.
I WISH I'D KNOWN HIM.
MY FOLKS SAID I MET HIM ONCE, BUT I DON'T REMEMBER. I WAS ONLY FOUR.
. . . UNLESS I'M REPRESSING MEMORIES OF SATANIC WHOOPEE CUSHION ABUSE . . .
VVRRRRR

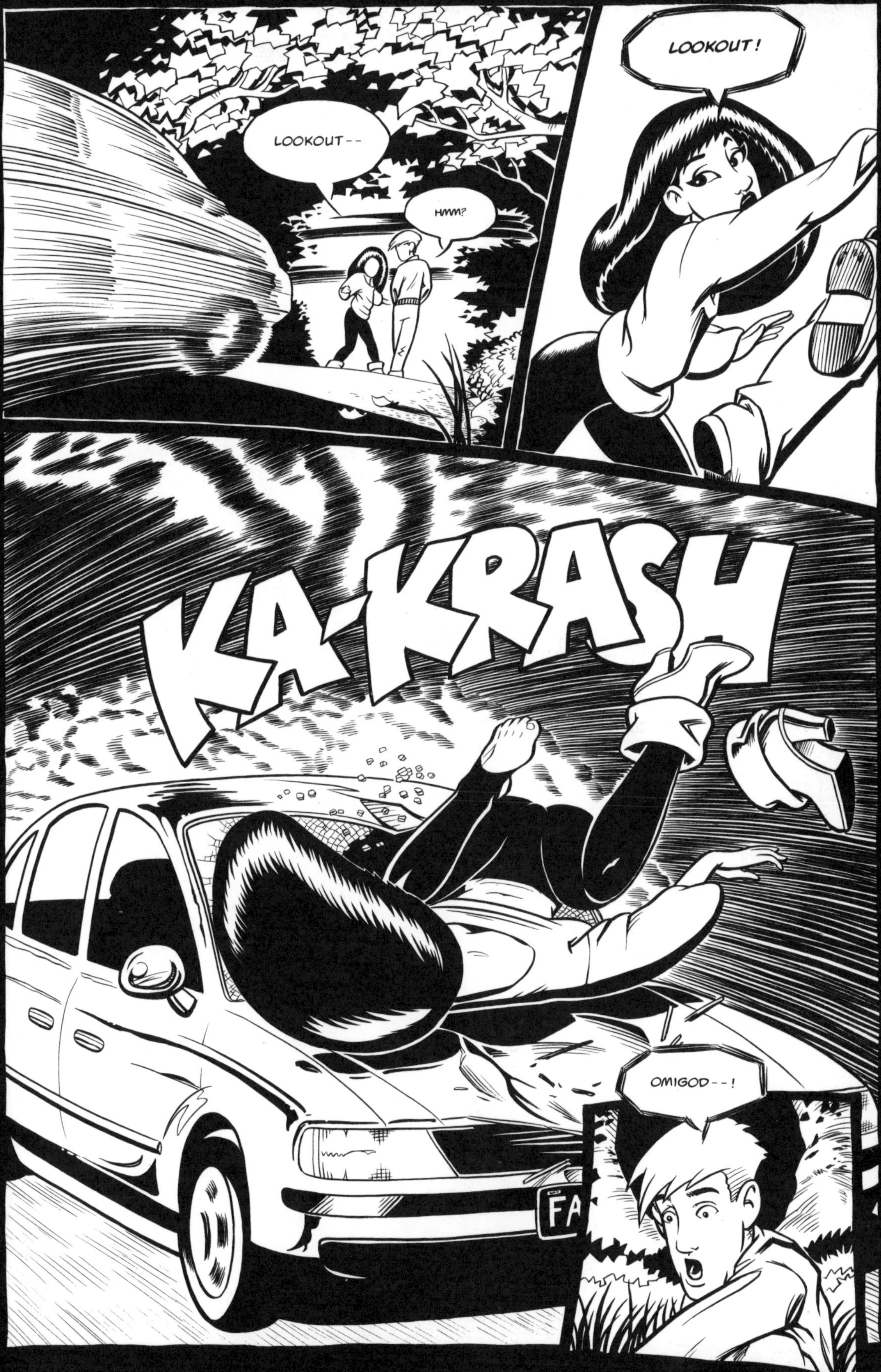
LOOKOUT--
HMM?
LOOKOUT!
KA-KRASH
FA
OMIGOD--!

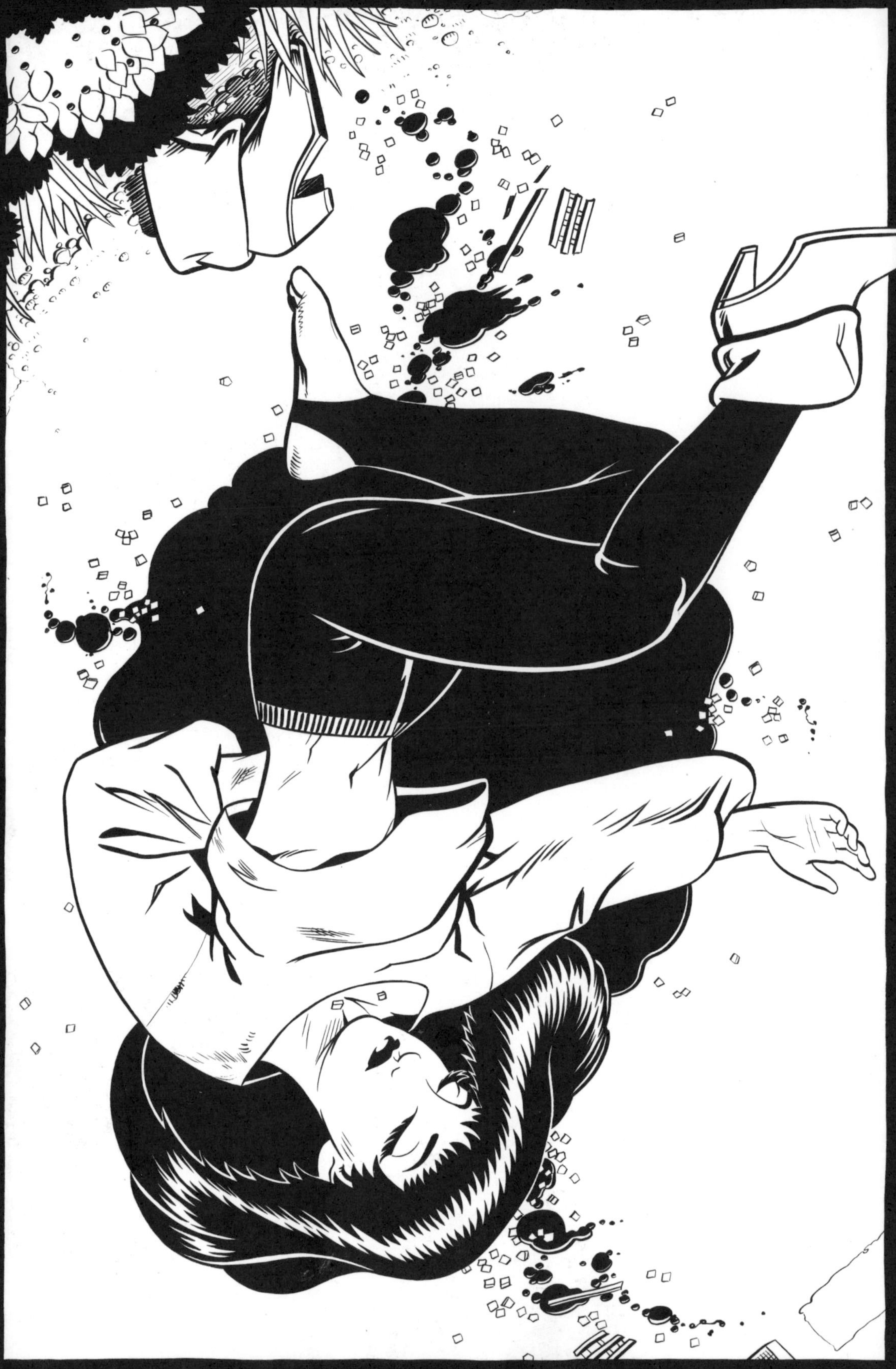

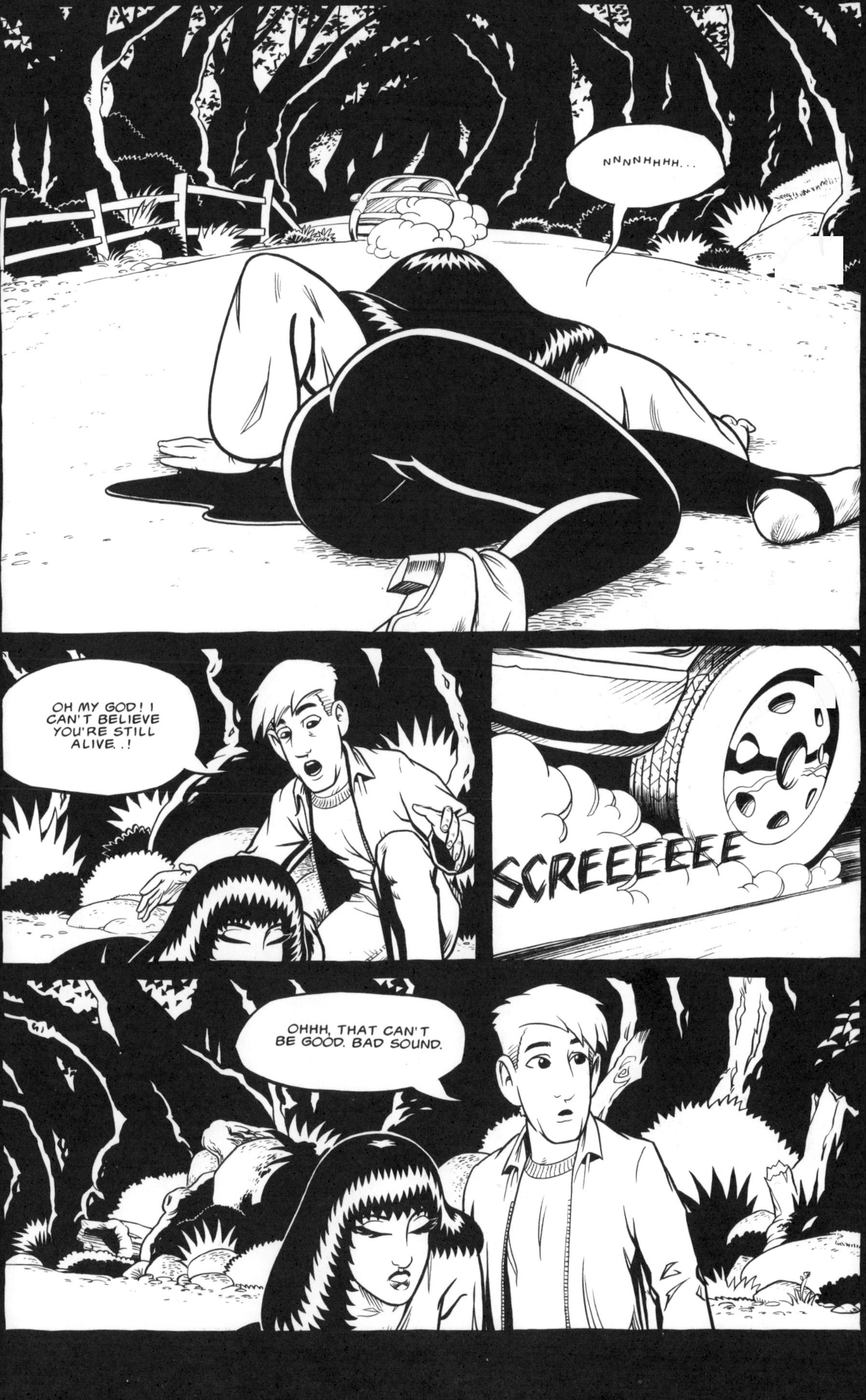
NNNNHHHH...
OH MY GOD! I CAN'T BELIEVE YOU'RE STILL ALIVE..!
SCREEEEEEE
OHHH, THAT CAN'T BE GOOD. BAD SOUND.

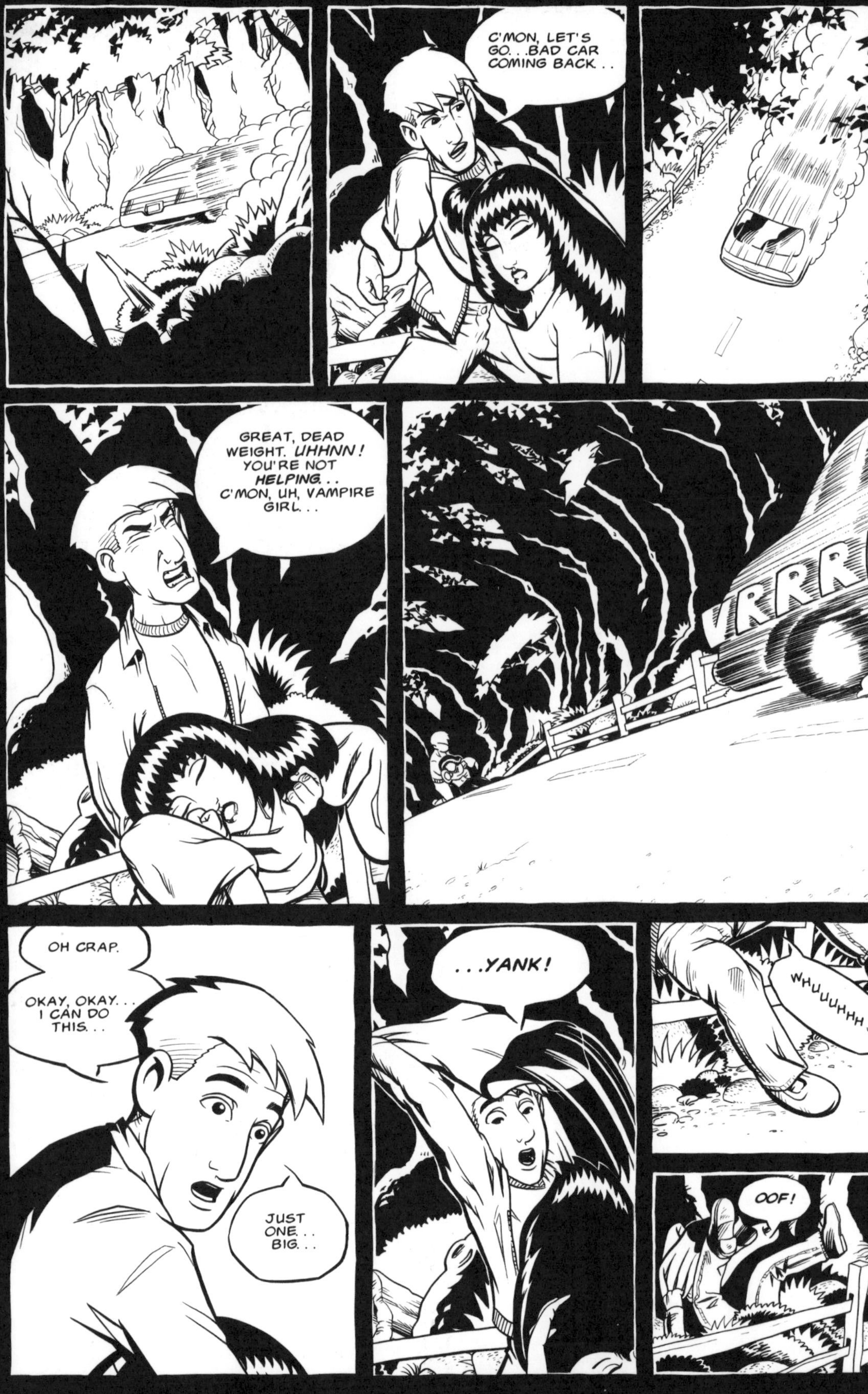
C'MON, LET'S GO. . .BAD CAR COMING BACK. . .
GREAT, DEAD WEIGHT. UHHNN! YOU'RE NOT HELPING. . . C'MON, UH, VAMPIRE GIRL. . .
VRRRR
OH CRAP.
OKAY, OKAY. . . I CAN DO THIS. . .
JUST ONE. . . BIG. . .
. . .YANK!
WHUUUHHH
OOF!

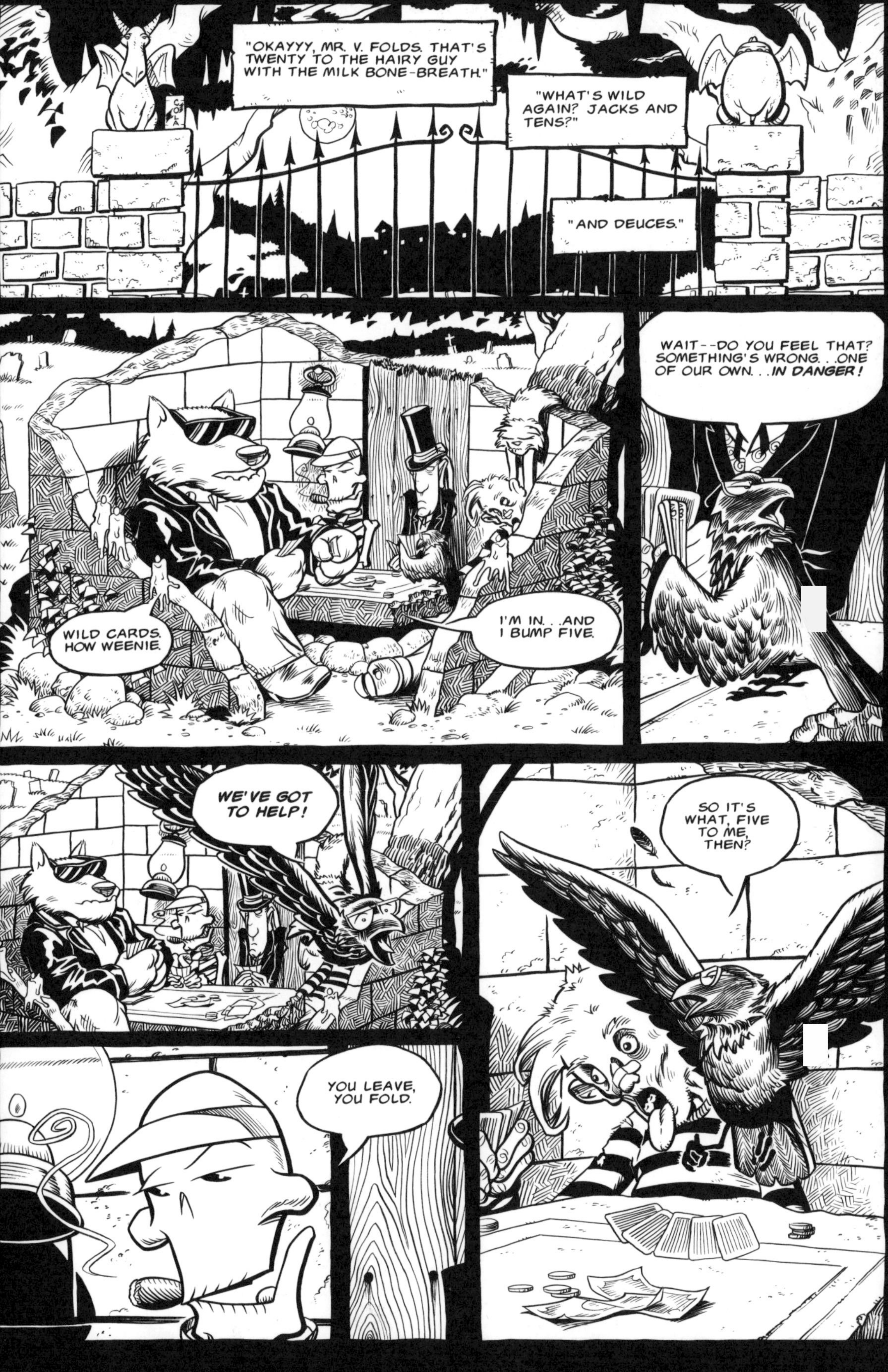
"OKAYYY, MR. V. FOLDS. THAT'S TWENTY TO THE HAIRY GUY WITH THE MILK BONE-BREATH."
"WHAT'S WILD AGAIN? JACKS AND TENS?"
"AND DEUCES."
WILD CARDS. HOW WEENIE.
I'M IN. . .AND I BUMP FIVE.
WAIT--DO YOU FEEL THAT? SOMETHING'S WRONG. . .ONE OF OUR OWN. . .IN DANGER!
WE'VE GOT TO HELP!
SO IT'S WHAT, FIVE TO ME, THEN?
YOU LEAVE, YOU FOLD.

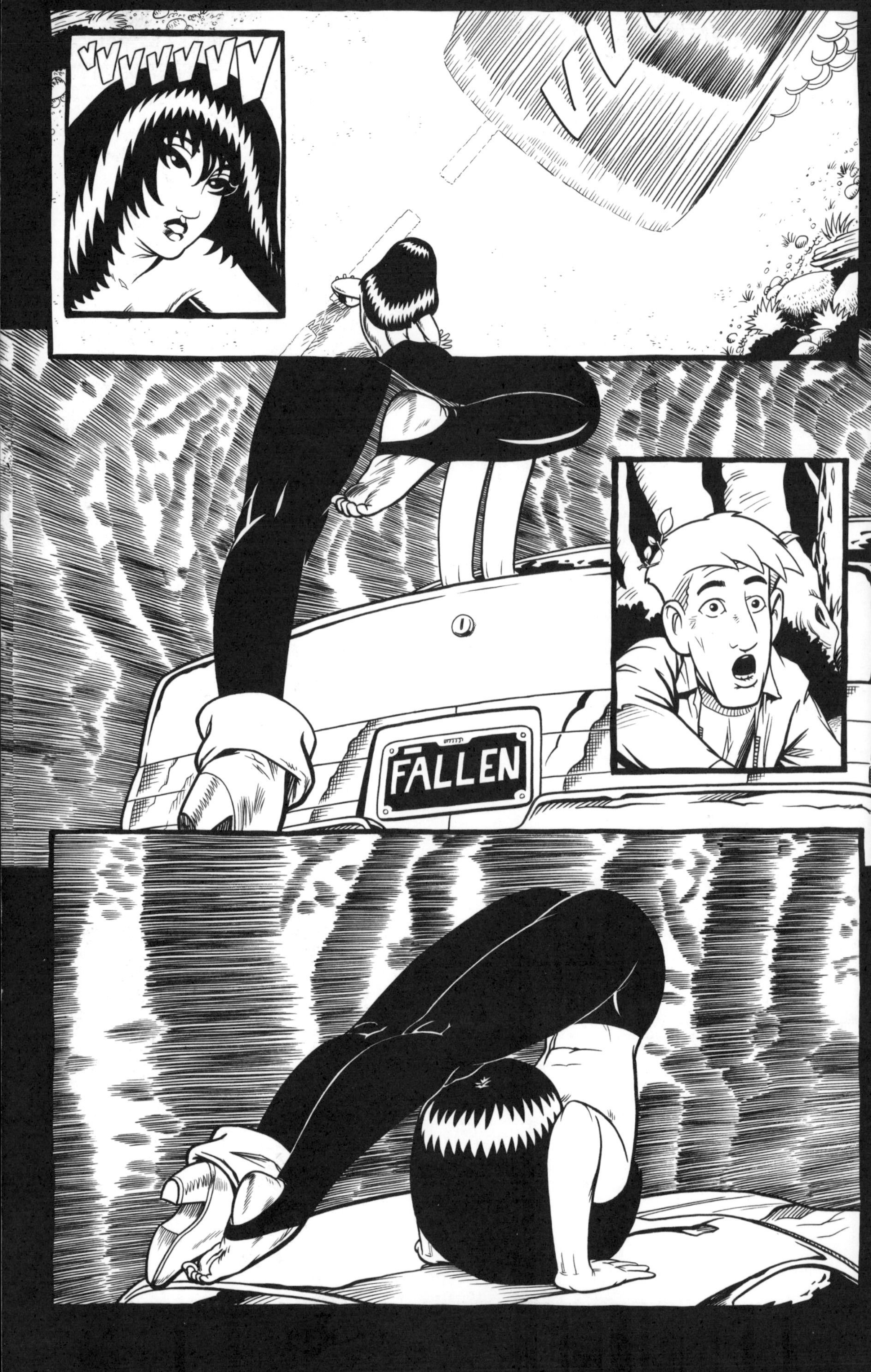

VVVVVVV
VVV
FALLEN

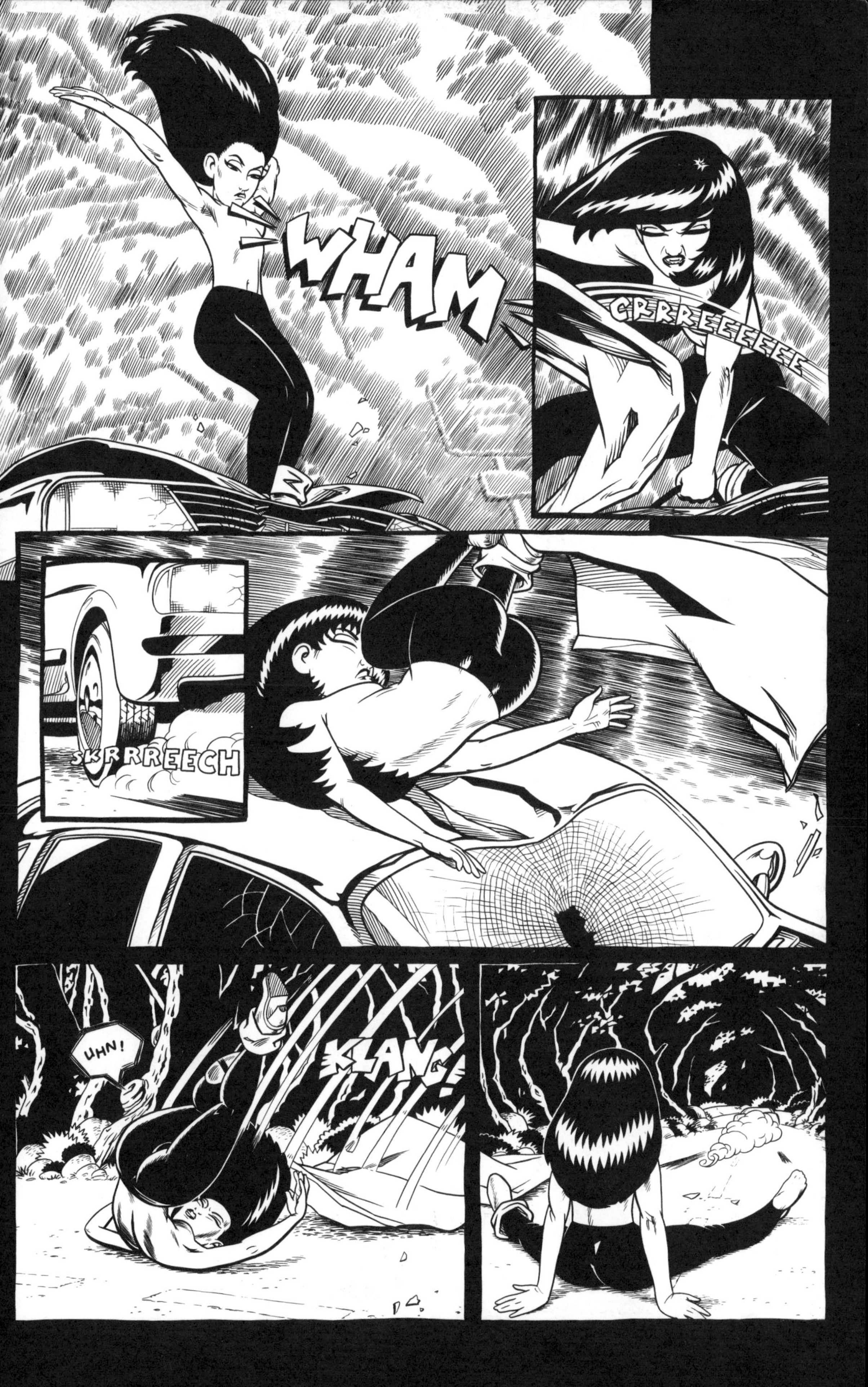
WHAM
CRRREEEEEEE
SKRRREECH
UHN!
KLANG!

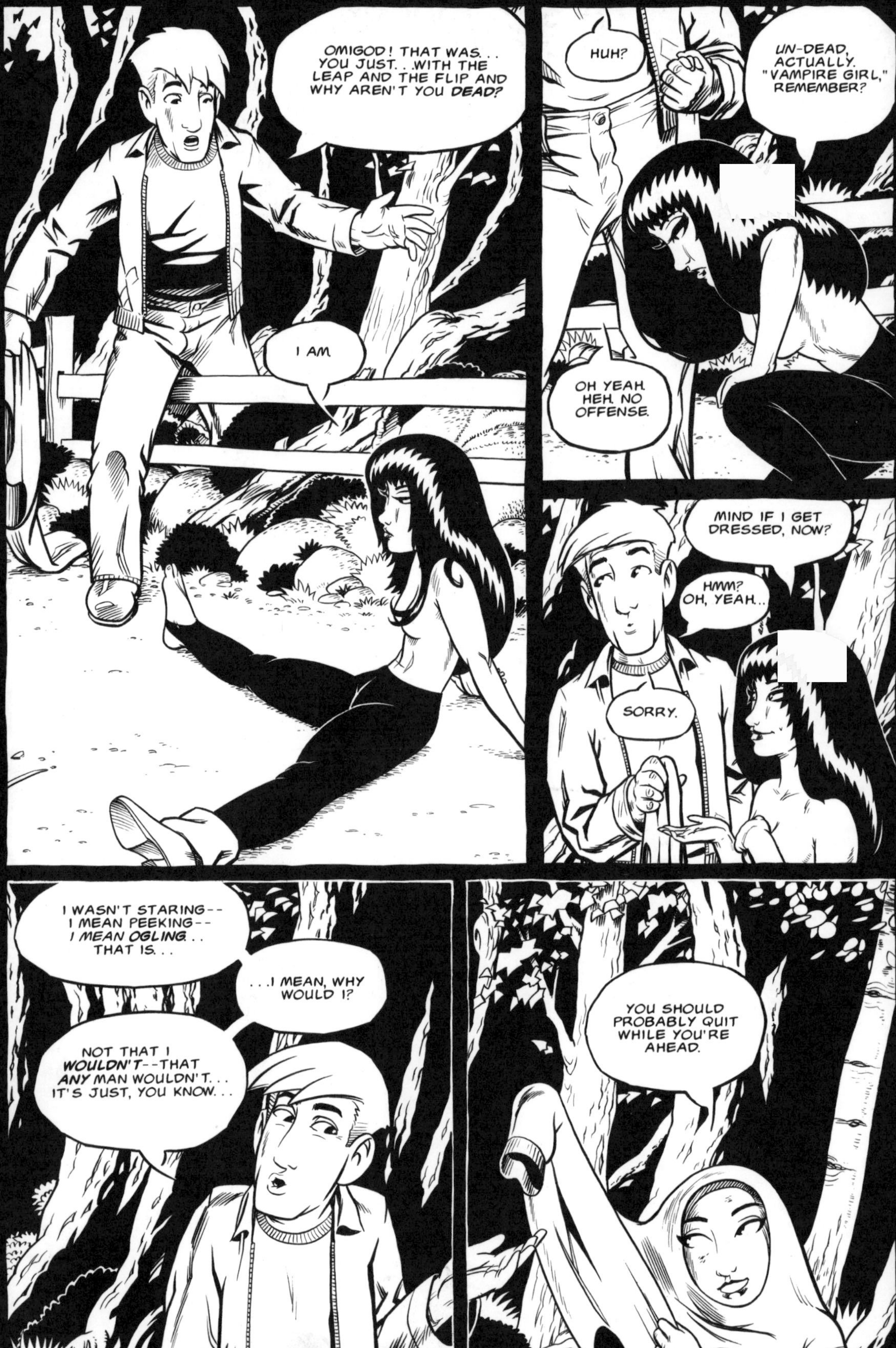
OMIGOD! THAT WAS. . . YOU JUST. . .WITH THE LEAP AND THE FLIP AND WHY AREN'T YOU *DEAD?*
I AM.
HUH?
UN-DEAD, ACTUALLY. "VAMPIRE GIRL," REMEMBER?
OH YEAH. HEH. NO OFFENSE.
MIND IF I GET DRESSED, NOW?
HMM? OH, YEAH. . .
SORRY.
I WASN'T STARING-- I MEAN PEEKING-- *I MEAN OGLING*. . . THAT IS. . .
. . .I MEAN, WHY WOULD I?
NOT THAT I ***WOULDN'T***--THAT ***ANY*** MAN WOULDN'T. . . IT'S JUST, YOU KNOW. . .
YOU SHOULD PROBABLY QUIT WHILE YOU'RE AHEAD.

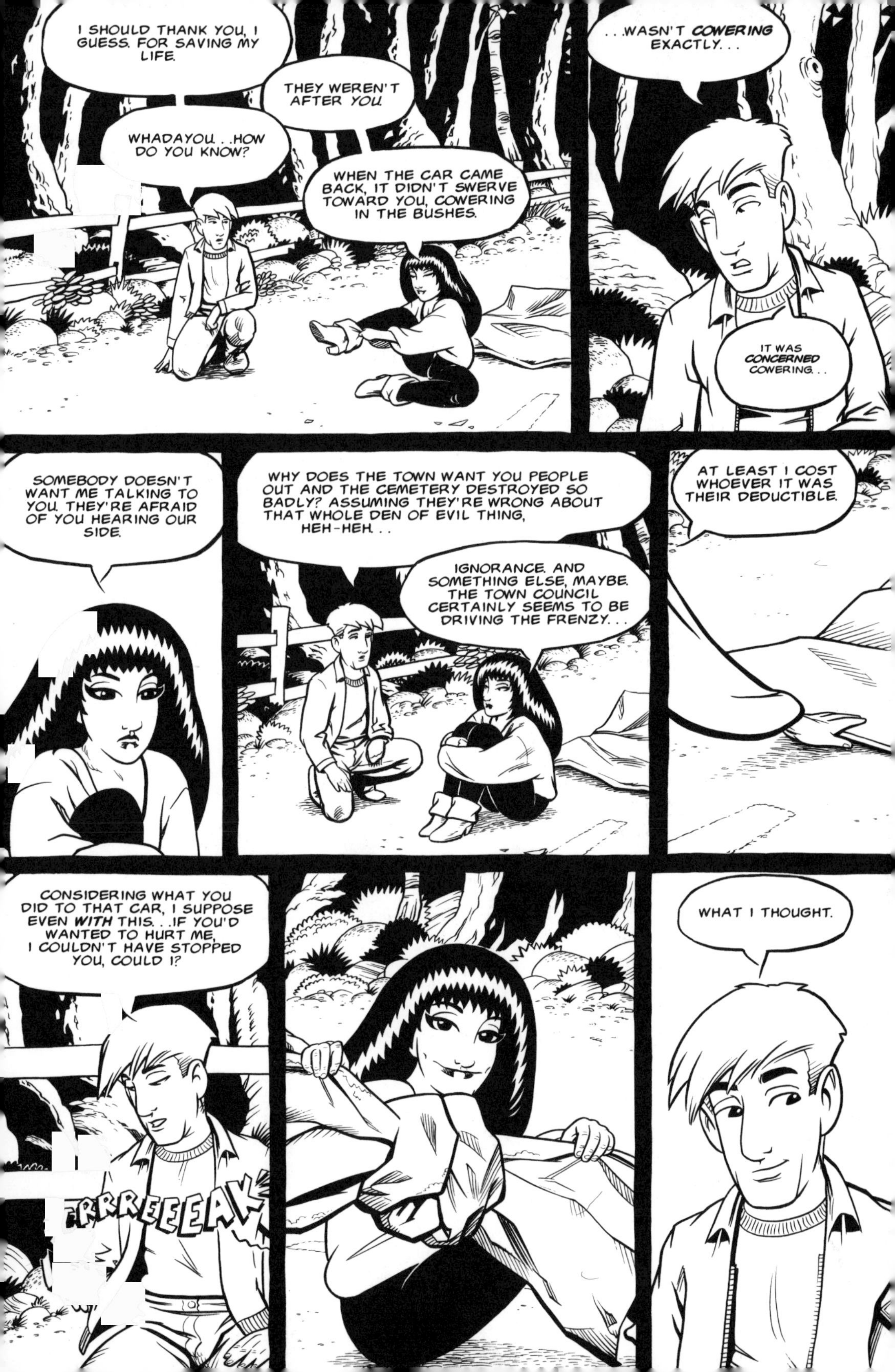
I SHOULD THANK YOU, I GUESS. FOR SAVING MY LIFE.
WHADAYOU. . .HOW DO YOU KNOW?
THEY WEREN'T AFTER *YOU.*
WHEN THE CAR CAME BACK, IT DIDN'T SWERVE TOWARD YOU, COWERING IN THE BUSHES.
. . .WASN'T ***COWERING*** EXACTLY. . .
IT WAS ***CONCERNED*** COWERING. . .
SOMEBODY DOESN'T WANT ME TALKING TO YOU. THEY'RE AFRAID OF YOU HEARING OUR SIDE.
WHY DOES THE TOWN WANT YOU PEOPLE OUT AND THE CEMETERY DESTROYED SO BADLY? ASSUMING THEY'RE WRONG ABOUT THAT WHOLE DEN OF EVIL THING, HEH-HEH. . .
IGNORANCE. AND SOMETHING ELSE, MAYBE. THE TOWN COUNCIL CERTAINLY SEEMS TO BE DRIVING THE FRENZY. . .
AT LEAST I COST WHOEVER IT WAS THEIR DEDUCTIBLE.
CONSIDERING WHAT YOU DID TO THAT CAR, I SUPPOSE EVEN ***WITH*** THIS. . .IF YOU'D WANTED TO HURT ME, I COULDN'T HAVE STOPPED YOU, COULD I?
RRRREEEEAK
WHAT I THOUGHT.

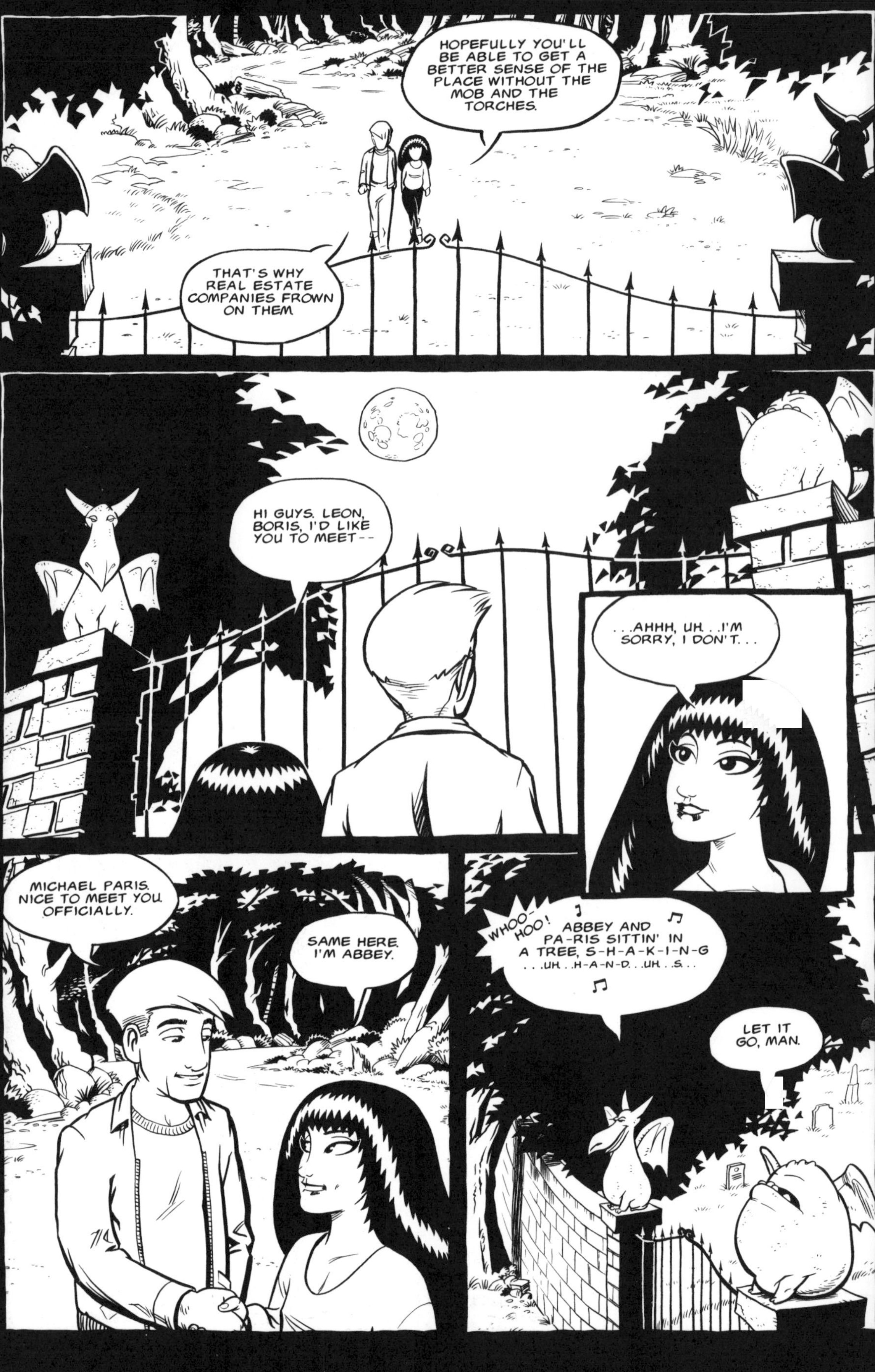
HOPEFULLY YOU'LL BE ABLE TO GET A BETTER SENSE OF THE PLACE WITHOUT THE MOB AND THE TORCHES.
THAT'S WHY REAL ESTATE COMPANIES FROWN ON THEM.
HI GUYS. LEON, BORIS, I'D LIKE YOU TO MEET--
...AHHH, UH...I'M SORRY, I DON'T...
MICHAEL PARIS. NICE TO MEET YOU. OFFICIALLY.
SAME HERE. I'M ABBEY.
WHOO-HOO!
ABBEY AND PA-RIS SITTIN' IN A TREE, S-H-A-K-I-N-G ...UH...H-A-N-D...UH...S...
LET IT GO, MAN.

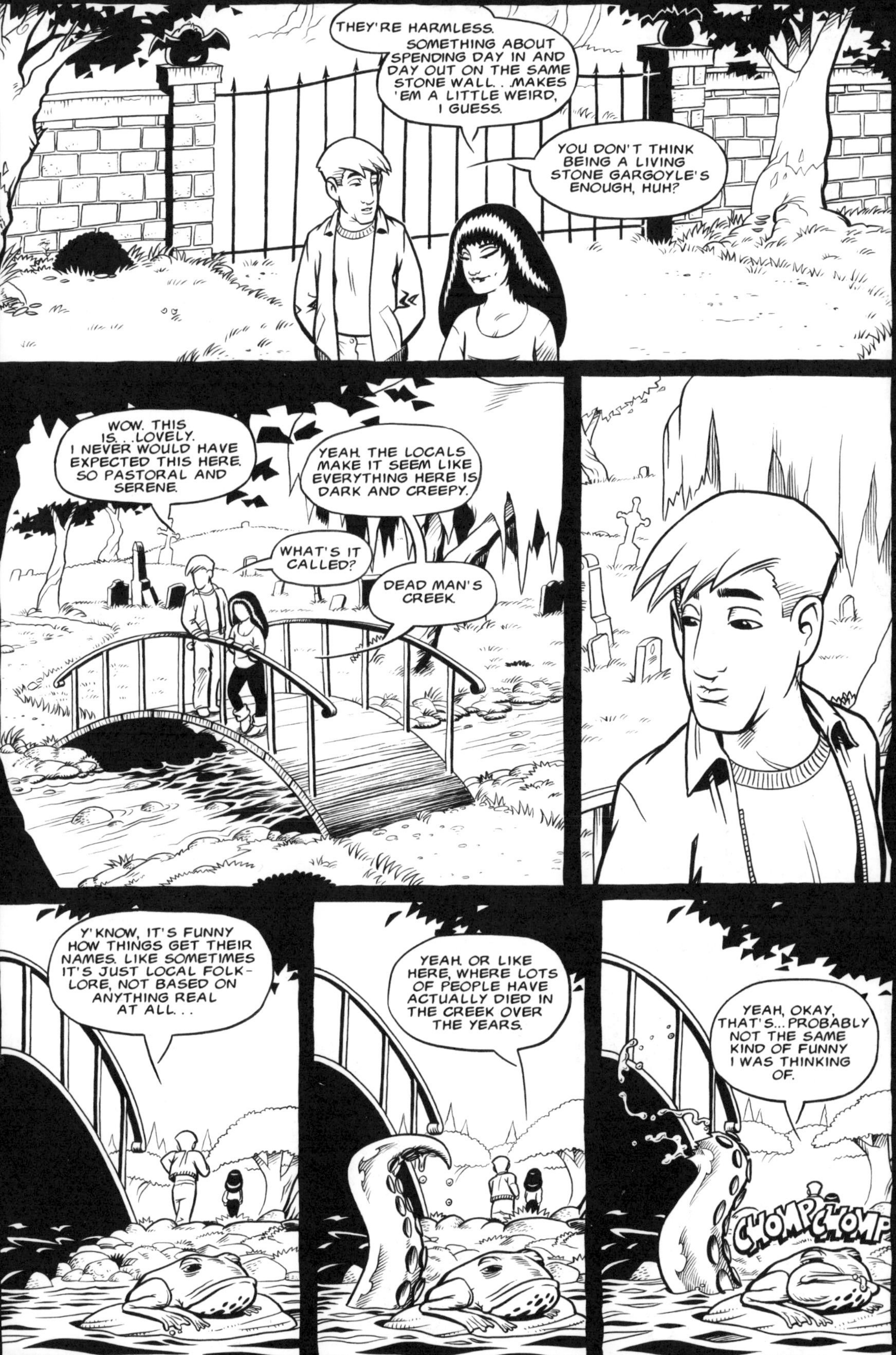
THEY'RE HARMLESS.
SOMETHING ABOUT SPENDING DAY IN AND DAY OUT ON THE SAME STONE WALL. . MAKES 'EM A LITTLE WEIRD, I GUESS.
YOU DON'T THINK BEING A LIVING STONE GARGOYLE'S ENOUGH, HUH?
WOW. THIS IS. . .LOVELY. I NEVER WOULD HAVE EXPECTED THIS HERE. SO PASTORAL AND SERENE.
YEAH. THE LOCALS MAKE IT SEEM LIKE EVERYTHING HERE IS DARK AND CREEPY.
WHAT'S IT CALLED?
DEAD MAN'S CREEK.
Y'KNOW, IT'S FUNNY HOW THINGS GET THEIR NAMES. LIKE SOMETIMES IT'S JUST LOCAL FOLK-LORE, NOT BASED ON ANYTHING REAL AT ALL. . .
YEAH. OR LIKE HERE, WHERE LOTS OF PEOPLE HAVE ACTUALLY DIED IN THE CREEK OVER THE YEARS.
YEAH, OKAY, THAT'S... PROBABLY NOT THE SAME KIND OF FUNNY I WAS THINKING OF.
CHOMP CHOMP

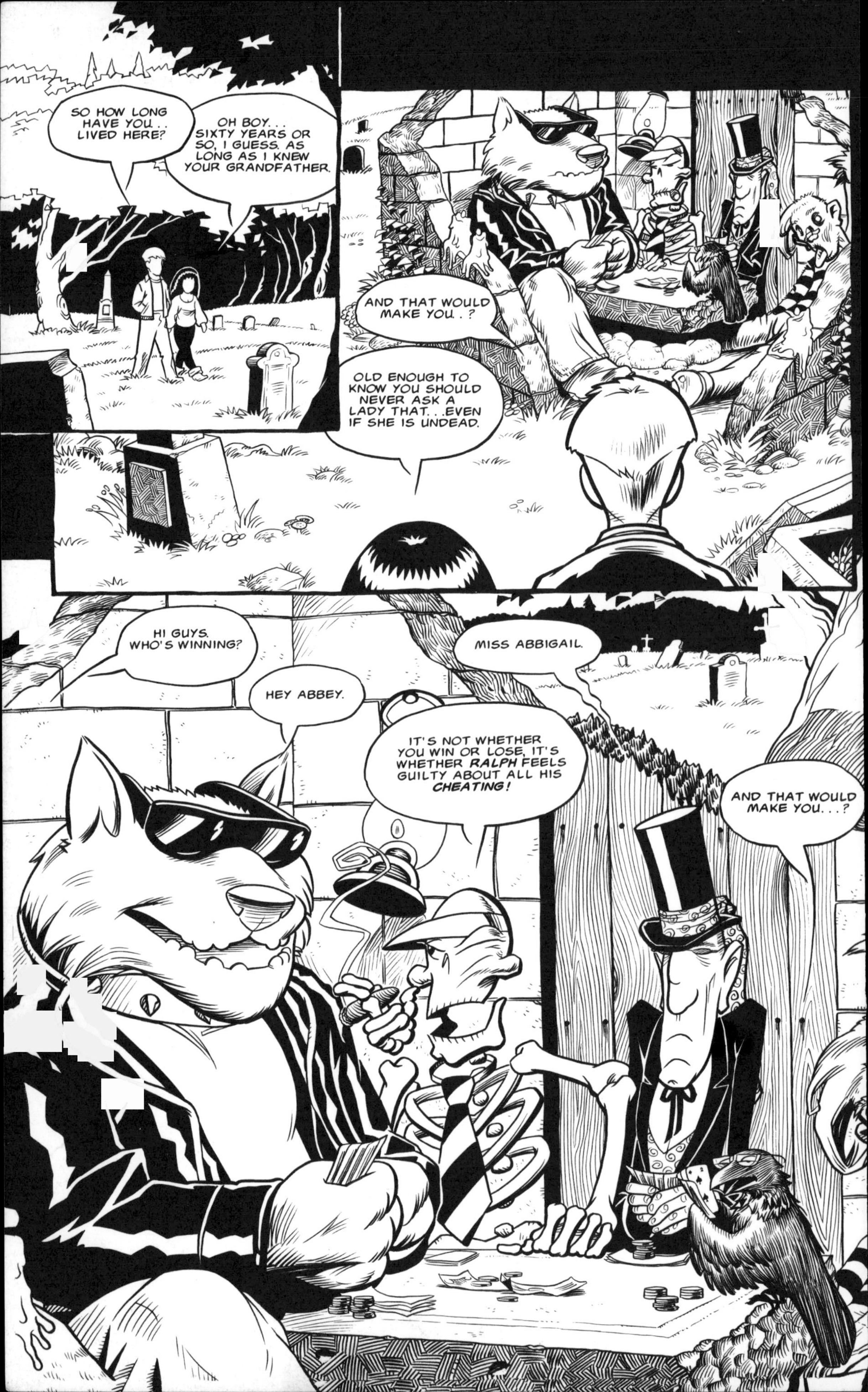

SO HOW LONG HAVE YOU.. LIVED HERE?
OH BOY... SIXTY YEARS OR SO, I GUESS. AS LONG AS I KNEW YOUR GRANDFATHER.
AND THAT WOULD MAKE YOU..?
OLD ENOUGH TO KNOW YOU SHOULD NEVER ASK A LADY THAT...EVEN IF SHE IS UNDEAD.
HI GUYS. WHO'S WINNING?
HEY ABBEY.
MISS ABBIGAIL.
IT'S NOT WHETHER YOU WIN OR LOSE, IT'S WHETHER RALPH FEELS GUILTY ABOUT ALL HIS CHEATING!
AND THAT WOULD MAKE YOU...?

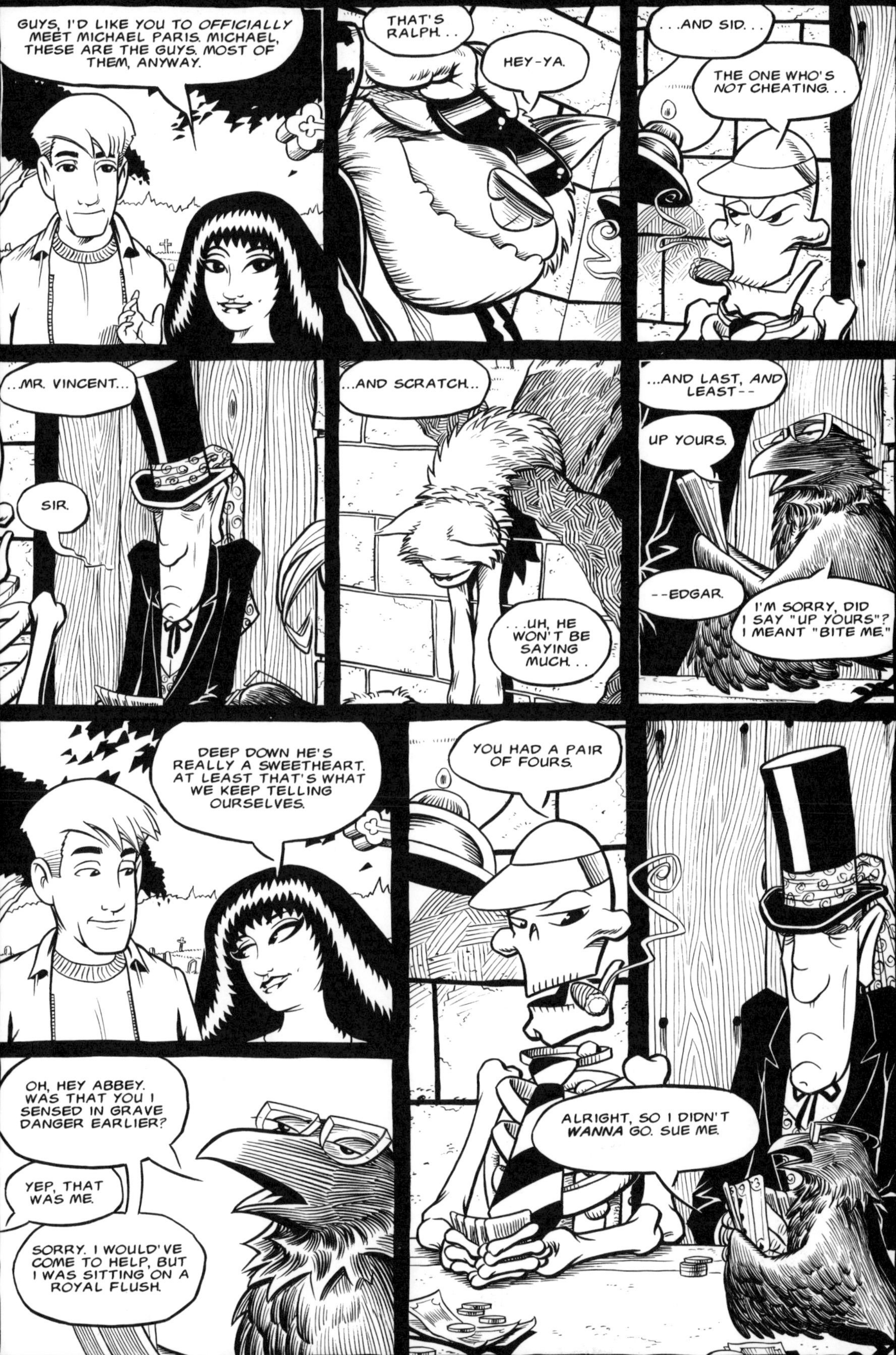
GUYS, I'D LIKE YOU TO *OFFICIALLY* MEET MICHAEL PARIS. MICHAEL, THESE ARE THE GUYS. MOST OF THEM, ANYWAY.
THAT'S RALPH. . .
HEY-YA.
. . .AND SID. . .
THE ONE WHO'S *NOT* CHEATING. . .
. . .MR. VINCENT. . .
SIR.
. . .AND SCRATCH. . .
. . .UH, HE WON'T BE SAYING MUCH. . .
. . .AND LAST, AND LEAST--
UP YOURS.
--EDGAR.
I'M SORRY, DID I SAY "UP YOURS"? I MEANT "BITE ME."
DEEP DOWN HE'S REALLY A SWEETHEART. AT LEAST THAT'S WHAT WE KEEP TELLING OURSELVES.
OH, HEY ABBEY. WAS THAT YOU I SENSED IN GRAVE DANGER EARLIER?
YEP, THAT WAS ME.
SORRY. I WOULD'VE COME TO HELP, BUT I WAS SITTING ON A ROYAL FLUSH.
YOU HAD A PAIR OF FOURS.
ALRIGHT, SO I DIDN'T *WANNA* GO. SUE ME.

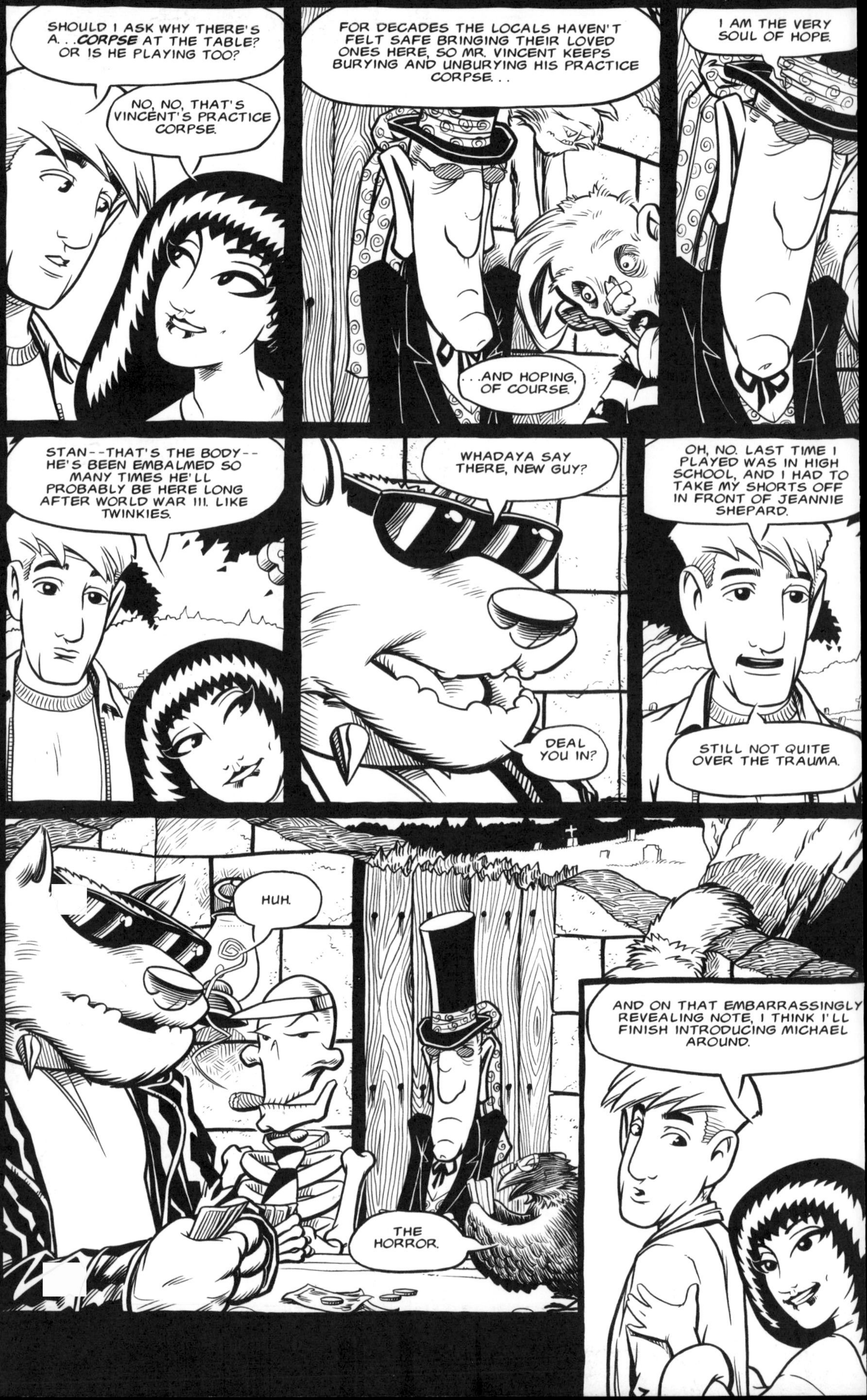
SHOULD I ASK WHY THERE'S A. . .CORPSE AT THE TABLE? OR IS HE PLAYING TOO?
NO, NO, THAT'S VINCENT'S PRACTICE CORPSE.
FOR DECADES THE LOCALS HAVEN'T FELT SAFE BRINGING THEIR LOVED ONES HERE, SO MR. VINCENT KEEPS BURYING AND UNBURYING HIS PRACTICE CORPSE. . .
. . .AND HOPING, OF COURSE.
I AM THE VERY SOUL OF HOPE.
STAN--THAT'S THE BODY--HE'S BEEN EMBALMED SO MANY TIMES HE'LL PROBABLY BE HERE LONG AFTER WORLD WAR III. LIKE TWINKIES.
WHADAYA SAY THERE, NEW GUY?
DEAL YOU IN?
OH, NO. LAST TIME I PLAYED WAS IN HIGH SCHOOL, AND I HAD TO TAKE MY SHORTS OFF IN FRONT OF JEANNIE SHEPARD.
STILL NOT QUITE OVER THE TRAUMA.
HUH.
THE HORROR.
AND ON THAT EMBARRASSINGLY REVEALING NOTE, I THINK I'LL FINISH INTRODUCING MICHAEL AROUND.

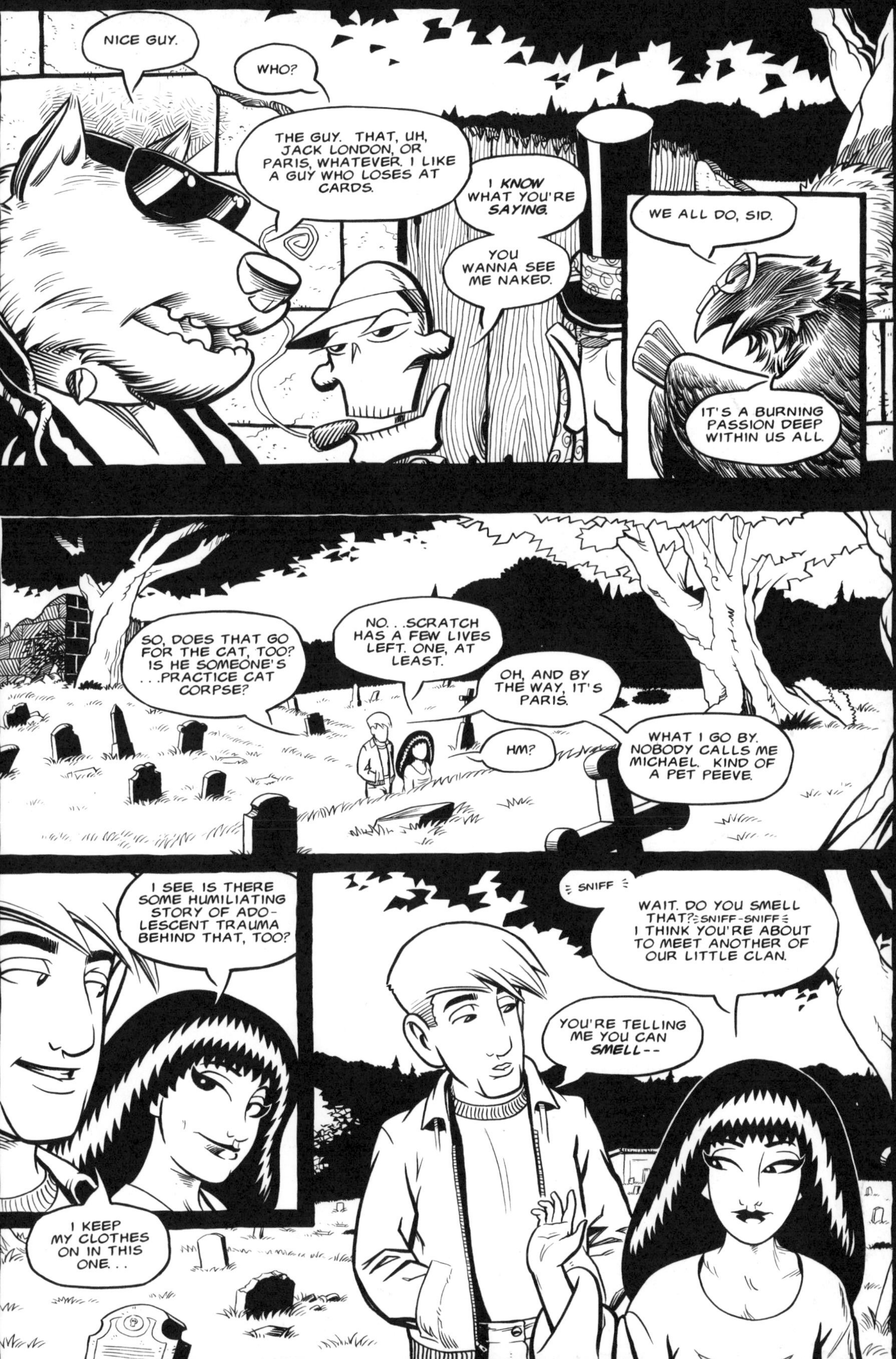
NICE GUY.
WHO?
THE GUY. THAT, UH, JACK LONDON, OR PARIS, WHATEVER. I LIKE A GUY WHO LOSES AT CARDS.
I *KNOW* WHAT YOU'RE *SAYING*.
YOU WANNA SEE ME NAKED.
WE ALL DO, SID.
IT'S A BURNING PASSION DEEP WITHIN US ALL.
SO, DOES THAT GO FOR THE CAT, TOO? IS HE SOMEONE'S . . .PRACTICE CAT CORPSE?
NO. . .SCRATCH HAS A FEW LIVES LEFT. ONE, AT LEAST.
OH, AND BY THE WAY, IT'S PARIS.
HM?
WHAT I GO BY. NOBODY CALLS ME MICHAEL. KIND OF A PET PEEVE.
I SEE. IS THERE SOME HUMILIATING STORY OF ADO-LESCENT TRAUMA BEHIND THAT, TOO?
I KEEP MY CLOTHES ON IN THIS ONE. . .
SNIFF
WAIT. DO YOU SMELL THAT? SNIFF-SNIFF I THINK YOU'RE ABOUT TO MEET ANOTHER OF OUR LITTLE CLAN.
YOU'RE TELLING ME YOU CAN *SMELL*--

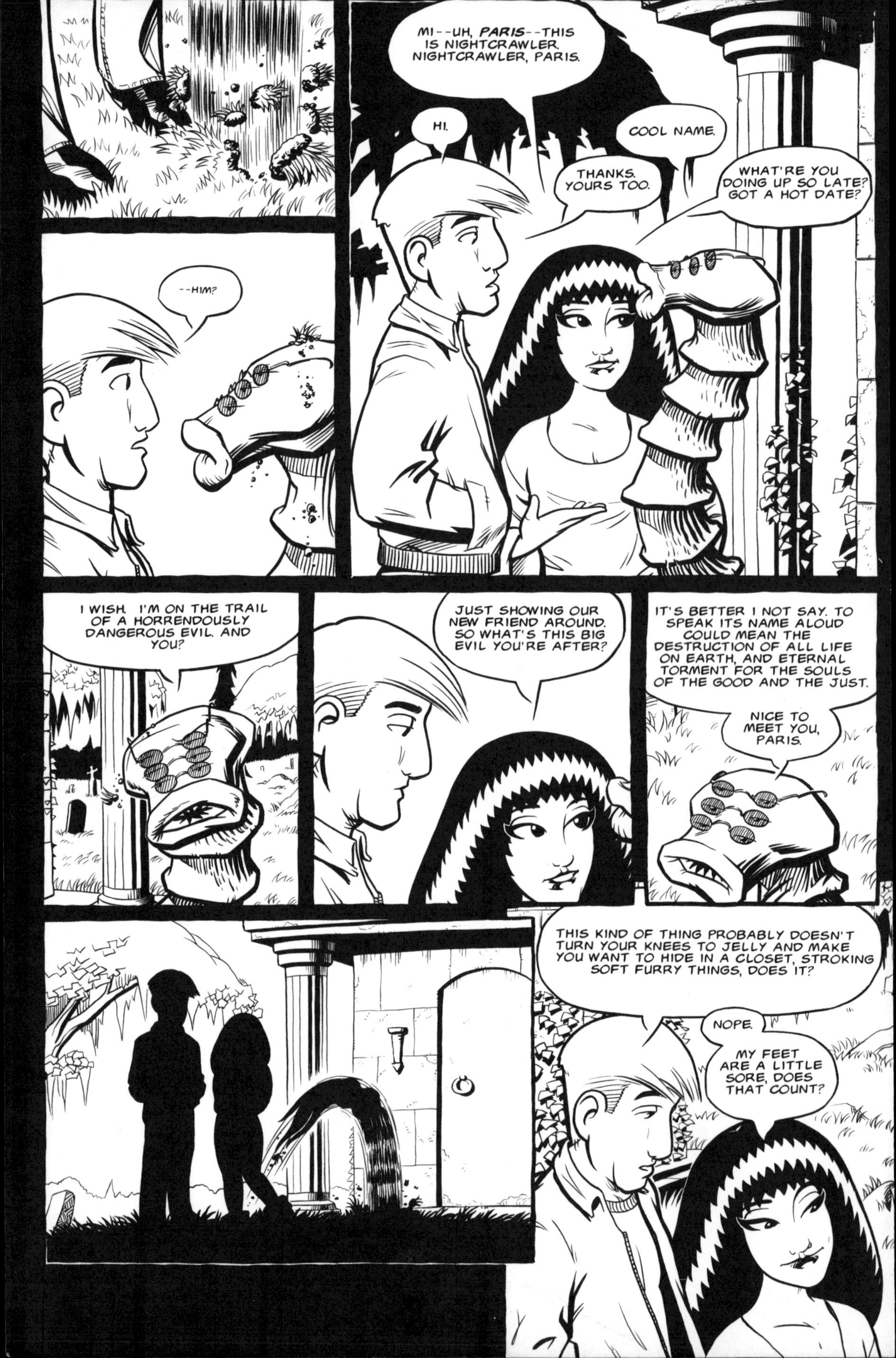
MI--UH, PARIS--THIS IS NIGHTCRAWLER. NIGHTCRAWLER, PARIS.
HI.
COOL NAME.
THANKS. YOURS TOO.
WHAT'RE YOU DOING UP SO LATE? GOT A HOT DATE?
--HIM?
I WISH. I'M ON THE TRAIL OF A HORRENDOUSLY DANGEROUS EVIL. AND YOU?
JUST SHOWING OUR NEW FRIEND AROUND. SO WHAT'S THIS BIG EVIL YOU'RE AFTER?
IT'S BETTER I NOT SAY. TO SPEAK ITS NAME ALOUD COULD MEAN THE DESTRUCTION OF ALL LIFE ON EARTH, AND ETERNAL TORMENT FOR THE SOULS OF THE GOOD AND THE JUST.
NICE TO MEET YOU, PARIS.
THIS KIND OF THING PROBABLY DOESN'T TURN YOUR KNEES TO JELLY AND MAKE YOU WANT TO HIDE IN A CLOSET, STROKING SOFT FURRY THINGS, DOES IT?
NOPE.
MY FEET ARE A LITTLE SORE, DOES THAT COUNT?

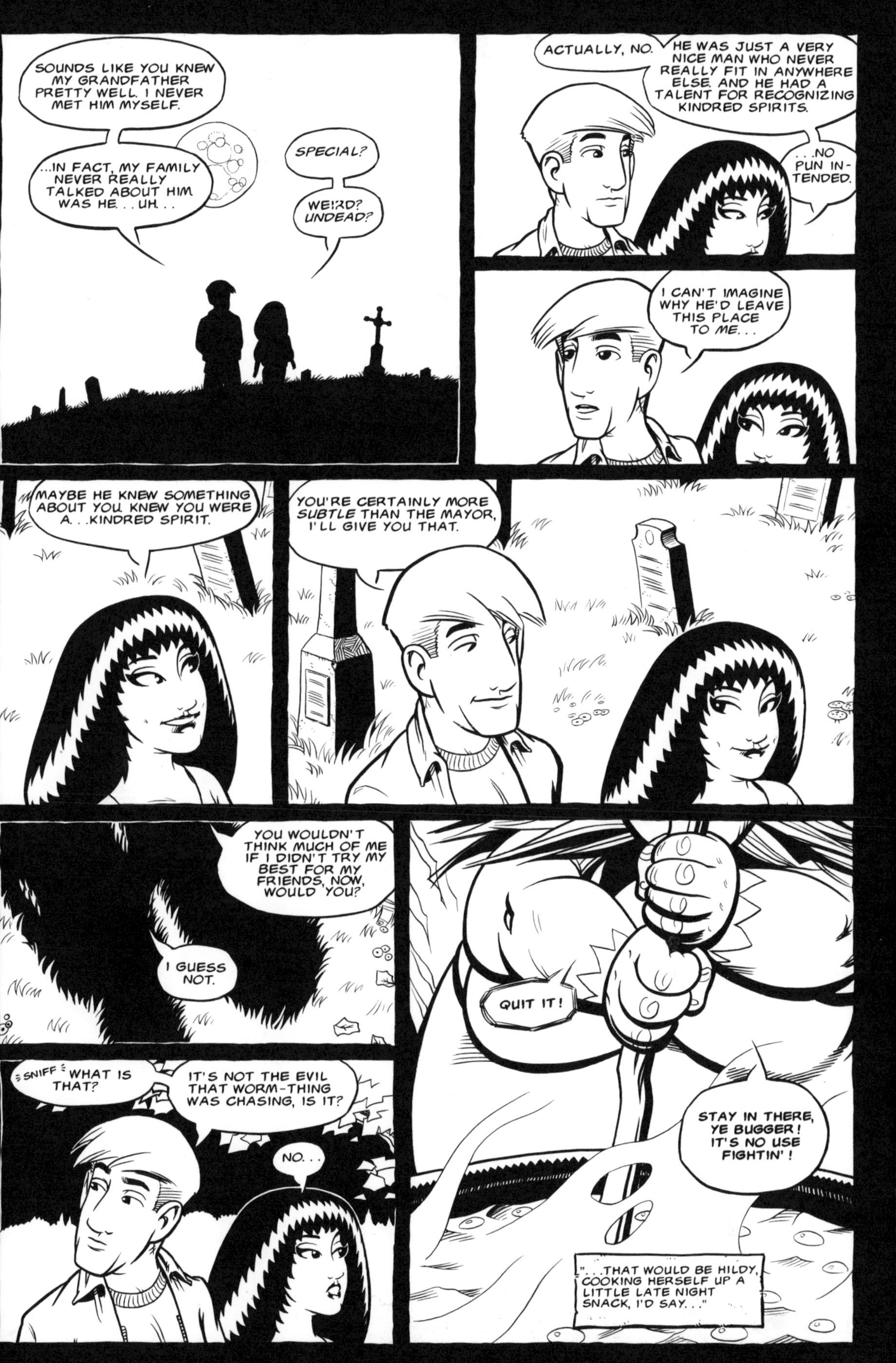
SOUNDS LIKE YOU KNEW MY GRANDFATHER PRETTY WELL. I NEVER MET HIM MYSELF.
...IN FACT, MY FAMILY NEVER REALLY TALKED ABOUT HIM WAS HE. . . UH. . .
SPECIAL?
WEIRD? UNDEAD?
ACTUALLY, NO.
HE WAS JUST A VERY NICE MAN WHO NEVER REALLY FIT IN ANYWHERE ELSE. AND HE HAD A TALENT FOR RECOGNIZING KINDRED SPIRITS.
. . .NO PUN IN-TENDED.
I CAN'T IMAGINE WHY HE'D LEAVE THIS PLACE TO ME. . .
MAYBE HE KNEW SOMETHING ABOUT YOU. KNEW YOU WERE A. . .KINDRED SPIRIT.
YOU'RE CERTAINLY MORE SUBTLE THAN THE MAYOR, I'LL GIVE YOU THAT.
YOU WOULDN'T THINK MUCH OF ME IF I DIDN'T TRY MY BEST FOR MY FRIENDS, NOW, WOULD YOU?
I GUESS NOT.
SNIFF WHAT IS THAT?
IT'S NOT THE EVIL THAT WORM-THING WAS CHASING, IS IT?
NO. . .
QUIT IT!
STAY IN THERE, YE BUGGER! IT'S NO USE FIGHTIN'!
". . .THAT WOULD BE HILDY, COOKING HERSELF UP A LITTLE LATE NIGHT SNACK, I'D SAY. . ."

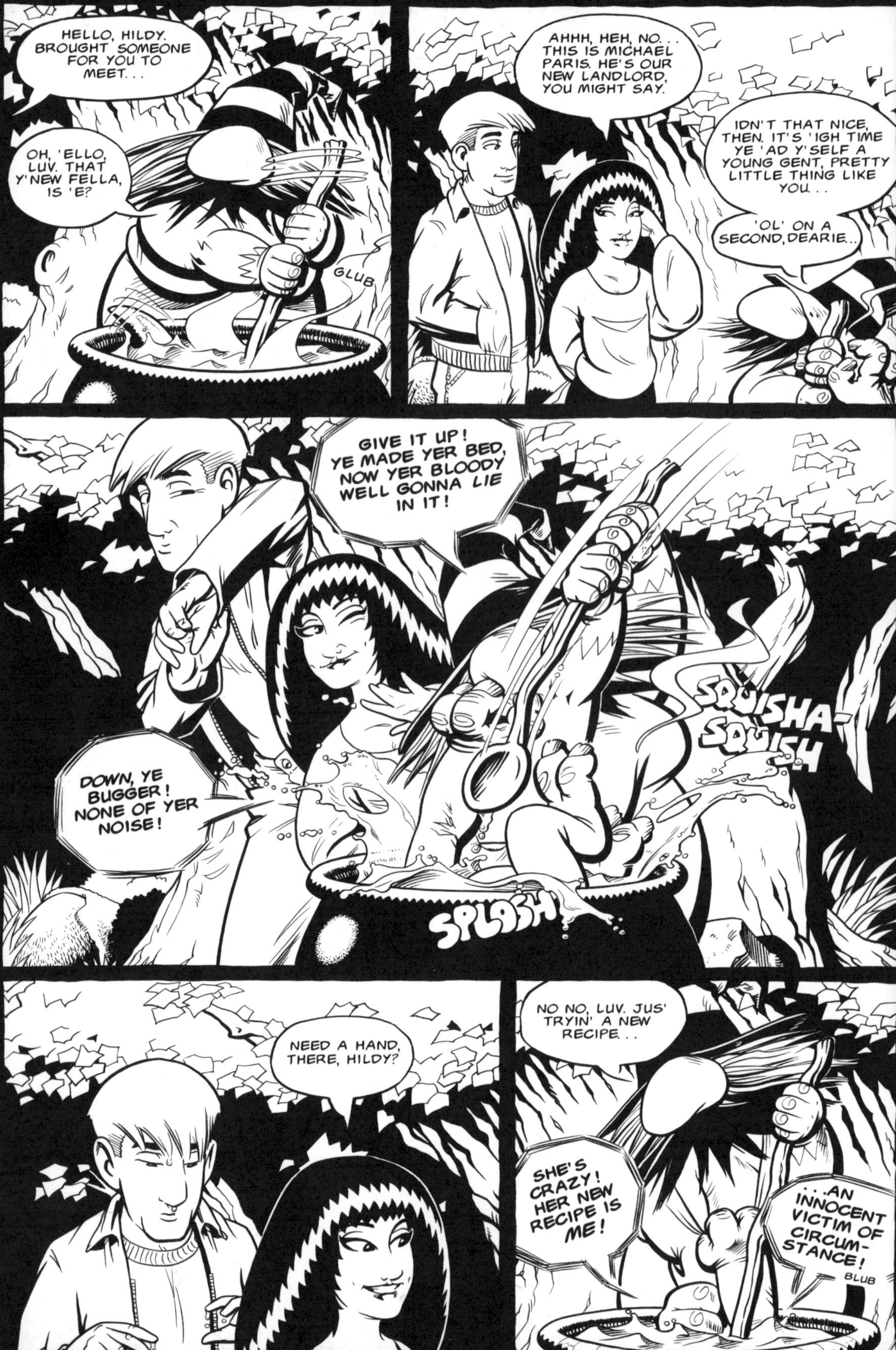
HELLO, HILDY. BROUGHT SOMEONE FOR YOU TO MEET. . .
OH, 'ELLO, LUV. THAT Y'NEW FELLA, IS 'E?
GLUB
AHHH, HEH, NO. . . THIS IS MICHAEL PARIS. HE'S OUR NEW LANDLORD, YOU MIGHT SAY.
IDN'T THAT NICE, THEN. IT'S 'IGH TIME YE 'AD Y'SELF A YOUNG GENT, PRETTY LITTLE THING LIKE YOU. . .
'OL' ON A SECOND, DEARIE. . .
GIVE IT UP! YE MADE YER BED, NOW YER BLOODY WELL GONNA LIE IN IT!
DOWN, YE BUGGER! NONE OF YER NOISE!
SQUISHA-SQUISH
SPLOSH
NEED A HAND, THERE, HILDY?
NO NO, LUV. JUS' TRYIN' A NEW RECIPE. . .
SHE'S CRAZY! HER NEW RECIPE IS ME!
. . .AN INNOCENT VICTIM OF CIRCUM-STANCE!
BLUB

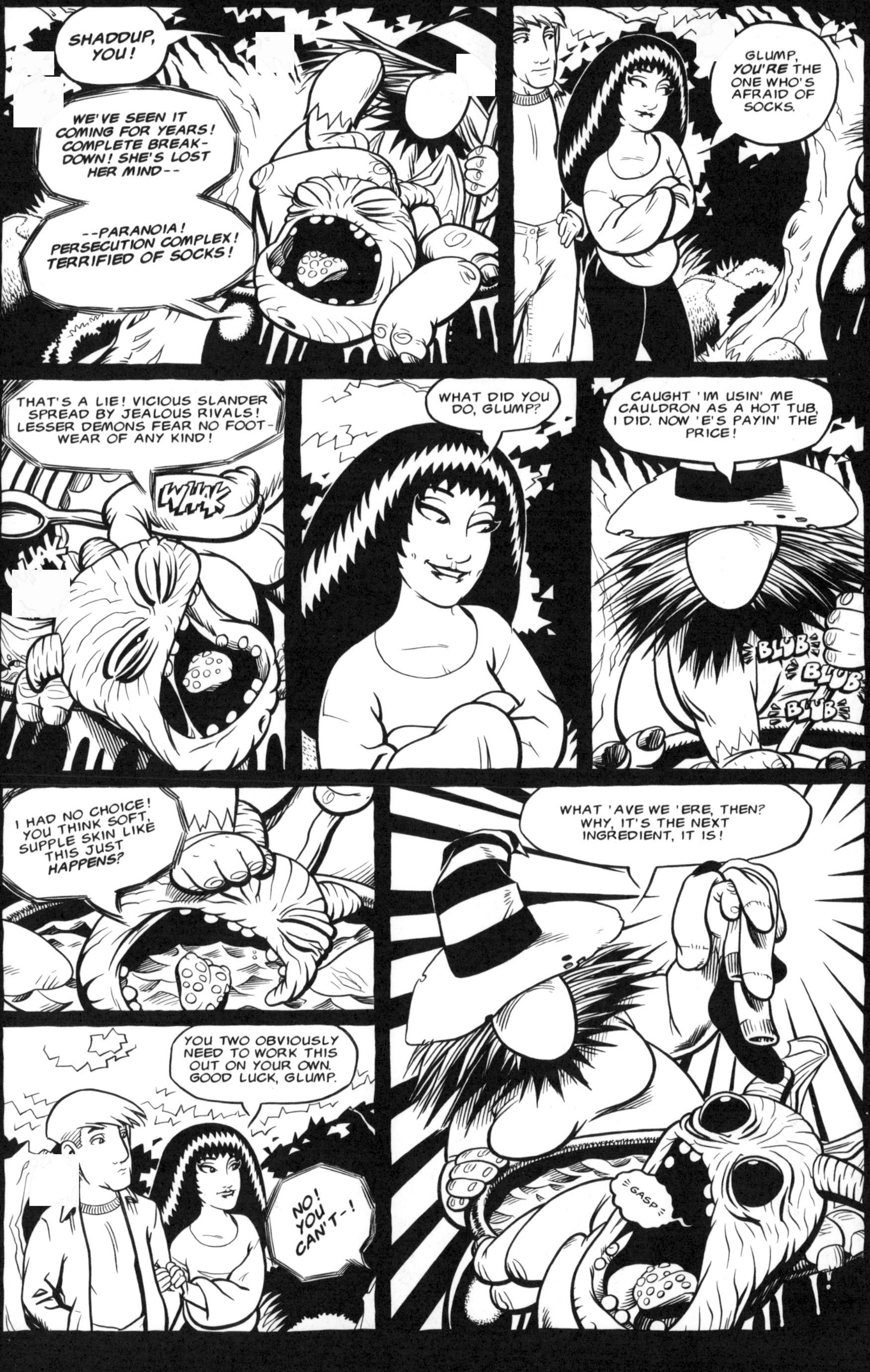
SHADDUP, YOU!
WE'VE SEEN IT COMING FOR YEARS! COMPLETE BREAK-DOWN! SHE'S LOST HER MIND--
--PARANOIA! PERSECUTION COMPLEX! TERRIFIED OF SOCKS!
GLUMP, YOU'RE THE ONE WHO'S AFRAID OF SOCKS.
THAT'S A LIE! VICIOUS SLANDER SPREAD BY JEALOUS RIVALS! LESSER DEMONS FEAR NO FOOT-WEAR OF ANY KIND!
WHAT DID YOU DO, GLUMP?
CAUGHT 'IM USIN' ME CAULDRON AS A HOT TUB, I DID. NOW 'E'S PAYIN' THE PRICE!
BLUB
BLUB
BLUB
I HAD NO CHOICE! YOU THINK SOFT, SUPPLE SKIN LIKE THIS JUST HAPPENS?
YOU TWO OBVIOUSLY NEED TO WORK THIS OUT ON YOUR OWN. GOOD LUCK, GLUMP.
NO! YOU CAN'T-!
WHAT 'AVE WE 'ERE, THEN? WHY, IT'S THE NEXT INGREDIENT, IT IS!
GASP

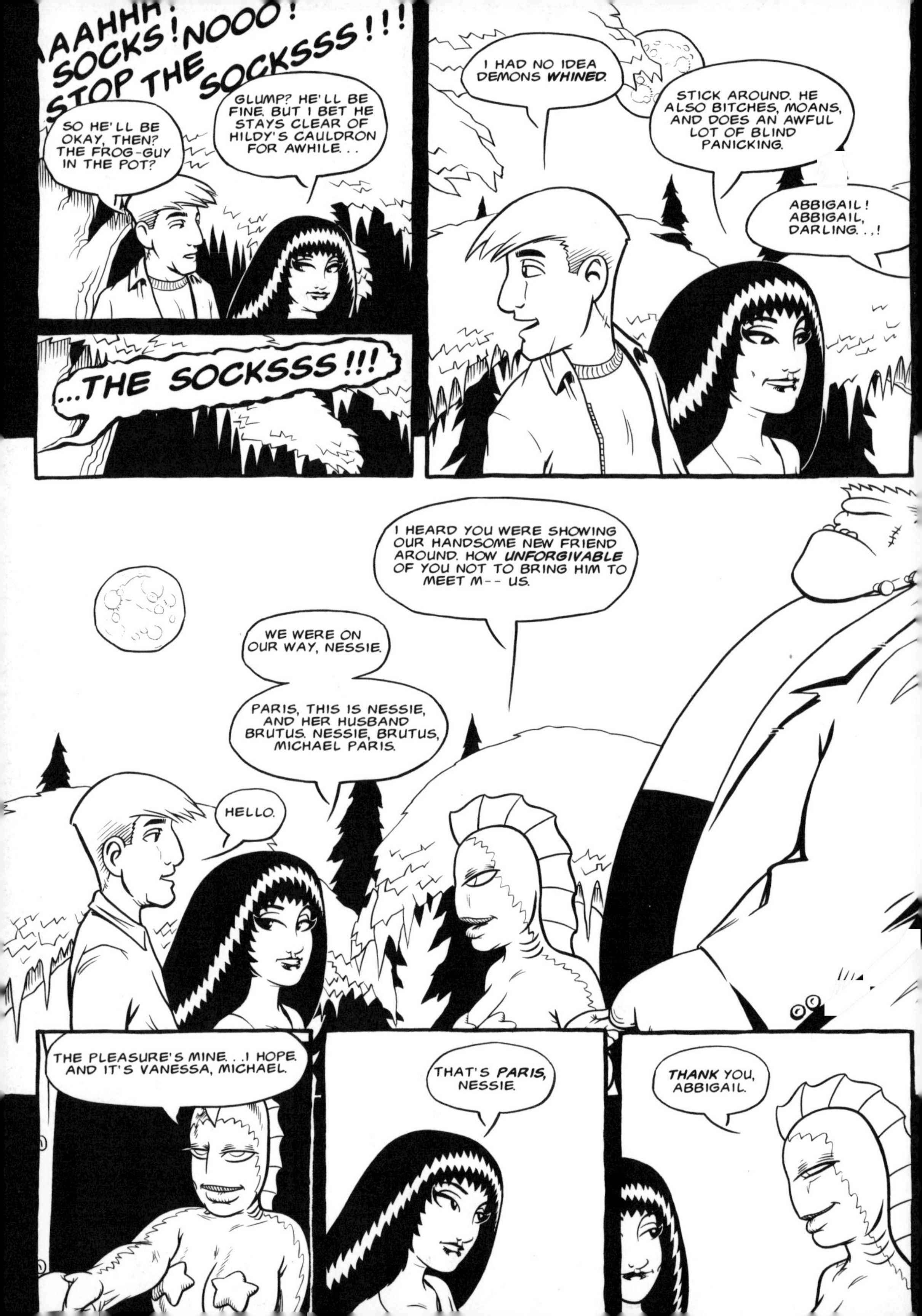
AAHHH! SOCKS! NOOO! STOP THE SOCKSSS!!!
SO HE'LL BE OKAY, THEN? THE FROG-GUY IN THE POT?
GLUMP? HE'LL BE FINE. BUT I BET HE STAYS CLEAR OF HILDY'S CAULDRON FOR AWHILE...
...THE SOCKSSS!!!
I HAD NO IDEA DEMONS WHINED.
STICK AROUND. HE ALSO BITCHES, MOANS, AND DOES AN AWFUL LOT OF BLIND PANICKING.
ABBIGAIL! ABBIGAIL, DARLING..,!
I HEARD YOU WERE SHOWING OUR HANDSOME NEW FRIEND AROUND. HOW UNFORGIVABLE OF YOU NOT TO BRING HIM TO MEET M-- US.
WE WERE ON OUR WAY, NESSIE.
PARIS, THIS IS NESSIE, AND HER HUSBAND BRUTUS. NESSIE, BRUTUS, MICHAEL PARIS.
HELLO.
THE PLEASURE'S MINE...I HOPE. AND IT'S VANESSA, MICHAEL.
THAT'S PARIS, NESSIE.
THANK YOU, ABBIGAIL.

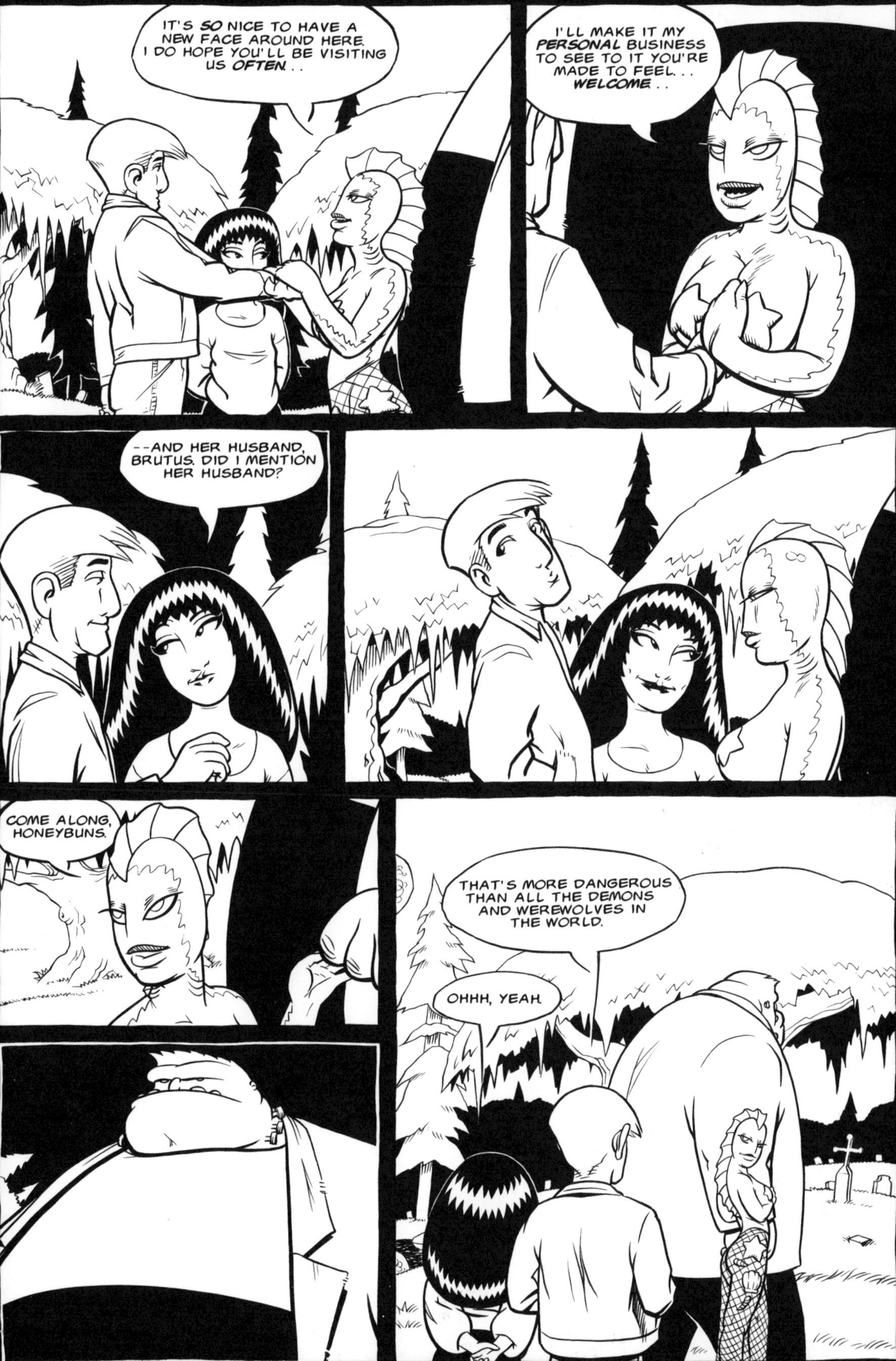
IT'S SO NICE TO HAVE A NEW FACE AROUND HERE. I DO HOPE YOU'LL BE VISITING US OFTEN . .
I'LL MAKE IT MY PERSONAL BUSINESS TO SEE TO IT YOU'RE MADE TO FEEL. . . WELCOME . .
--AND HER HUSBAND, BRUTUS. DID I MENTION HER HUSBAND?
COME ALONG, HONEYBUNS.
THAT'S MORE DANGEROUS THAN ALL THE DEMONS AND WEREWOLVES IN THE WORLD.
OHHH, YEAH.

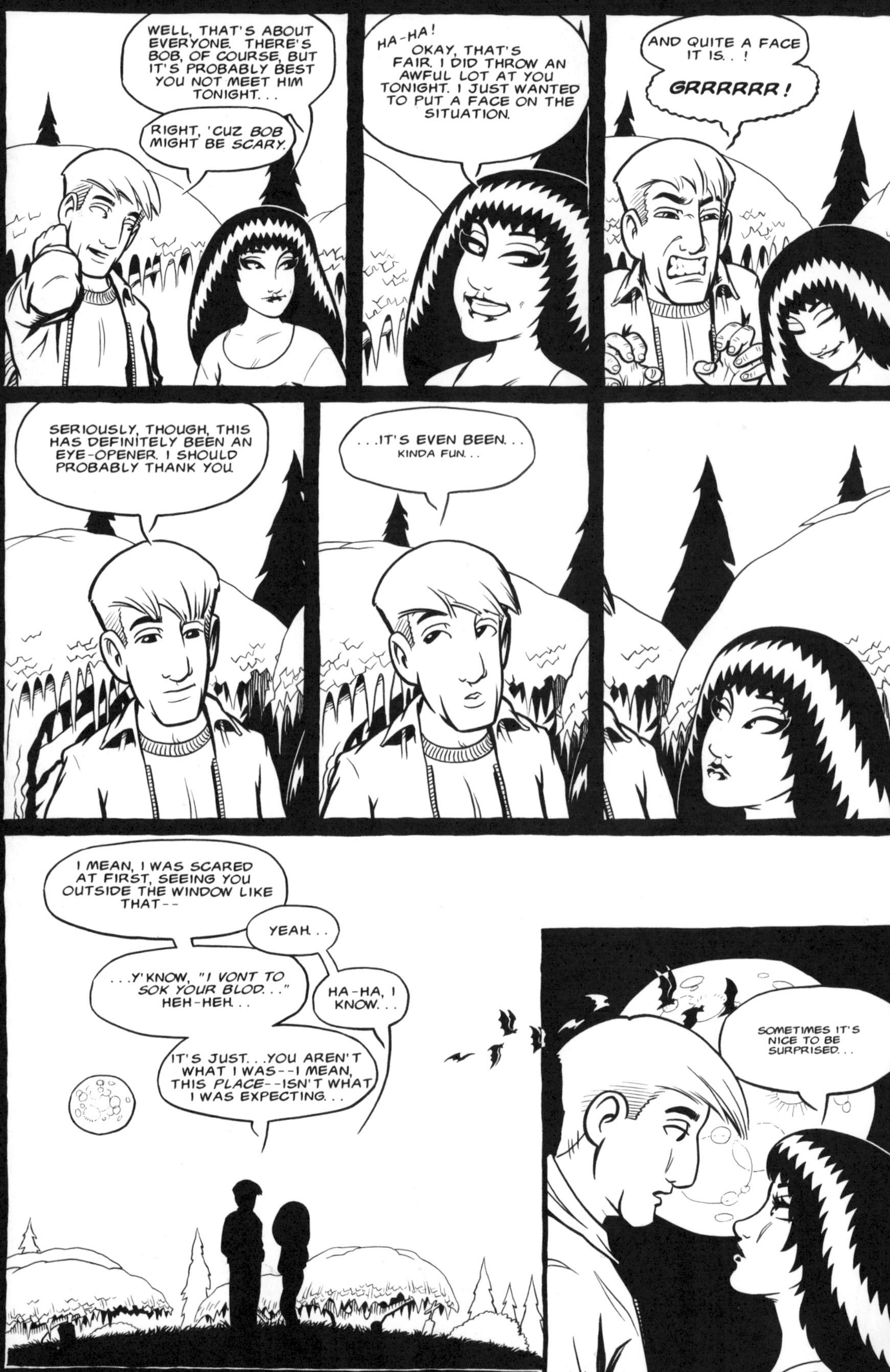
WELL, THAT'S ABOUT EVERYONE. THERE'S BOB, OF COURSE, BUT IT'S PROBABLY BEST YOU NOT MEET HIM TONIGHT...
RIGHT, 'CUZ BOB MIGHT BE SCARY.
HA-HA!
OKAY, THAT'S FAIR. I DID THROW AN AWFUL LOT AT YOU TONIGHT. I JUST WANTED TO PUT A FACE ON THE SITUATION.
AND QUITE A FACE IT IS..!
GRRRRRR!
SERIOUSLY, THOUGH, THIS HAS DEFINITELY BEEN AN EYE-OPENER. I SHOULD PROBABLY THANK YOU.
...IT'S EVEN BEEN... KINDA FUN...
I MEAN, I WAS SCARED AT FIRST, SEEING YOU OUTSIDE THE WINDOW LIKE THAT--
YEAH..
...Y'KNOW, "I VONT TO SOK YOUR BLOD..." HEH-HEH..
HA-HA, I KNOW...
IT'S JUST...YOU AREN'T WHAT I WAS--I MEAN, THIS PLACE--ISN'T WHAT I WAS EXPECTING...
SOMETIMES IT'S NICE TO BE SURPRISED...

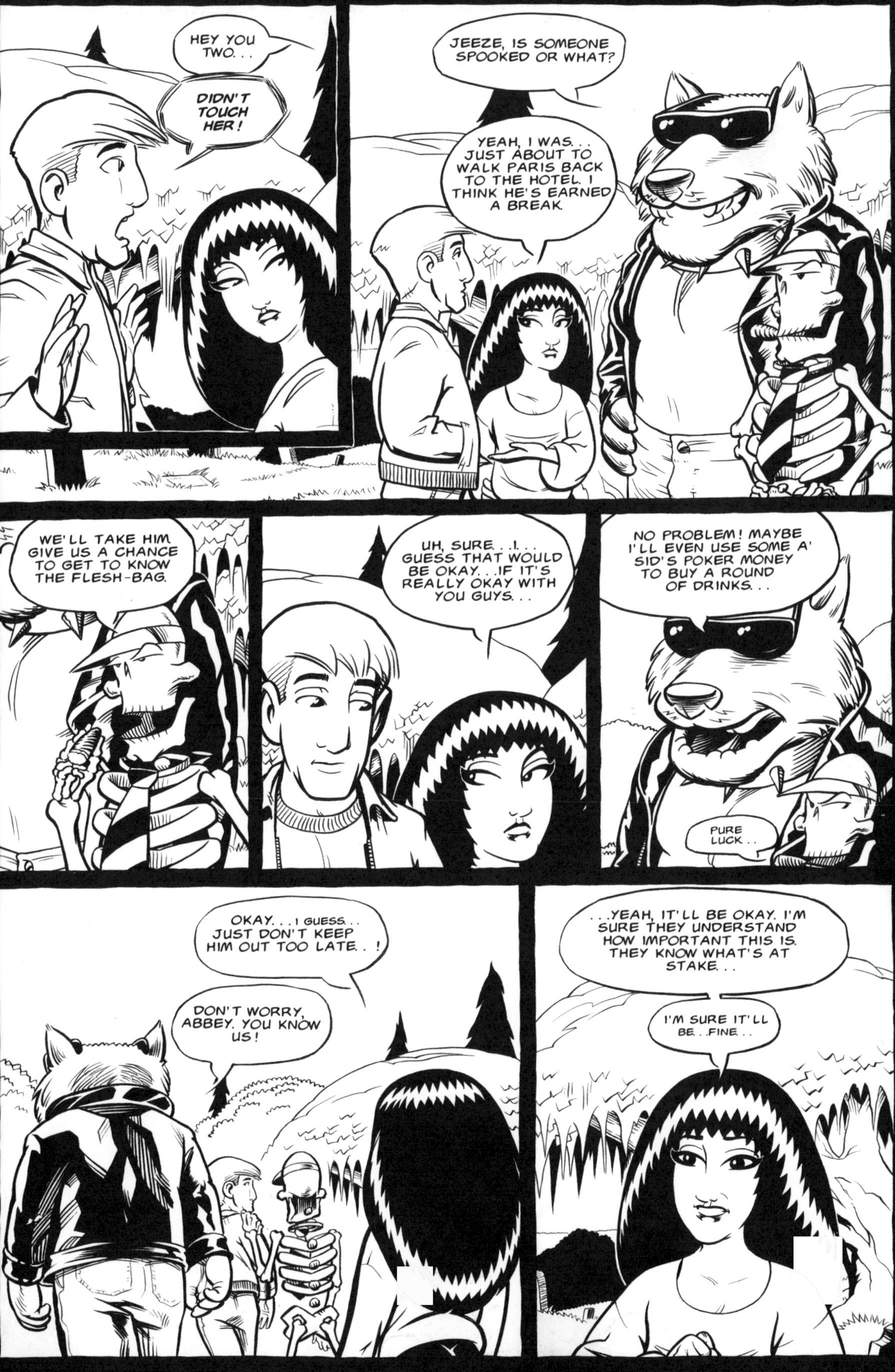
HEY YOU TWO. . .
DIDN'T TOUCH HER!
JEEZE, IS SOMEONE SPOOKED OR WHAT?
YEAH, I WAS. . . JUST ABOUT TO WALK PARIS BACK TO THE HOTEL. I THINK HE'S EARNED A BREAK.
WE'LL TAKE HIM. GIVE US A CHANCE TO GET TO KNOW THE FLESH-BAG.
UH, SURE. . .I. . . GUESS THAT WOULD BE OKAY. . .IF IT'S REALLY OKAY WITH YOU GUYS. . .
NO PROBLEM! MAYBE I'LL EVEN USE SOME A' SID'S POKER MONEY TO BUY A ROUND OF DRINKS. . .
PURE LUCK. .
OKAY. . . I GUESS. . . JUST DON'T KEEP HIM OUT TOO LATE. . !
DON'T WORRY, ABBEY. YOU KNOW US!
. . .YEAH, IT'LL BE OKAY. I'M SURE THEY UNDERSTAND HOW IMPORTANT THIS IS. THEY KNOW WHAT'S AT STAKE. . .
I'M SURE IT'LL BE. . FINE. . .

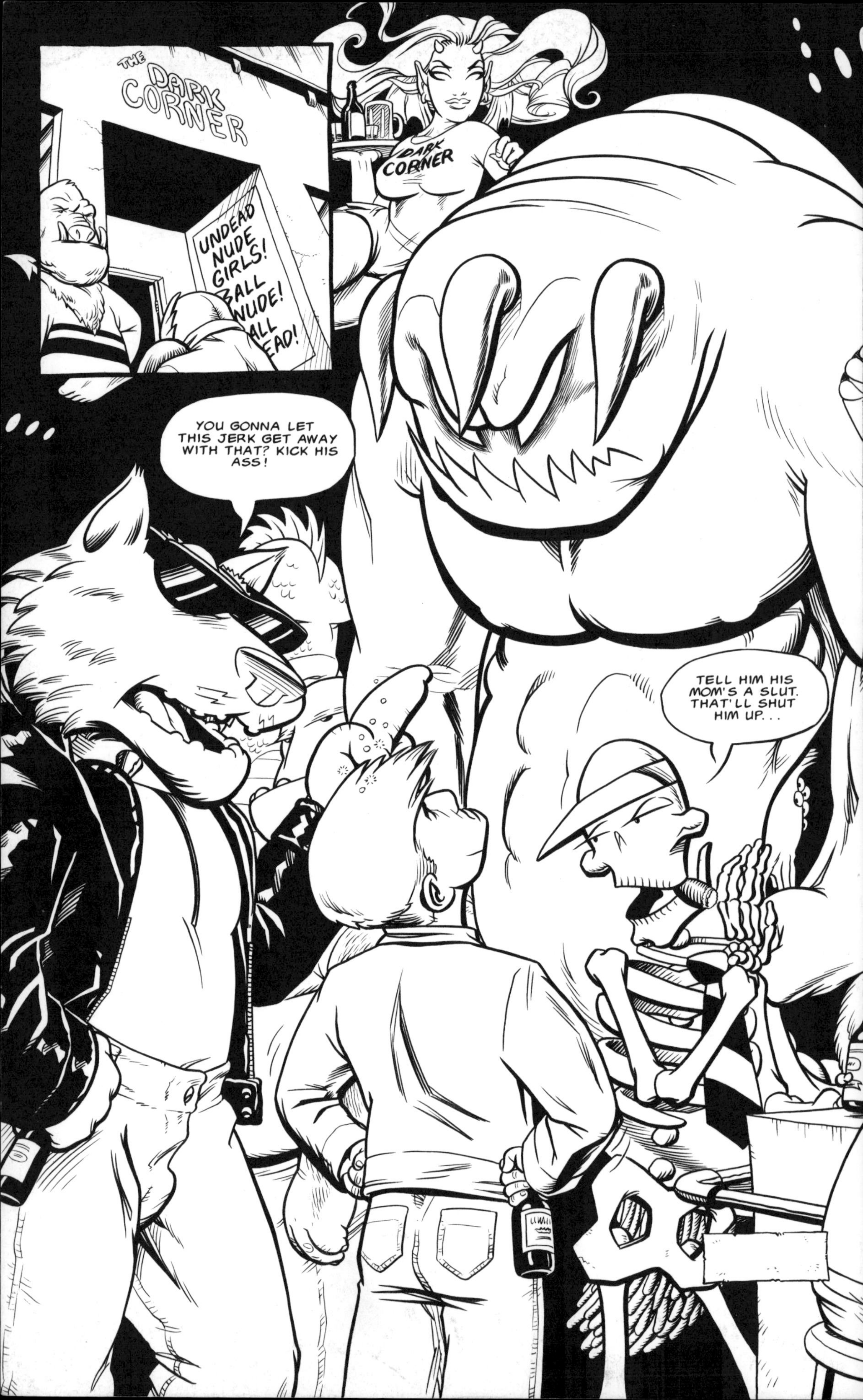
THE DARK CORNER
UNDEAD NUDE GIRLS! ALL NUDE! ALL DEAD!
DARK CORNER
YOU GONNA LET THIS JERK GET AWAY WITH THAT? KICK HIS ASS!
TELL HIM HIS MOM'S A SLUT. THAT'LL SHUT HIM UP...

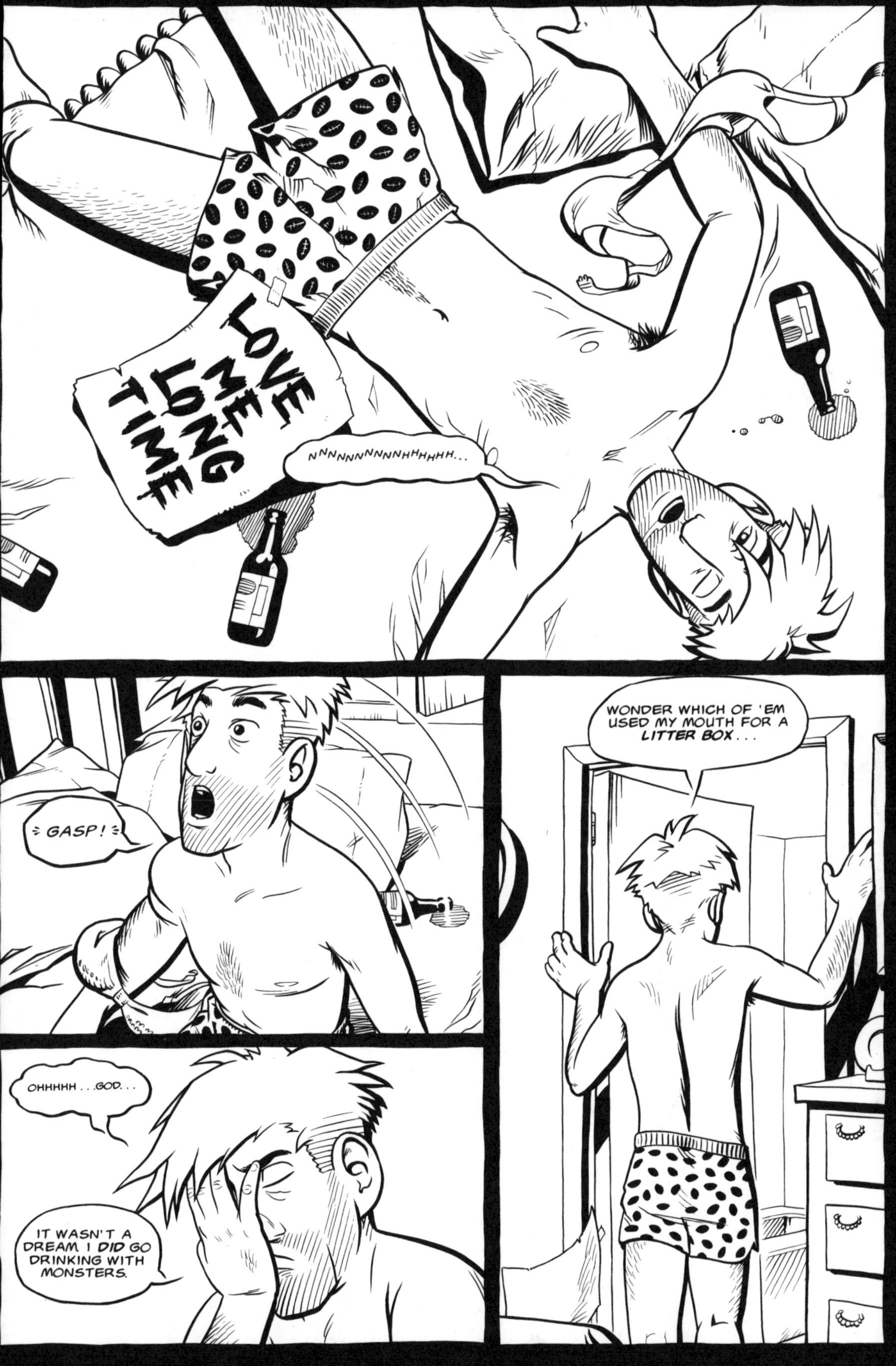
LOVE ME LONG TIME
NNNNNNNNNNHHHHHH...
GASP!
WONDER WHICH OF 'EM USED MY MOUTH FOR A LITTER BOX...
OHHHHH...GOD...
IT WASN'T A DREAM. I DID GO DRINKING WITH MONSTERS.

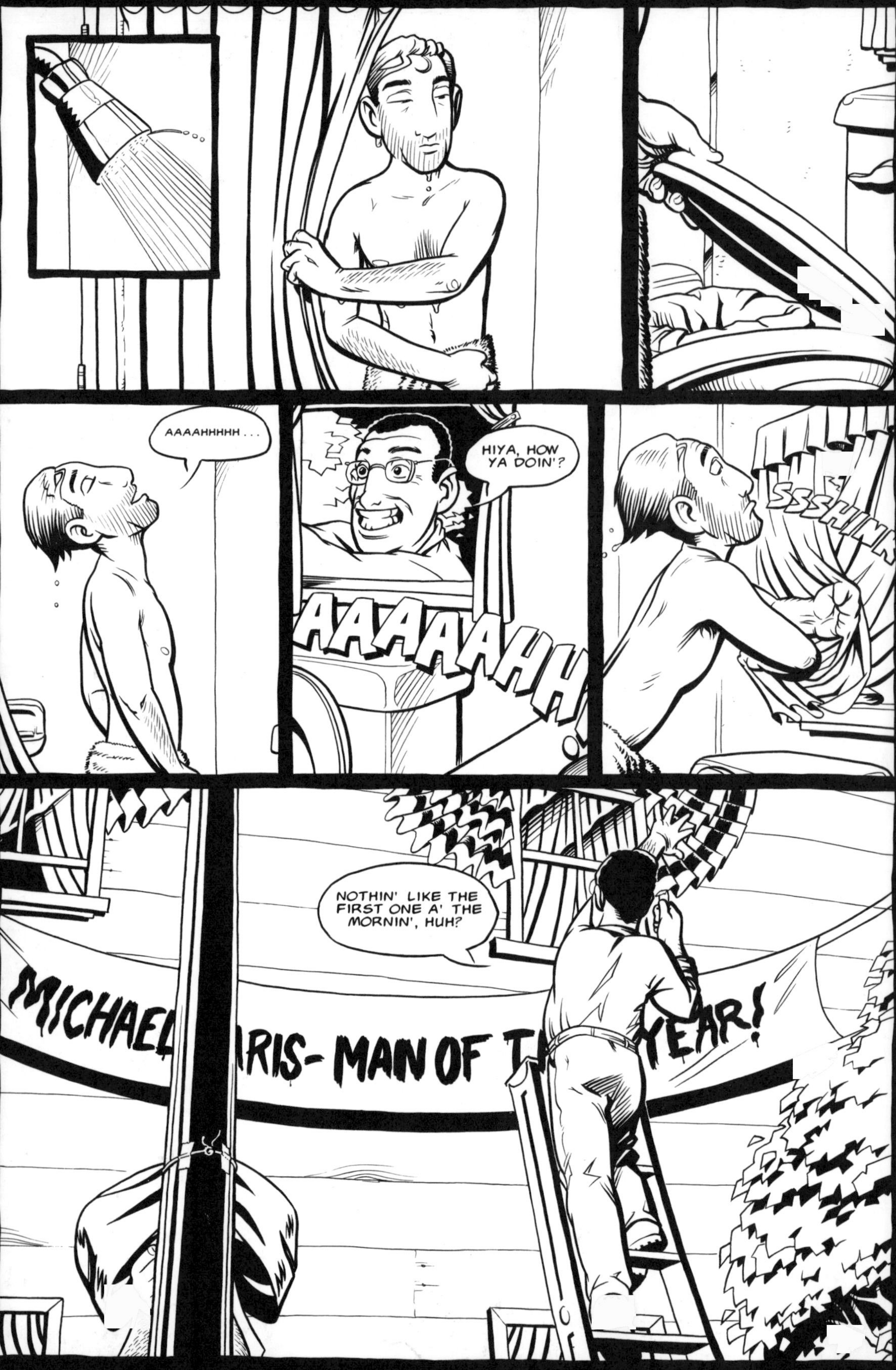
AAAAHHHHH . . .
HIYA, HOW YA DOIN'?
AAAAAAAHH
SSSHINK
NOTHIN' LIKE THE FIRST ONE A' THE MORNIN', HUH?
MICHAEL ARIS- MAN OF T YEAR!

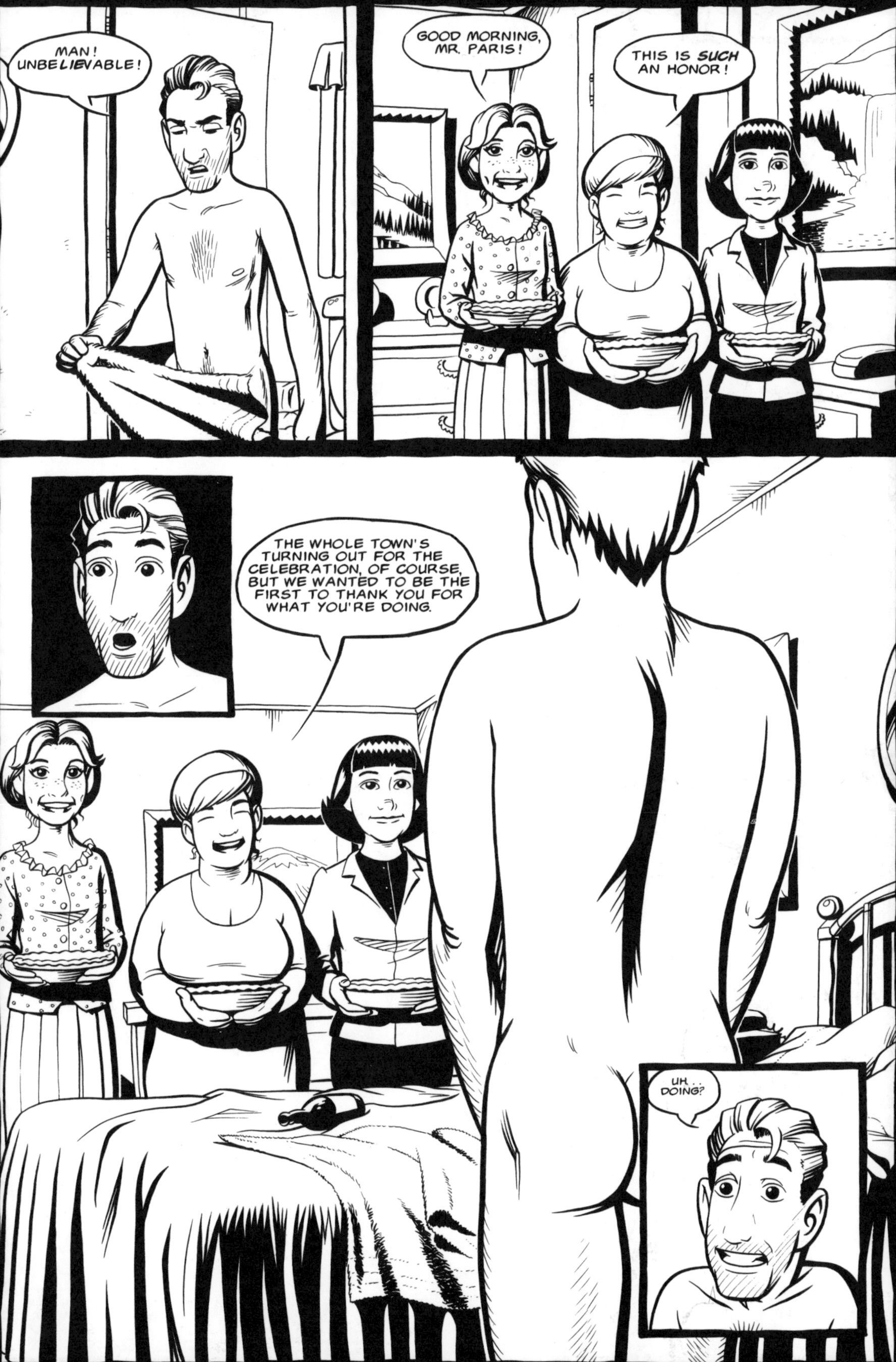
MAN! UNBELIEVABLE!
GOOD MORNING, MR. PARIS!
THIS IS SUCH AN HONOR!
THE WHOLE TOWN'S TURNING OUT FOR THE CELEBRATION, OF COURSE, BUT WE WANTED TO BE THE FIRST TO THANK YOU FOR WHAT YOU'RE DOING.
UH.. DOING?

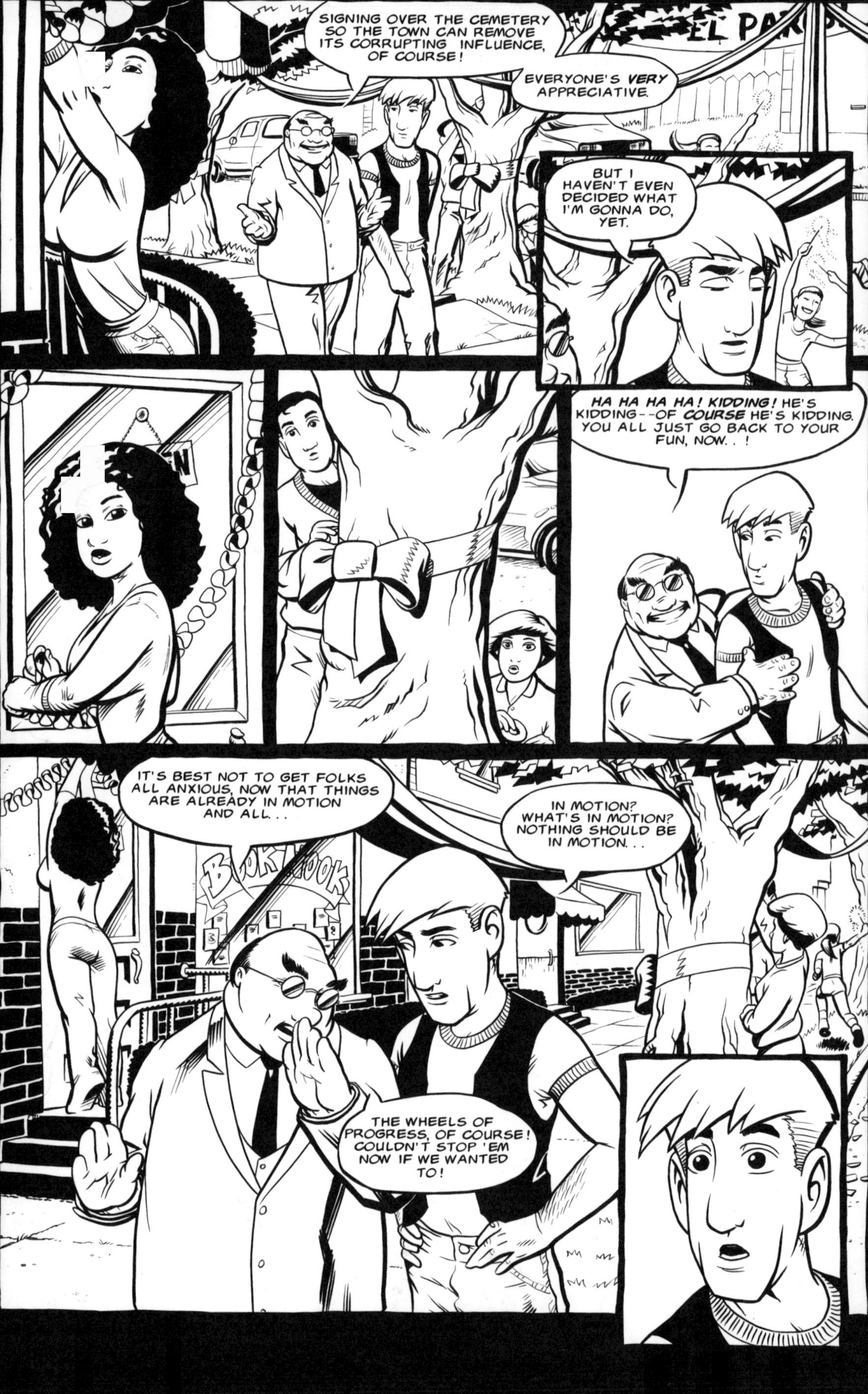

SIGNING OVER THE CEMETERY SO THE TOWN CAN REMOVE ITS CORRUPTING INFLUENCE, OF COURSE!
EVERYONE'S VERY APPRECIATIVE.
BUT I HAVEN'T EVEN DECIDED WHAT I'M GONNA DO, YET.
HA HA HA HA! KIDDING! HE'S KIDDING--OF COURSE HE'S KIDDING. YOU ALL JUST GO BACK TO YOUR FUN, NOW.. !
IT'S BEST NOT TO GET FOLKS ALL ANXIOUS, NOW THAT THINGS ARE ALREADY IN MOTION AND ALL...
IN MOTION? WHAT'S IN MOTION? NOTHING SHOULD BE IN MOTION...
THE WHEELS OF PROGRESS, OF COURSE! COULDN'T STOP 'EM NOW IF WE WANTED TO!

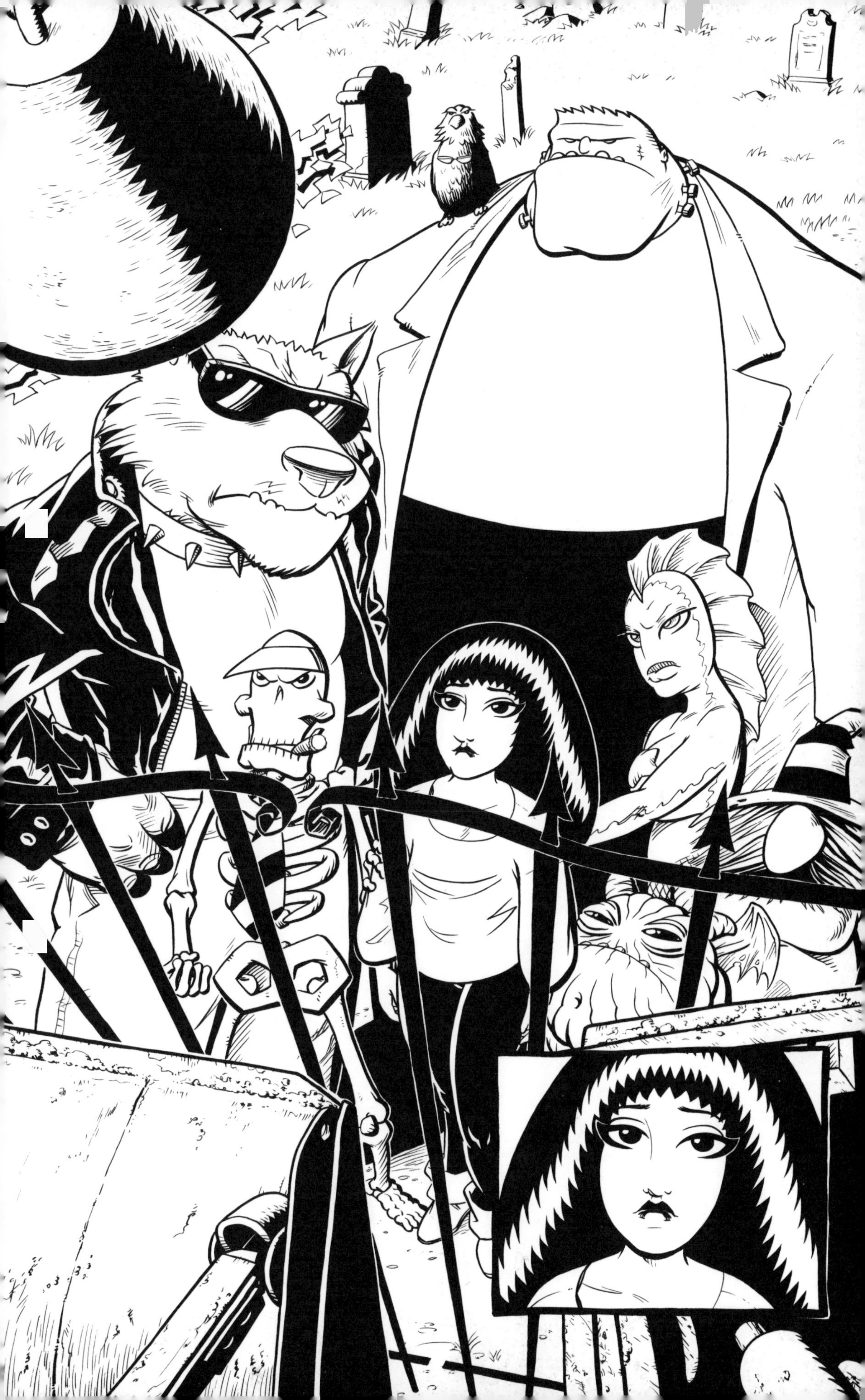

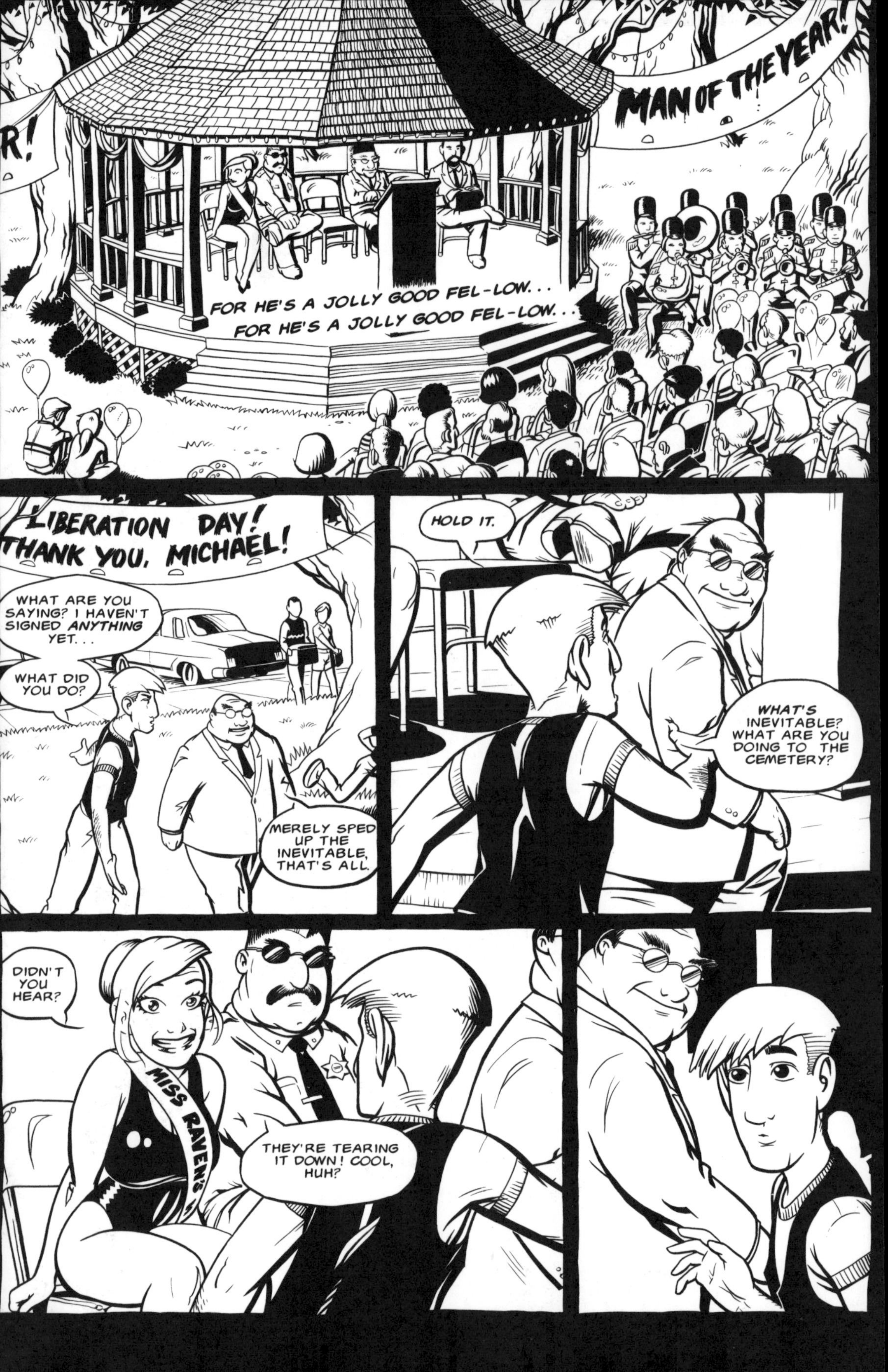
MAN OF THE YEAR!
R!
FOR HE'S A JOLLY GOOD FEL-LOW...
FOR HE'S A JOLLY GOOD FEL-LOW...
LIBERATION DAY! THANK YOU, MICHAEL!
WHAT ARE YOU SAYING? I HAVEN'T SIGNED *ANYTHING* YET...
WHAT DID YOU DO?
MERELY SPED UP THE INEVITABLE, THAT'S ALL.
HOLD IT.
WHAT'S INEVITABLE? WHAT ARE YOU DOING TO THE CEMETERY?
DIDN'T YOU HEAR?
MISS RAVEN'S
THEY'RE TEARING IT DOWN! COOL, HUH?

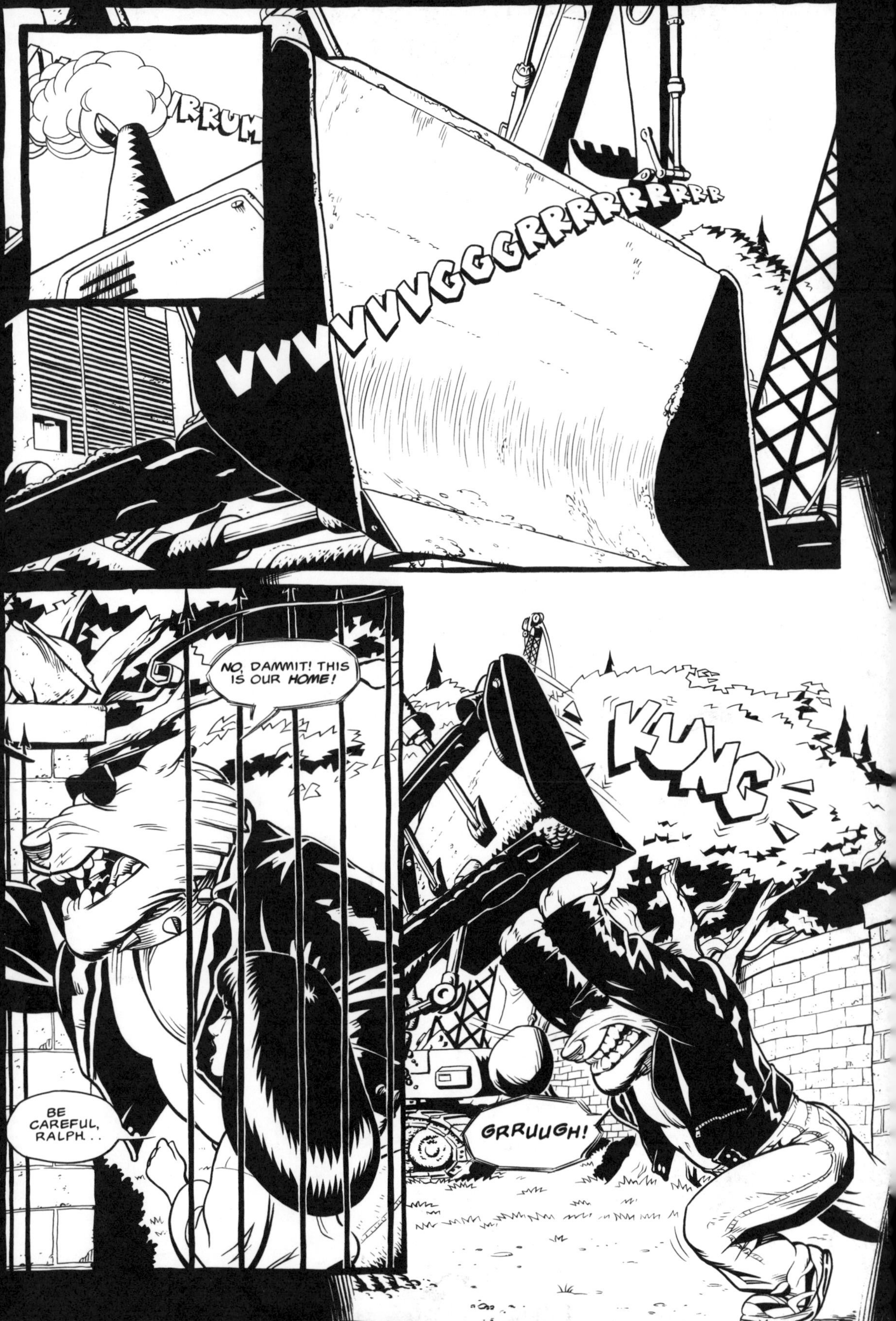
VRRUM
VVVVVVVVGGRRRRRRRRR
NO, DAMMIT! THIS IS OUR HOME!
KUNG
BE CAREFUL, RALPH. . .
GRRUUGH!

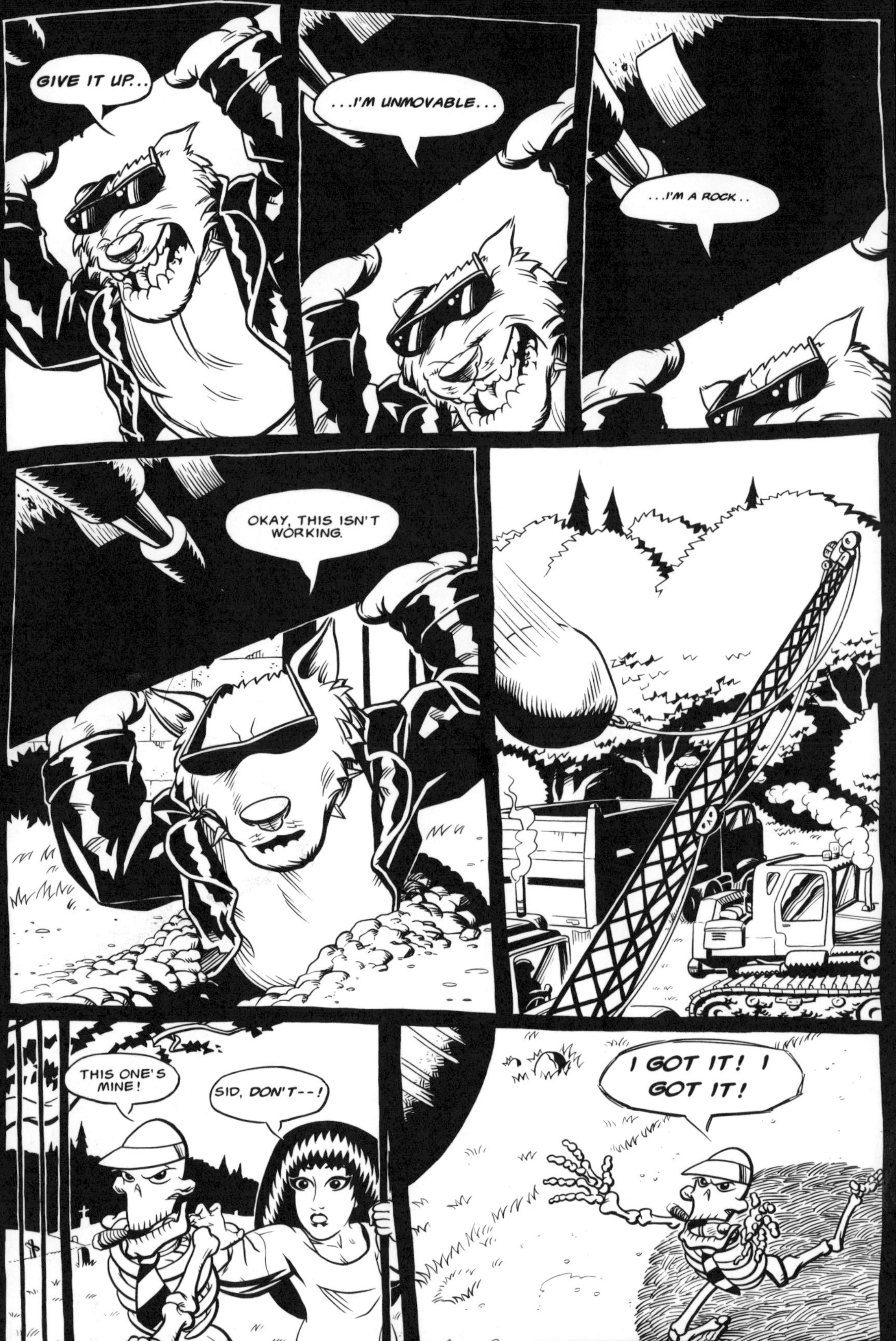
GIVE IT UP...
...I'M UNMOVABLE...
...I'M A ROCK..
OKAY, THIS ISN'T WORKING.
THIS ONE'S MINE!
SID, DON'T--!
I GOT IT! I GOT IT!

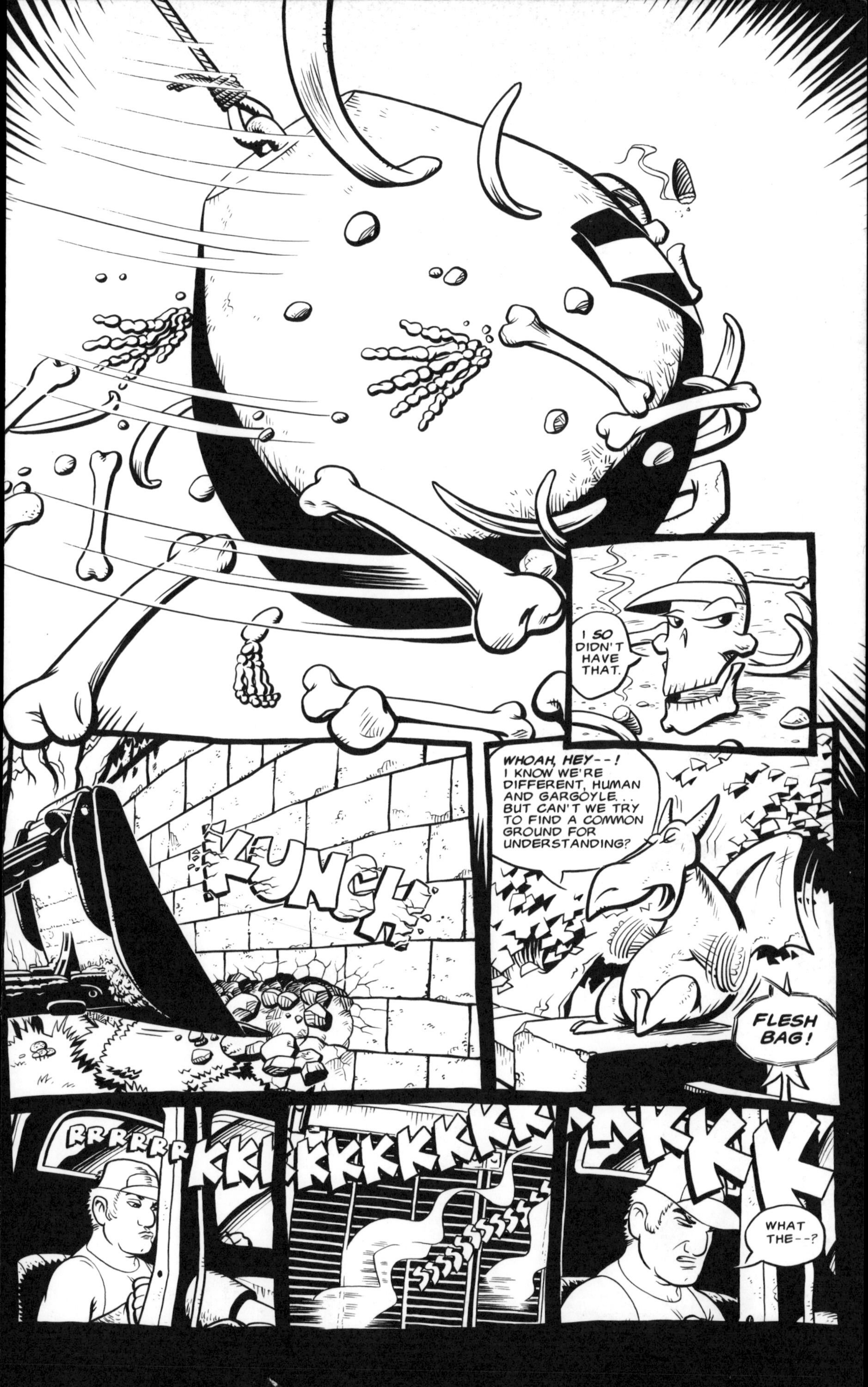
I SO DIDN'T HAVE THAT.
KUNCH
WHOAH, HEY--! I KNOW WE'RE DIFFERENT, HUMAN AND GARGOYLE.. BUT CAN'T WE TRY TO FIND A COMMON GROUND FOR UNDERSTANDING?
FLESH BAG!
RRRRRRRKKKKKKKKKKKKKKKK
WHAT THE--?

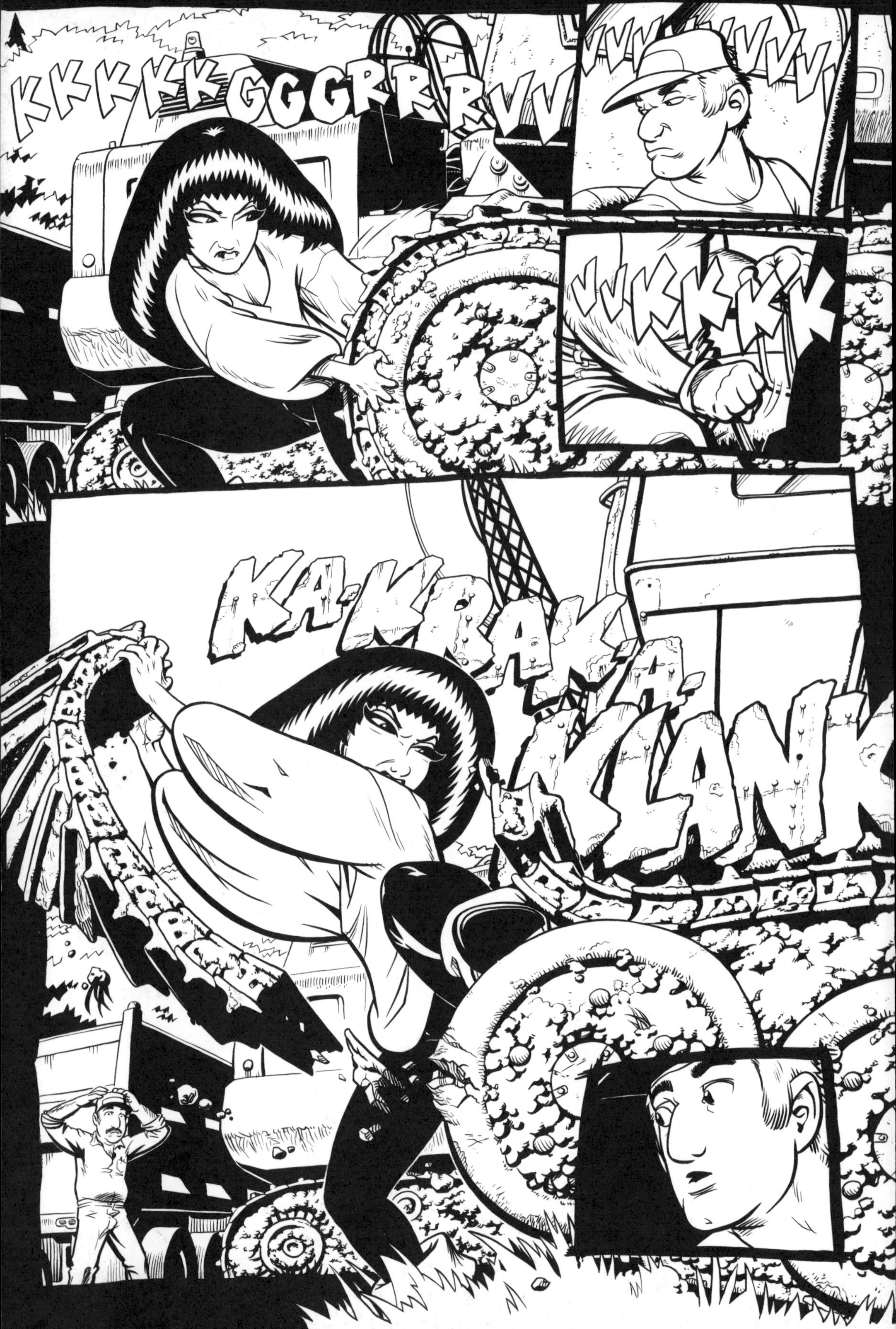
KKKKKGGGRRRVVV
VVKKKKK
KA-KRAK-A-KLANK

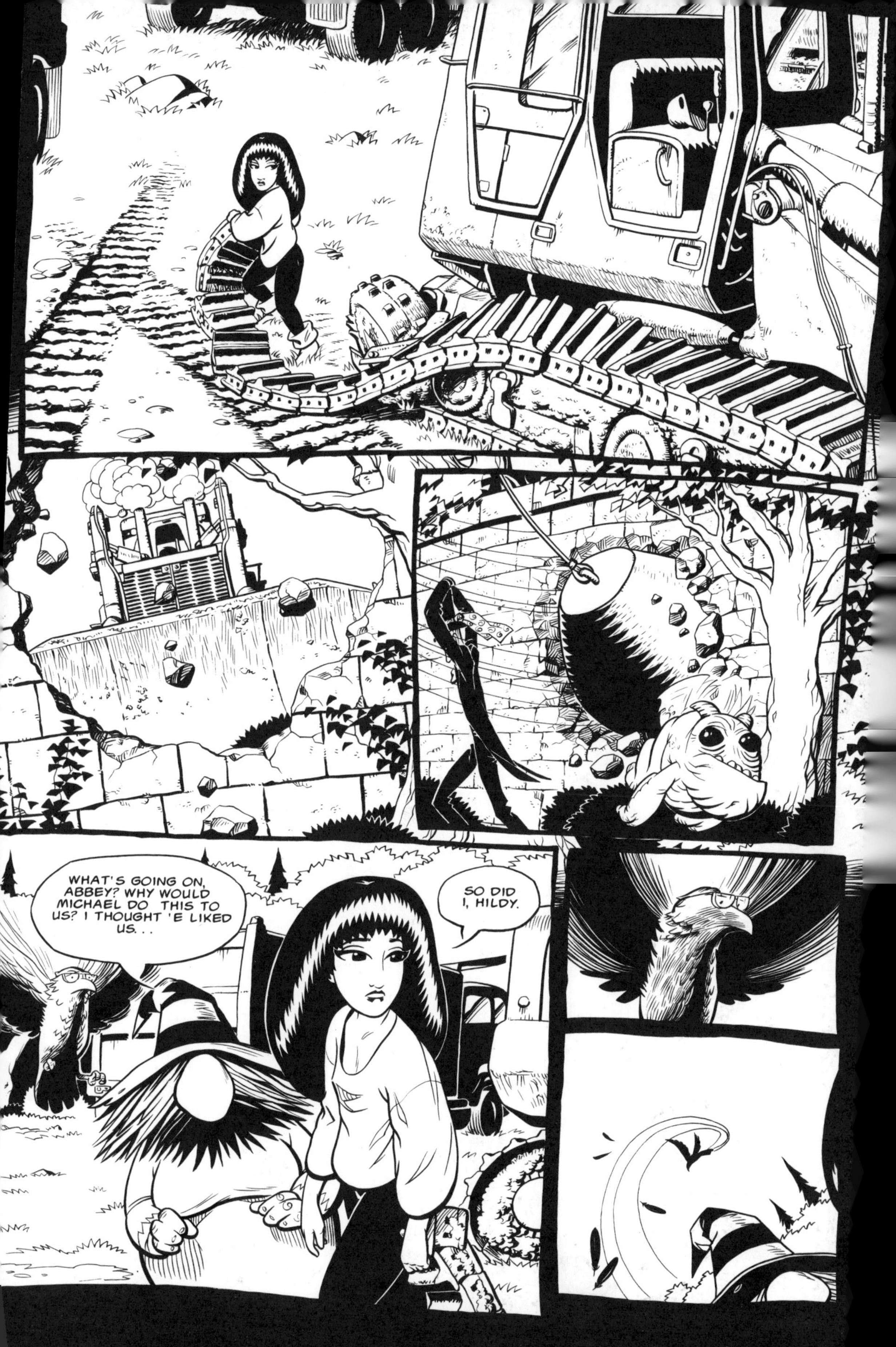
WHAT'S GOING ON, ABBEY? WHY WOULD MICHAEL DO THIS TO US? I THOUGHT 'E LIKED US. . .
SO DID I, HILDY.

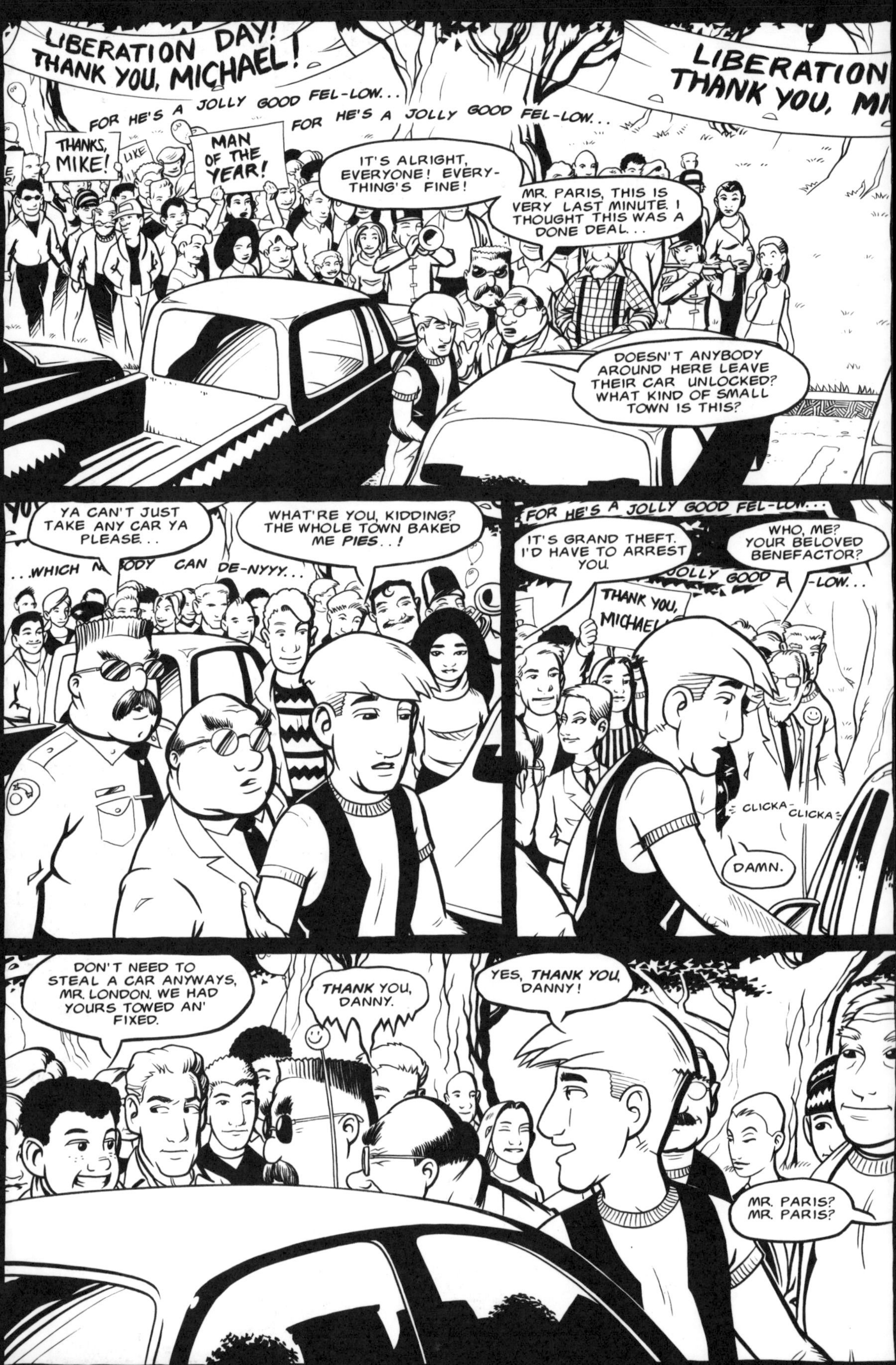
LIBERATION DAY! THANK YOU, MICHAEL!
LIBERATION
THANK YOU, MI
FOR HE'S A JOLLY GOOD FEL-LOW...
FOR HE'S A JOLLY GOOD FEL-LOW...
THANKS, MIKE!
MAN OF THE YEAR!
IT'S ALRIGHT, EVERYONE! EVERYTHING'S FINE!
MR. PARIS, THIS IS VERY LAST MINUTE. I THOUGHT THIS WAS A DONE DEAL...
DOESN'T ANYBODY AROUND HERE LEAVE THEIR CAR UNLOCKED? WHAT KIND OF SMALL TOWN IS THIS?
YA CAN'T JUST TAKE ANY CAR YA PLEASE...
...WHICH N BODY CAN DE-NYYY...
WHAT'RE YOU, KIDDING? THE WHOLE TOWN BAKED ME PIES..!
FOR HE'S A JOLLY GOOD FEL-LOW...
IT'S GRAND THEFT. I'D HAVE TO ARREST YOU.
WHO, ME? YOUR BELOVED BENEFACTOR?
JOLLY GOOD F -LOW...
THANK YOU, MICHAEL
CLICKA-CLICKA
DAMN.
DON'T NEED TO STEAL A CAR ANYWAYS, MR. LONDON. WE HAD YOURS TOWED AN' FIXED.
THANK YOU, DANNY.
YES, THANK YOU, DANNY!
MR. PARIS? MR. PARIS?

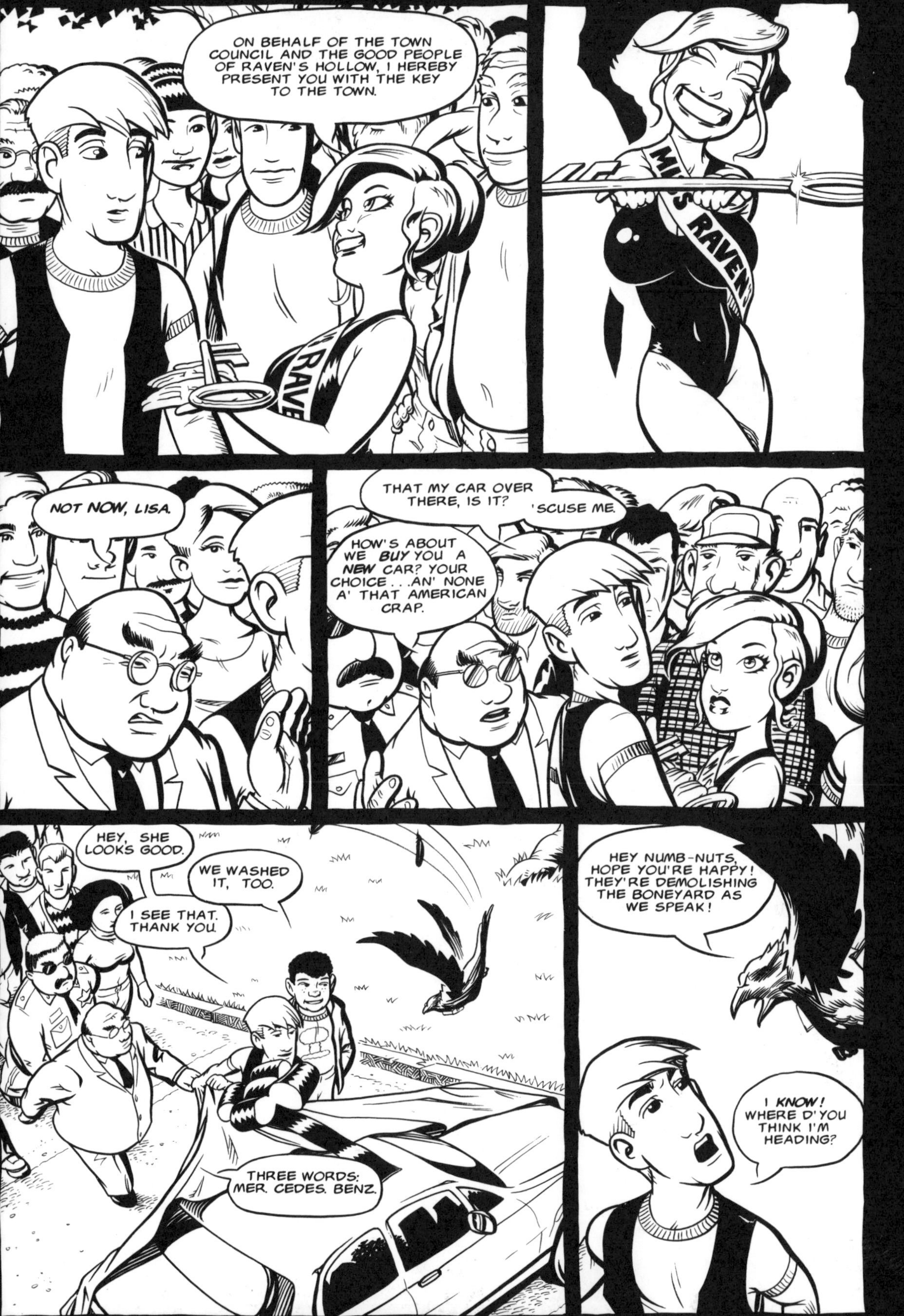
ON BEHALF OF THE TOWN COUNCIL AND THE GOOD PEOPLE OF RAVEN'S HOLLOW, I HEREBY PRESENT YOU WITH THE KEY TO THE TOWN.
MISS RAVEN
NOT NOW, LISA.
THAT MY CAR OVER THERE, IS IT?
'SCUSE ME.
HOW'S ABOUT WE BUY YOU A NEW CAR? YOUR CHOICE...AN' NONE A' THAT AMERICAN CRAP.
HEY, SHE LOOKS GOOD.
WE WASHED IT, TOO.
I SEE THAT. THANK YOU.
THREE WORDS: MER. CEDES. BENZ.
HEY NUMB-NUTS, HOPE YOU'RE HAPPY! THEY'RE DEMOLISHING THE BONEYARD AS WE SPEAK!
I KNOW! WHERE D'YOU THINK I'M HEADING?

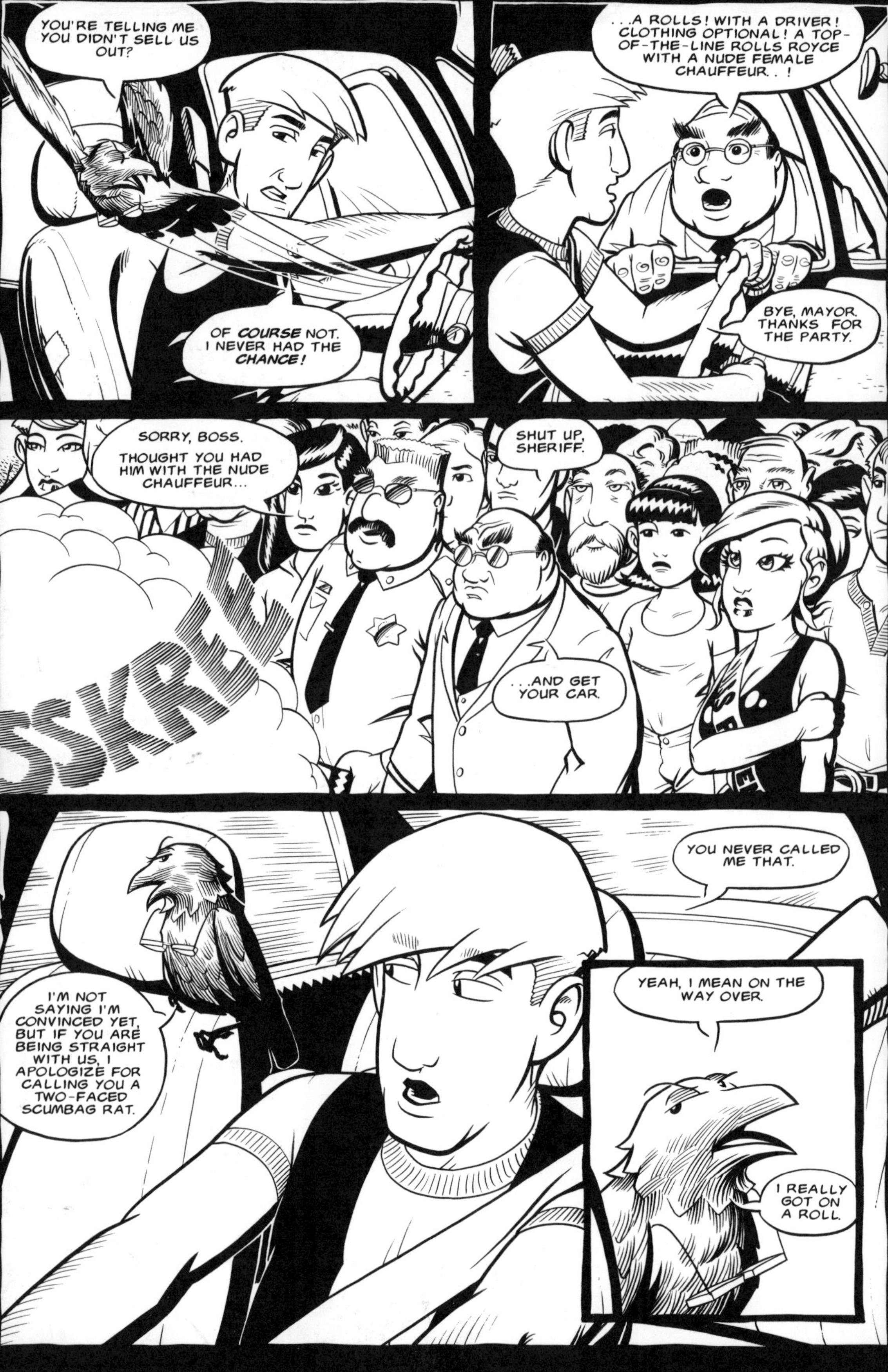

YOU'RE TELLING ME YOU DIDN'T SELL US OUT?
OF COURSE NOT. I NEVER HAD THE CHANCE!
...A ROLLS! WITH A DRIVER! CLOTHING OPTIONAL! A TOP-OF-THE-LINE ROLLS ROYCE WITH A NUDE FEMALE CHAUFFEUR..!
BYE, MAYOR. THANKS FOR THE PARTY.
SORRY, BOSS.
THOUGHT YOU HAD HIM WITH THE NUDE CHAUFFEUR...
SSKREE
SHUT UP, SHERIFF.
...AND GET YOUR CAR.
YOU NEVER CALLED ME THAT.
I'M NOT SAYING I'M CONVINCED YET, BUT IF YOU ARE BEING STRAIGHT WITH US, I APOLOGIZE FOR CALLING YOU A TWO-FACED SCUMBAG RAT.
YEAH, I MEAN ON THE WAY OVER.
I REALLY GOT ON A ROLL.

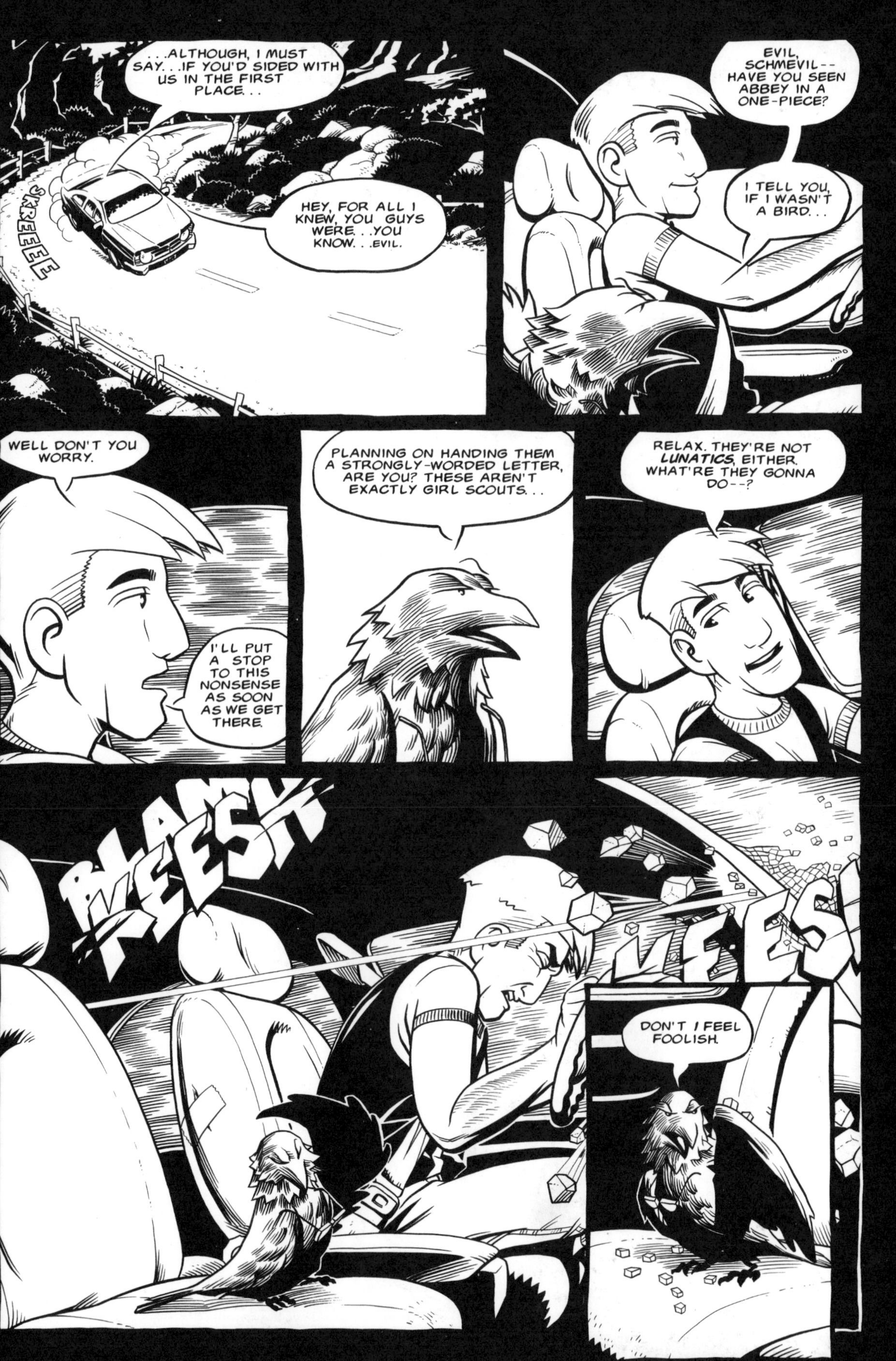
...ALTHOUGH, I MUST SAY...IF YOU'D SIDED WITH US IN THE FIRST PLACE...
SKREEEEE
HEY, FOR ALL I KNEW, YOU GUYS WERE...YOU KNOW...EVIL.
EVIL, SCHMEVIL-- HAVE YOU SEEN ABBEY IN A ONE-PIECE?
I TELL YOU, IF I WASN'T A BIRD...
WELL DON'T YOU WORRY.
I'LL PUT A STOP TO THIS NONSENSE AS SOON AS WE GET THERE.
PLANNING ON HANDING THEM A STRONGLY-WORDED LETTER, ARE YOU? THESE AREN'T EXACTLY GIRL SCOUTS...
RELAX. THEY'RE NOT LUNATICS, EITHER. WHAT'RE THEY GONNA DO--?
BLAM
FEESH
FEESH
DON'T I FEEL FOOLISH.

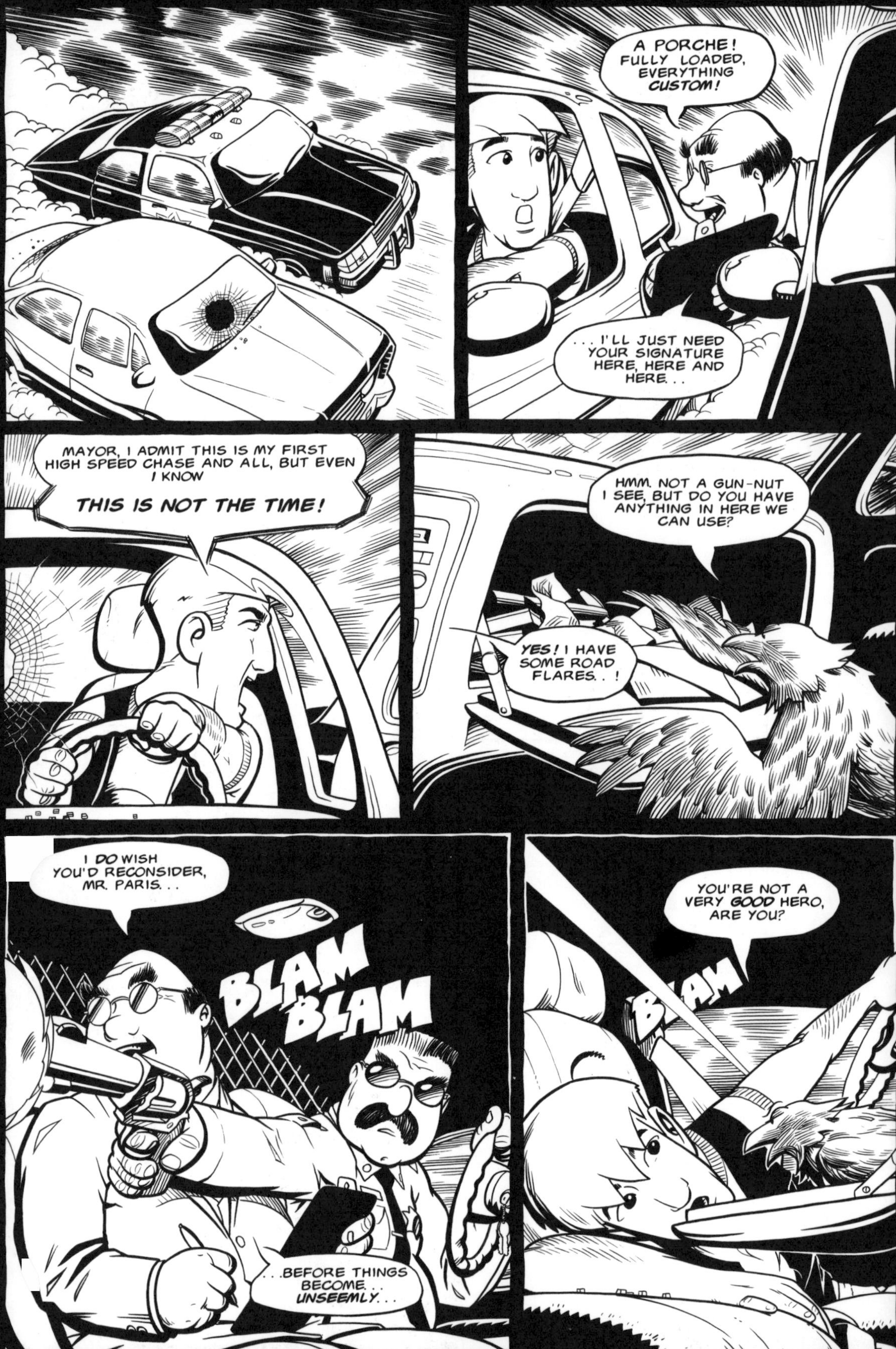
A PORCHE! FULLY LOADED, EVERYTHING CUSTOM!
. . . I'LL JUST NEED YOUR SIGNATURE HERE, HERE AND HERE. . .
MAYOR, I ADMIT THIS IS MY FIRST HIGH SPEED CHASE AND ALL, BUT EVEN I KNOW
THIS IS NOT THE TIME!
HMM. NOT A GUN-NUT I SEE, BUT DO YOU HAVE ANYTHING IN HERE WE CAN USE?
YES! I HAVE SOME ROAD FLARES. . !
I DO WISH YOU'D RECONSIDER, MR. PARIS. . .
BLAM
BLAM
. . .BEFORE THINGS BECOME. . . UNSEEMLY. . .
YOU'RE NOT A VERY GOOD HERO, ARE YOU?
BLAM

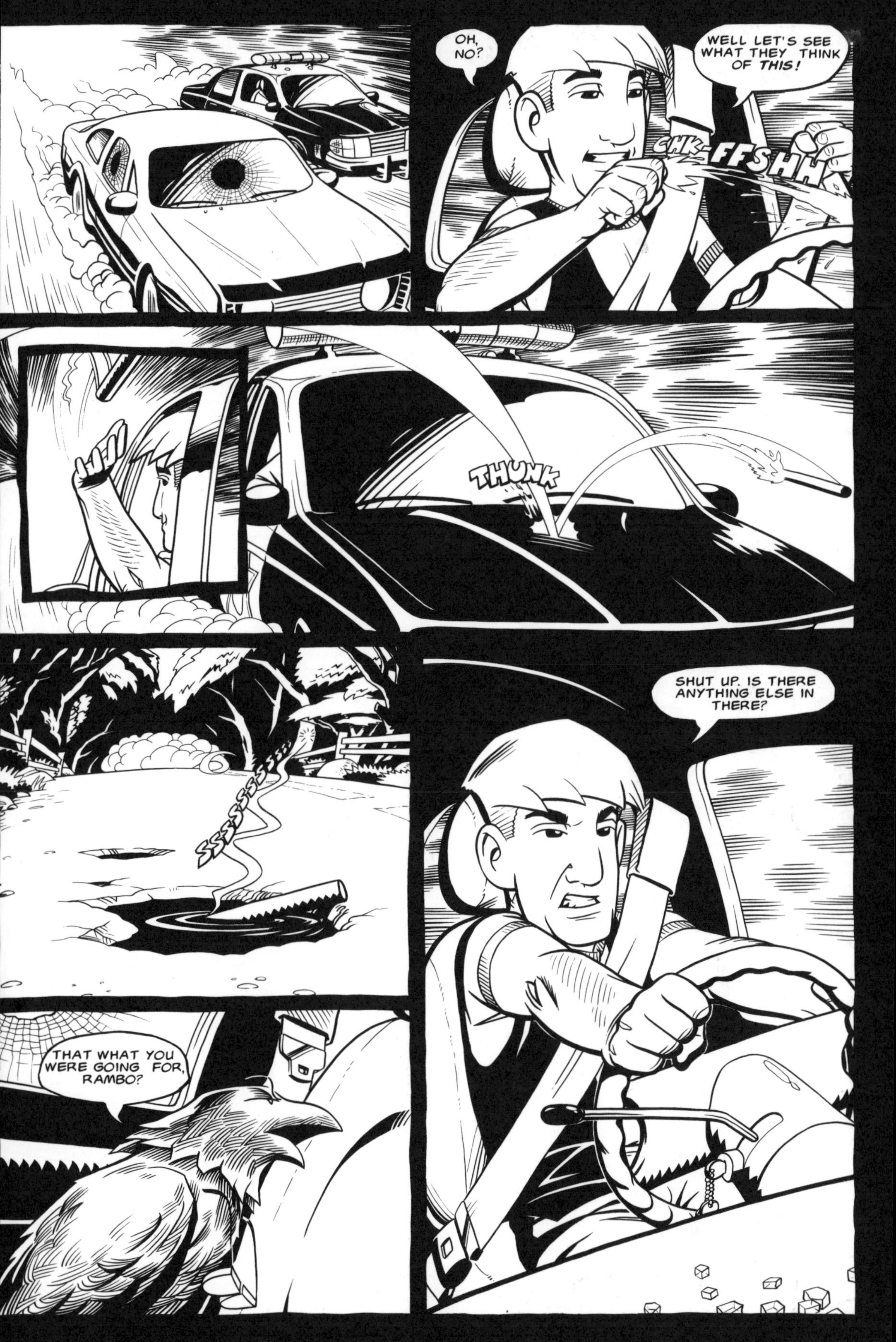
OH, NO?
WELL LET'S SEE WHAT THEY THINK OF THIS!
CHK-FFSHH
THUNK
SSSSSSSS
SHUT UP. IS THERE ANYTHING ELSE IN THERE?
THAT WHAT YOU WERE GOING FOR, RAMBO?

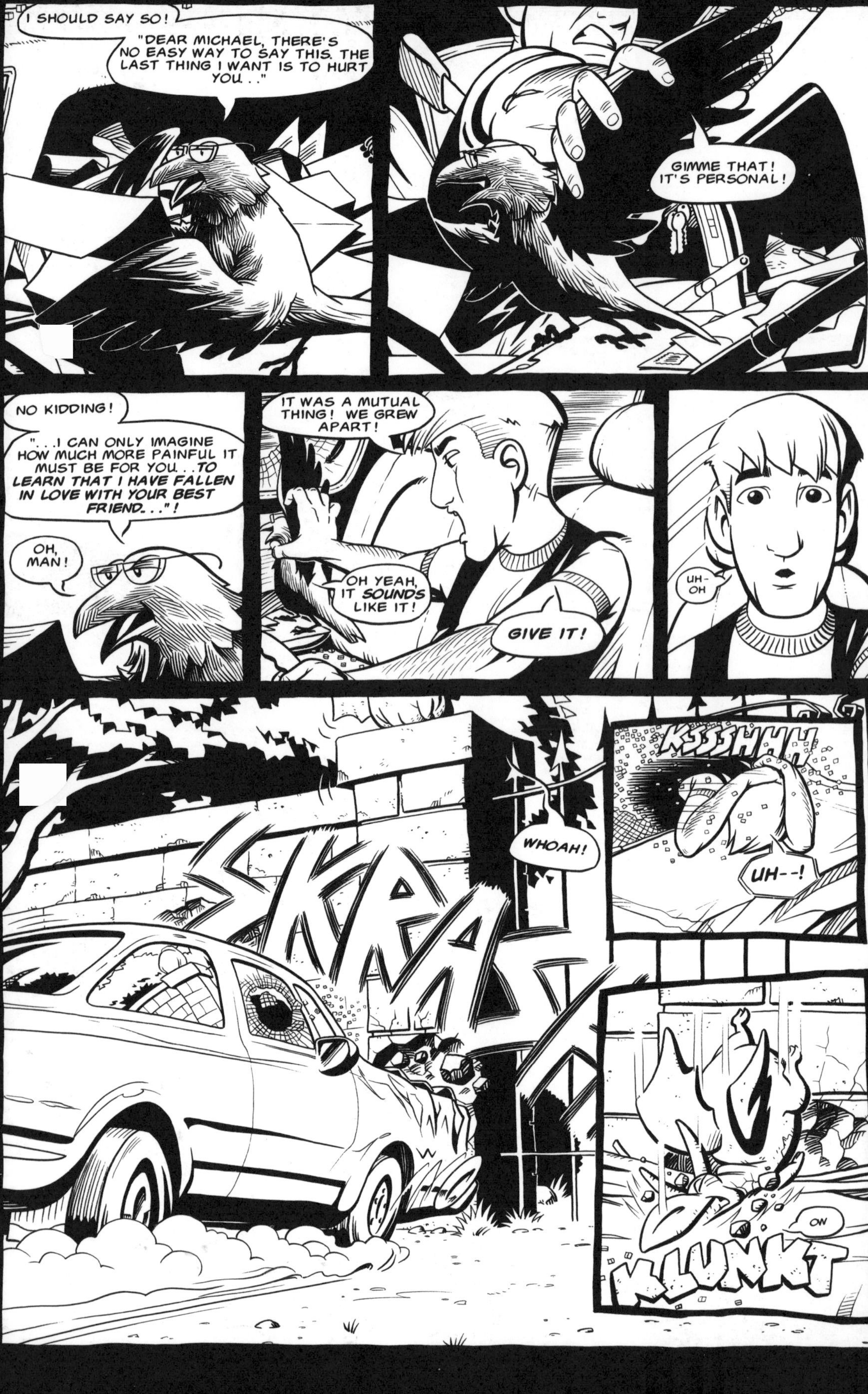
I SHOULD SAY SO!
"DEAR MICHAEL, THERE'S NO EASY WAY TO SAY THIS. THE LAST THING I WANT IS TO HURT YOU. . ."
GIMME THAT! IT'S PERSONAL!
NO KIDDING!
". . . I CAN ONLY IMAGINE HOW MUCH MORE PAINFUL IT MUST BE FOR YOU. . . TO LEARN THAT I HAVE FALLEN IN LOVE WITH YOUR BEST FRIEND. . ."!
OH, MAN!
IT WAS A MUTUAL THING! WE GREW APART!
OH YEAH, IT SOUNDS LIKE IT!
GIVE IT!
UH-OH
SKRASH
WHOAH!
KSSSHHH
UH--!
OW
KLUNKT

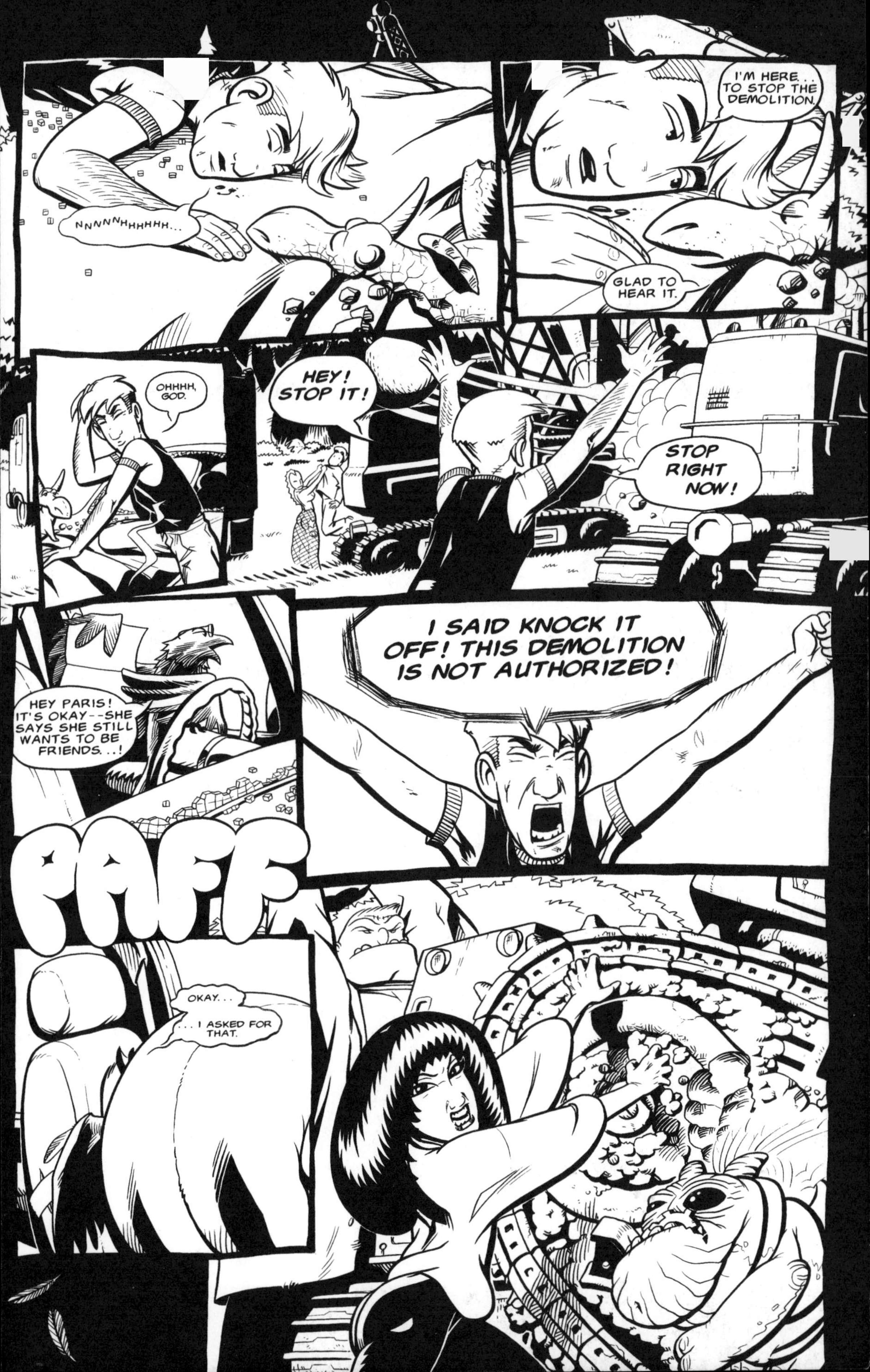
NNNNNHHHHHH...
I'M HERE... TO STOP THE DEMOLITION.
GLAD TO HEAR IT.
OHHHH, GOD.
HEY! STOP IT!
STOP RIGHT NOW!
HEY PARIS! IT'S OKAY--SHE SAYS SHE STILL WANTS TO BE FRIENDS...!
I SAID KNOCK IT OFF! THIS DEMOLITION IS NOT AUTHORIZED!
PAFF
OKAY...
...I ASKED FOR THAT.

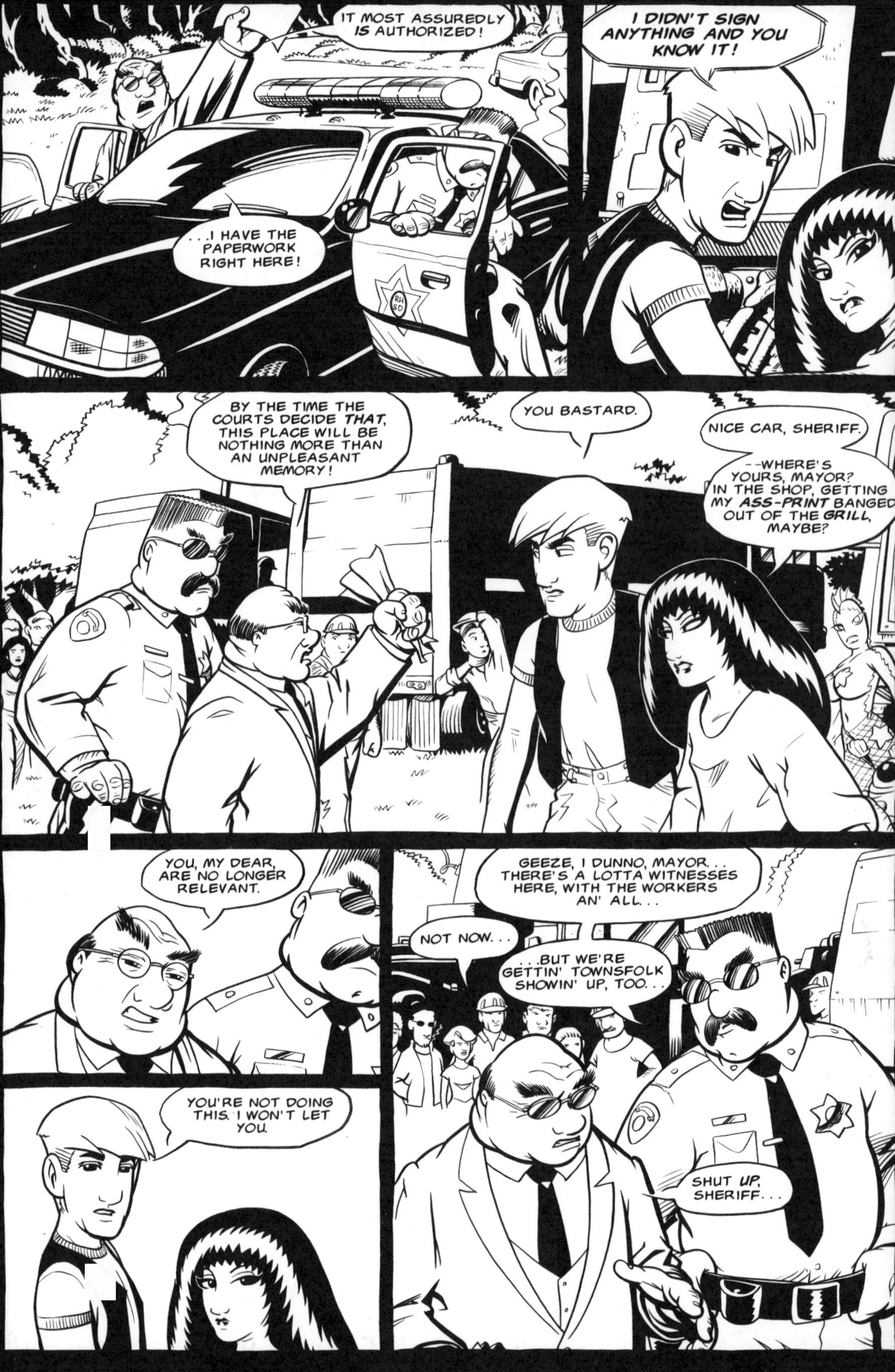
IT MOST ASSUREDLY IS AUTHORIZED!
...I HAVE THE PAPERWORK RIGHT HERE!
I DIDN'T SIGN ANYTHING AND YOU KNOW IT!
BY THE TIME THE COURTS DECIDE THAT, THIS PLACE WILL BE NOTHING MORE THAN AN UNPLEASANT MEMORY!
YOU BASTARD.
NICE CAR, SHERIFF.
--WHERE'S YOURS, MAYOR? IN THE SHOP, GETTING MY ASS-PRINT BANGED OUT OF THE GRILL, MAYBE?
YOU, MY DEAR, ARE NO LONGER RELEVANT.
YOU'RE NOT DOING THIS. I WON'T LET YOU.
GEEZE, I DUNNO, MAYOR... THERE'S A LOTTA WITNESSES HERE, WITH THE WORKERS AN' ALL...
NOT NOW...
...BUT WE'RE GETTIN' TOWNSFOLK SHOWIN' UP, TOO...
SHUT UP, SHERIFF...

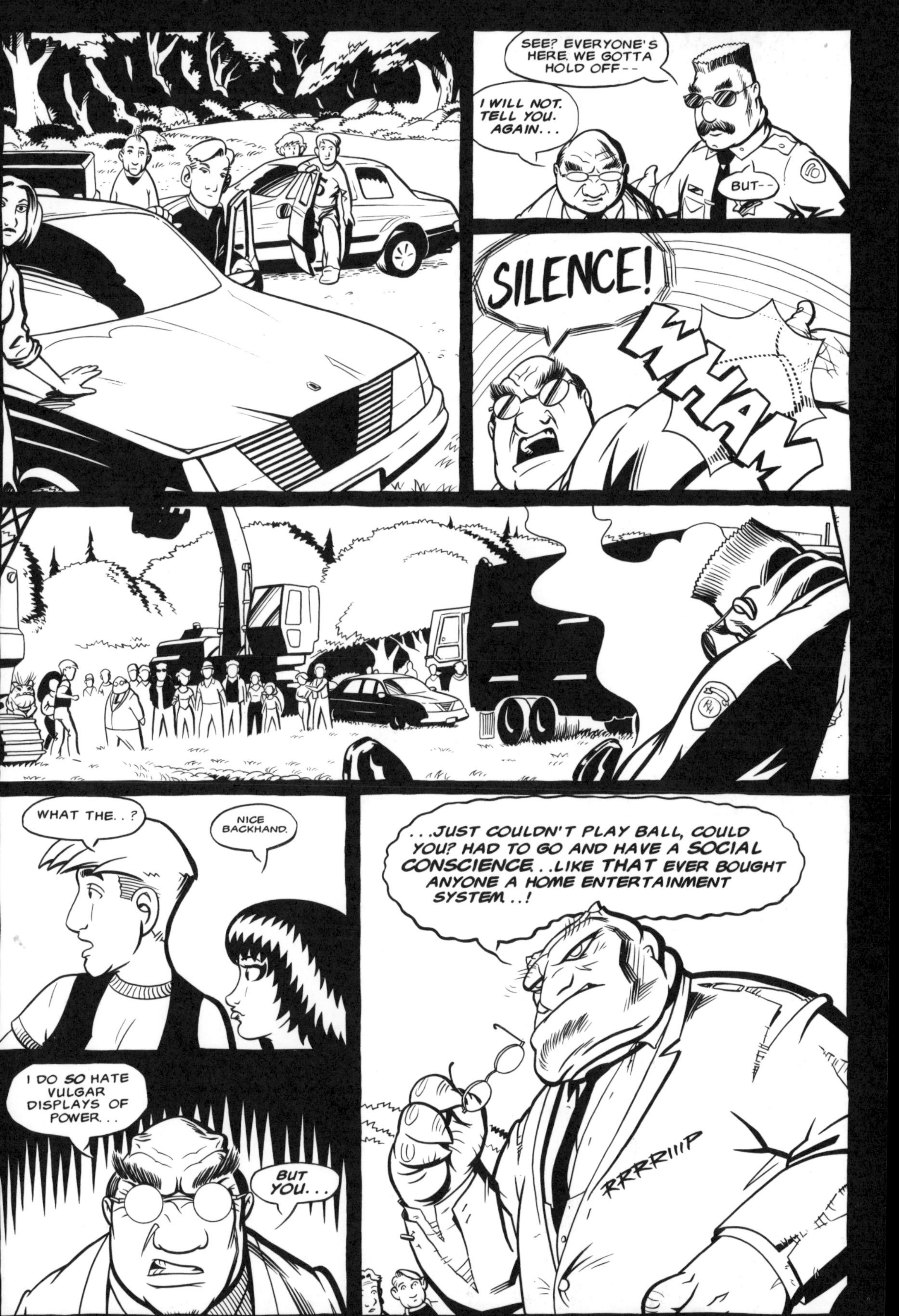
SEE? EVERYONE'S HERE. WE GOTTA HOLD OFF--
I WILL NOT. TELL YOU. AGAIN...
BUT--
SILENCE!
WHAM
WHAT THE..?
NICE BACKHAND.
...JUST COULDN'T PLAY BALL, COULD YOU? HAD TO GO AND HAVE A SOCIAL CONSCIENCE...LIKE THAT EVER BOUGHT ANYONE A HOME ENTERTAINMENT SYSTEM..!
I DO SO HATE VULGAR DISPLAYS OF POWER...
BUT YOU...
RRRRIIIP

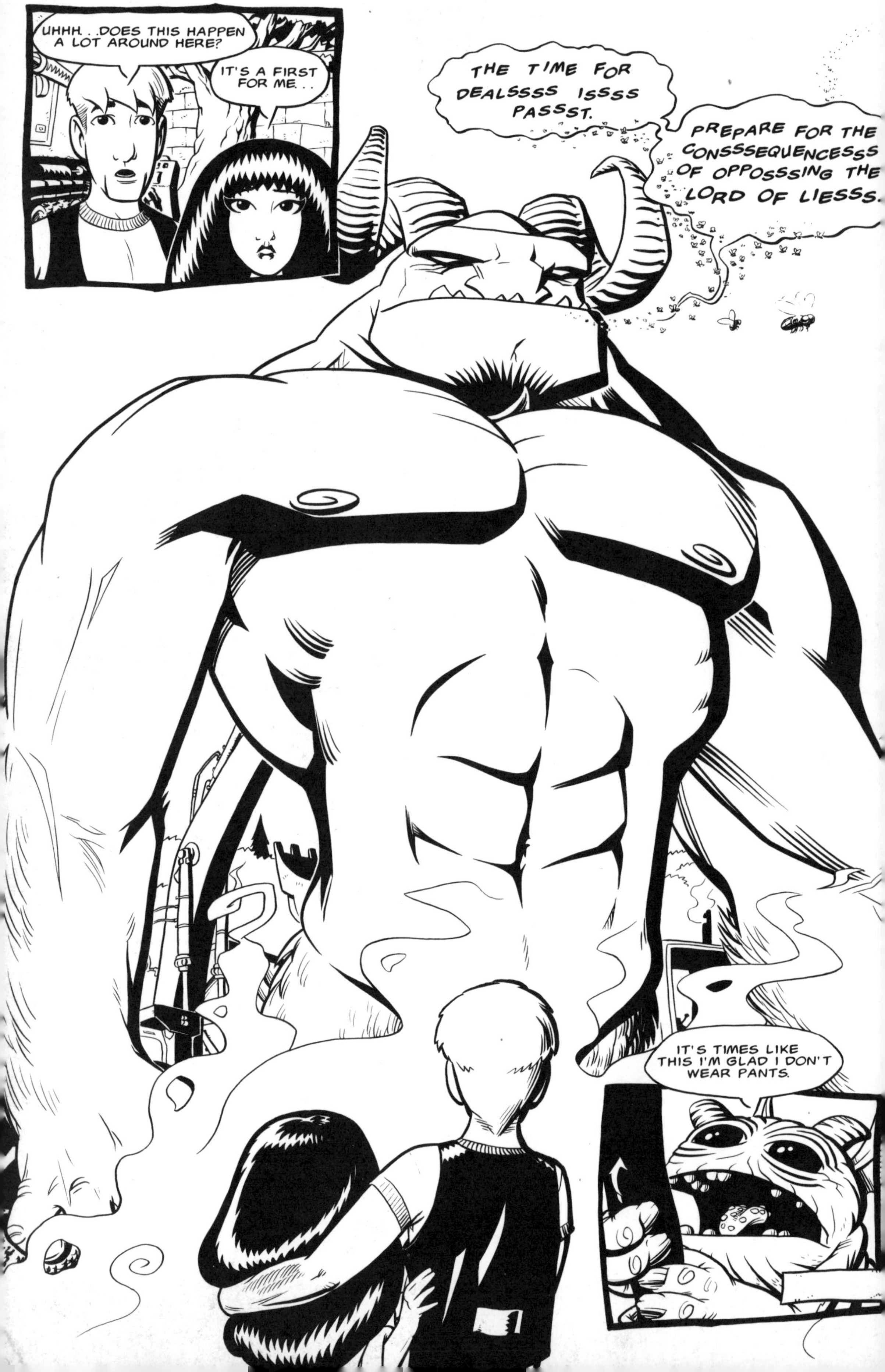
UHHH. . .DOES THIS HAPPEN A LOT AROUND HERE?
IT'S A FIRST FOR ME. . .
THE TIME FOR DEALSSSS ISSSS PASSST.
PREPARE FOR THE CONSSSEQUENCESSS OF OPPOSSSING THE LORD OF LIESSS.
IT'S TIMES LIKE THIS I'M GLAD I DON'T WEAR PANTS.

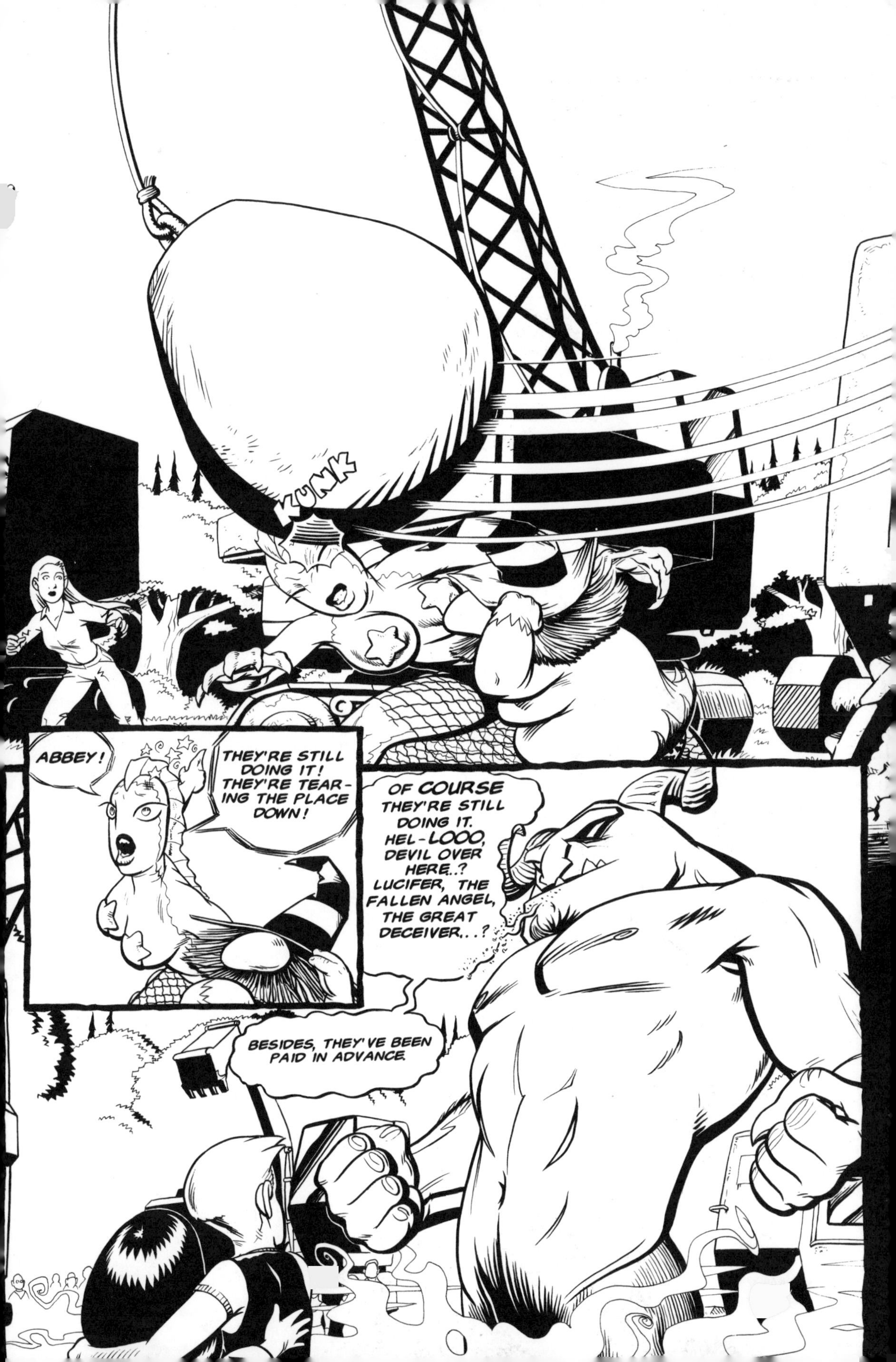
KUNK
ABBEY!
THEY'RE STILL DOING IT! THEY'RE TEARING THE PLACE DOWN!
OF COURSE THEY'RE STILL DOING IT. HEL-LOOO, DEVIL OVER HERE..? LUCIFER, THE FALLEN ANGEL, THE GREAT DECEIVER...?
BESIDES, THEY'VE BEEN PAID IN ADVANCE.

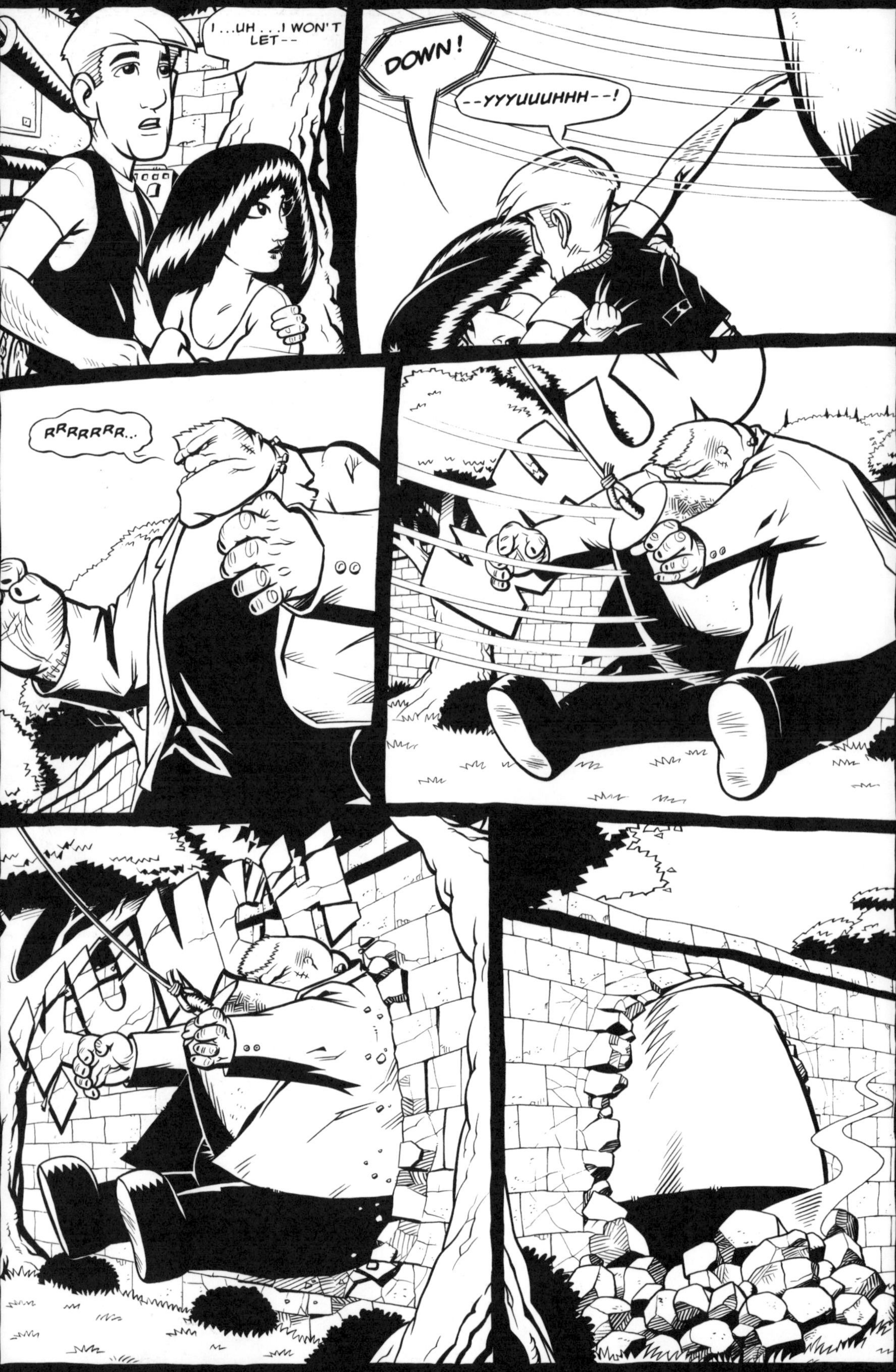

I...UH...I WON'T LET--
DOWN!
--YYYUUUHHH--!
RRRRRRR...

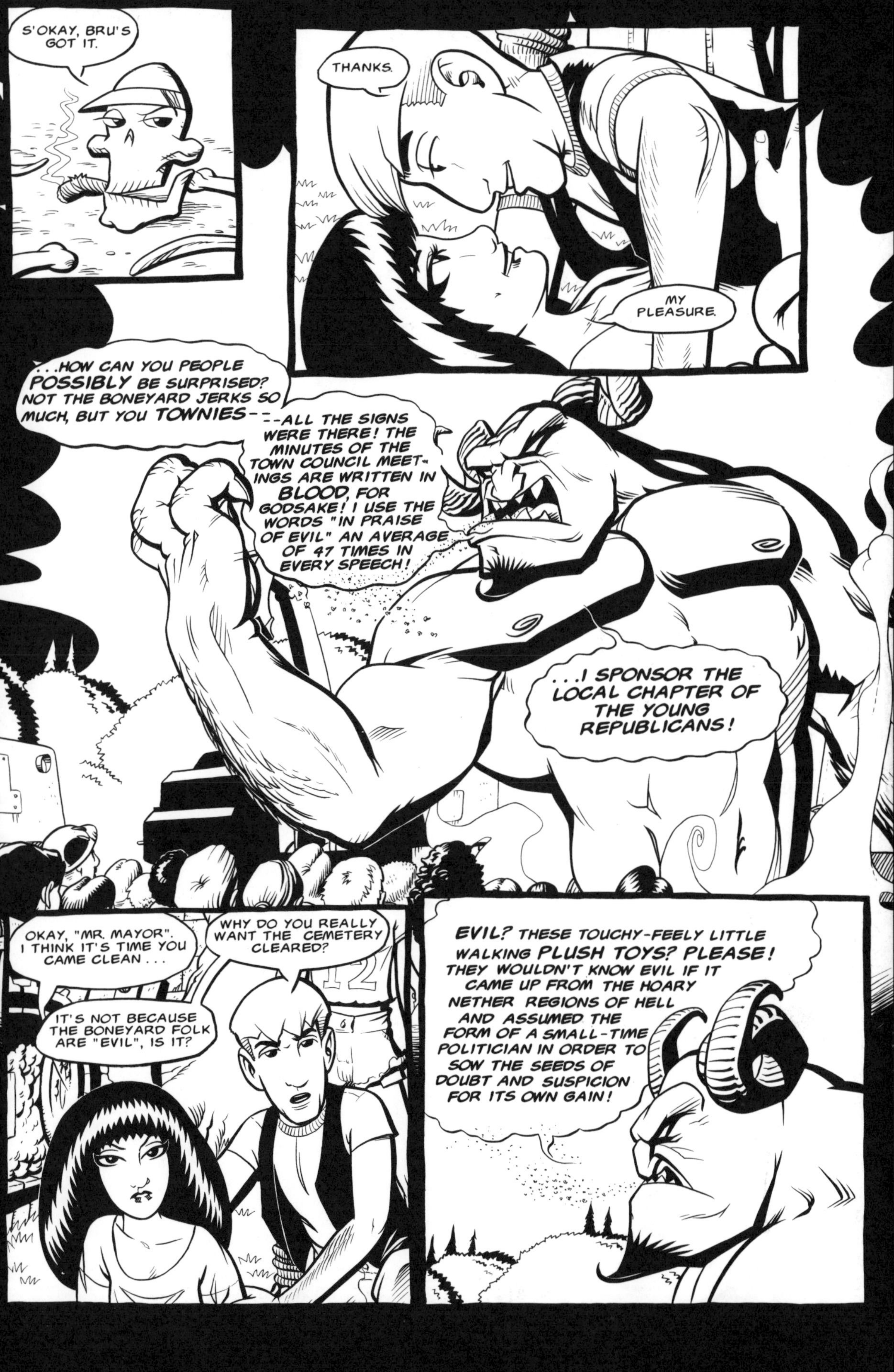
S'OKAY, BRU'S GOT IT.
THANKS.
MY PLEASURE.
...HOW CAN YOU PEOPLE POSSIBLY BE SURPRISED? NOT THE BONEYARD JERKS SO MUCH, BUT YOU TOWNIES--
--ALL THE SIGNS WERE THERE! THE MINUTES OF THE TOWN COUNCIL MEETINGS ARE WRITTEN IN BLOOD, FOR GODSAKE! I USE THE WORDS "IN PRAISE OF EVIL" AN AVERAGE OF 47 TIMES IN EVERY SPEECH!
...I SPONSOR THE LOCAL CHAPTER OF THE YOUNG REPUBLICANS!
OKAY, "MR. MAYOR". I THINK IT'S TIME YOU CAME CLEAN...
WHY DO YOU REALLY WANT THE CEMETERY CLEARED?
IT'S NOT BECAUSE THE BONEYARD FOLK ARE "EVIL", IS IT?
EVIL? THESE TOUCHY-FEELY LITTLE WALKING PLUSH TOYS? PLEASE! THEY WOULDN'T KNOW EVIL IF IT CAME UP FROM THE HOARY NETHER REGIONS OF HELL AND ASSUMED THE FORM OF A SMALL-TIME POLITICIAN IN ORDER TO SOW THE SEEDS OF DOUBT AND SUSPICION FOR ITS OWN GAIN!

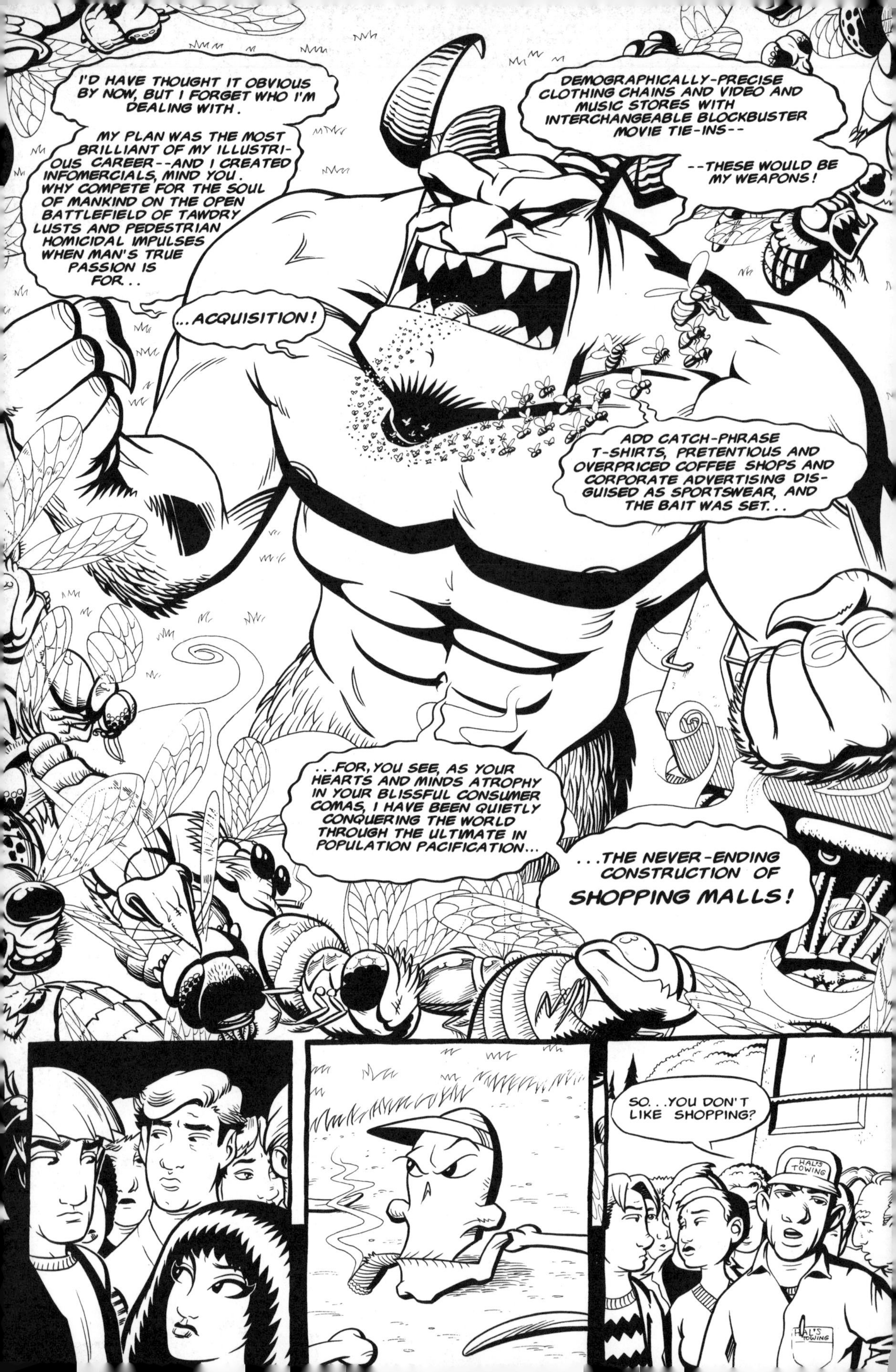
I'D HAVE THOUGHT IT OBVIOUS BY NOW, BUT I FORGET WHO I'M DEALING WITH.
MY PLAN WAS THE MOST BRILLIANT OF MY ILLUSTRI-OUS CAREER--AND I CREATED INFOMERCIALS, MIND YOU. WHY COMPETE FOR THE SOUL OF MANKIND ON THE OPEN BATTLEFIELD OF TAWDRY LUSTS AND PEDESTRIAN HOMICIDAL IMPULSES WHEN MAN'S TRUE PASSION IS FOR..
...ACQUISITION!
DEMOGRAPHICALLY-PRECISE CLOTHING CHAINS AND VIDEO AND MUSIC STORES WITH INTERCHANGEABLE BLOCKBUSTER MOVIE TIE-INS--
--THESE WOULD BE MY WEAPONS!
ADD CATCH-PHRASE T-SHIRTS, PRETENTIOUS AND OVERPRICED COFFEE SHOPS AND CORPORATE ADVERTISING DIS-GUISED AS SPORTSWEAR, AND THE BAIT WAS SET...
...FOR, YOU SEE, AS YOUR HEARTS AND MINDS ATROPHY IN YOUR BLISSFUL CONSUMER COMAS, I HAVE BEEN QUIETLY CONQUERING THE WORLD THROUGH THE ULTIMATE IN POPULATION PACIFICATION...
...THE NEVER-ENDING CONSTRUCTION OF SHOPPING MALLS!
SO...YOU DON'T LIKE SHOPPING?
HAL'S TOWING
HAL'S TOWING

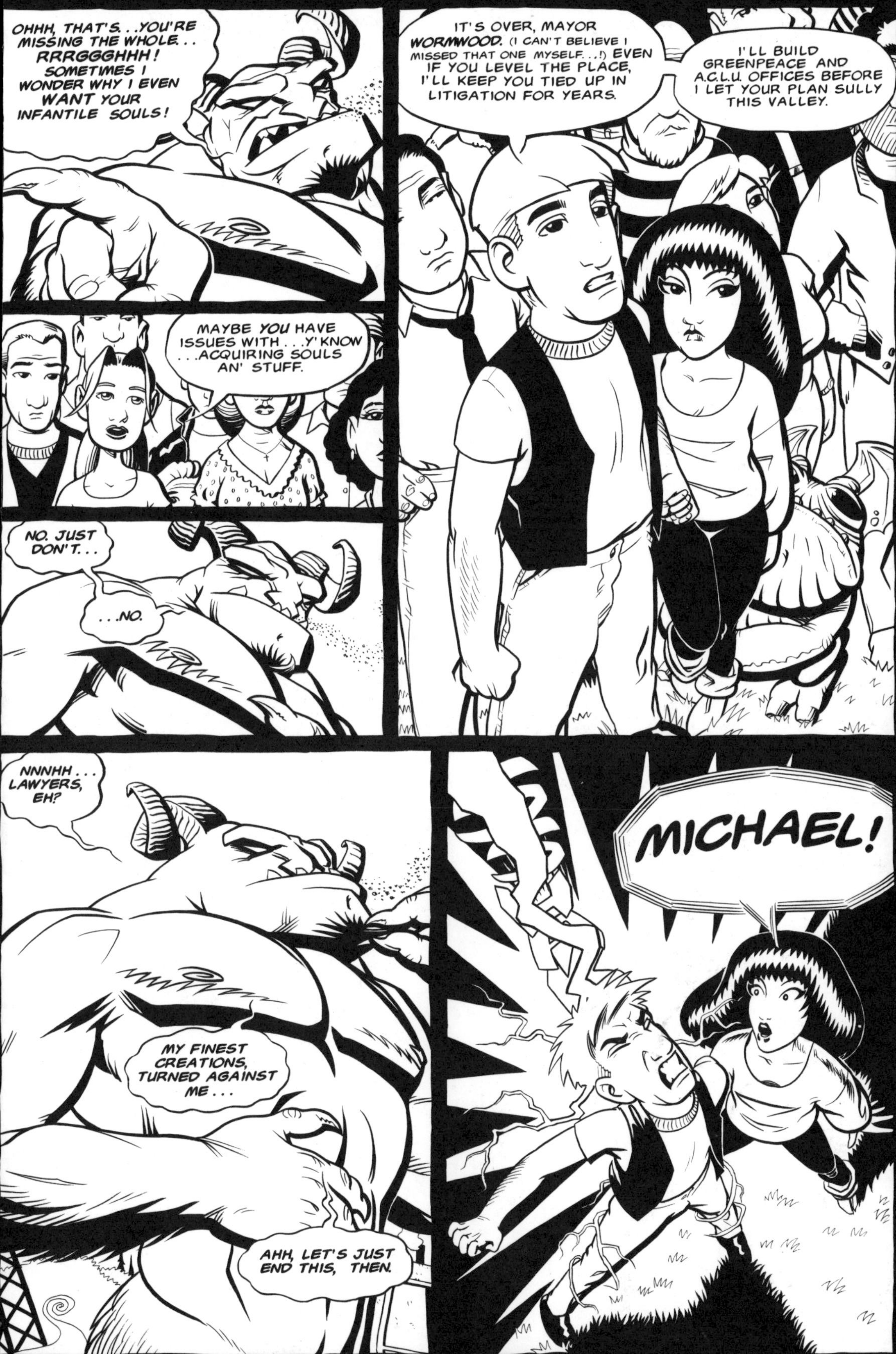
OHHH, THAT'S...YOU'RE MISSING THE WHOLE... RRRGGGHHH! SOMETIMES I WONDER WHY I EVEN WANT YOUR INFANTILE SOULS!
MAYBE YOU HAVE ISSUES WITH...Y'KNOW ...ACQUIRING SOULS AN' STUFF.
NO. JUST DON'T...
...NO.
IT'S OVER, MAYOR WORMWOOD. (I CAN'T BELIEVE I MISSED THAT ONE MYSELF...!) EVEN IF YOU LEVEL THE PLACE, I'LL KEEP YOU TIED UP IN LITIGATION FOR YEARS.
I'LL BUILD GREENPEACE AND A.C.L.U. OFFICES BEFORE I LET YOUR PLAN SULLY THIS VALLEY.
NNNHH... LAWYERS, EH?
MY FINEST CREATIONS, TURNED AGAINST ME...
AHH, LET'S JUST END THIS, THEN.
MICHAEL!

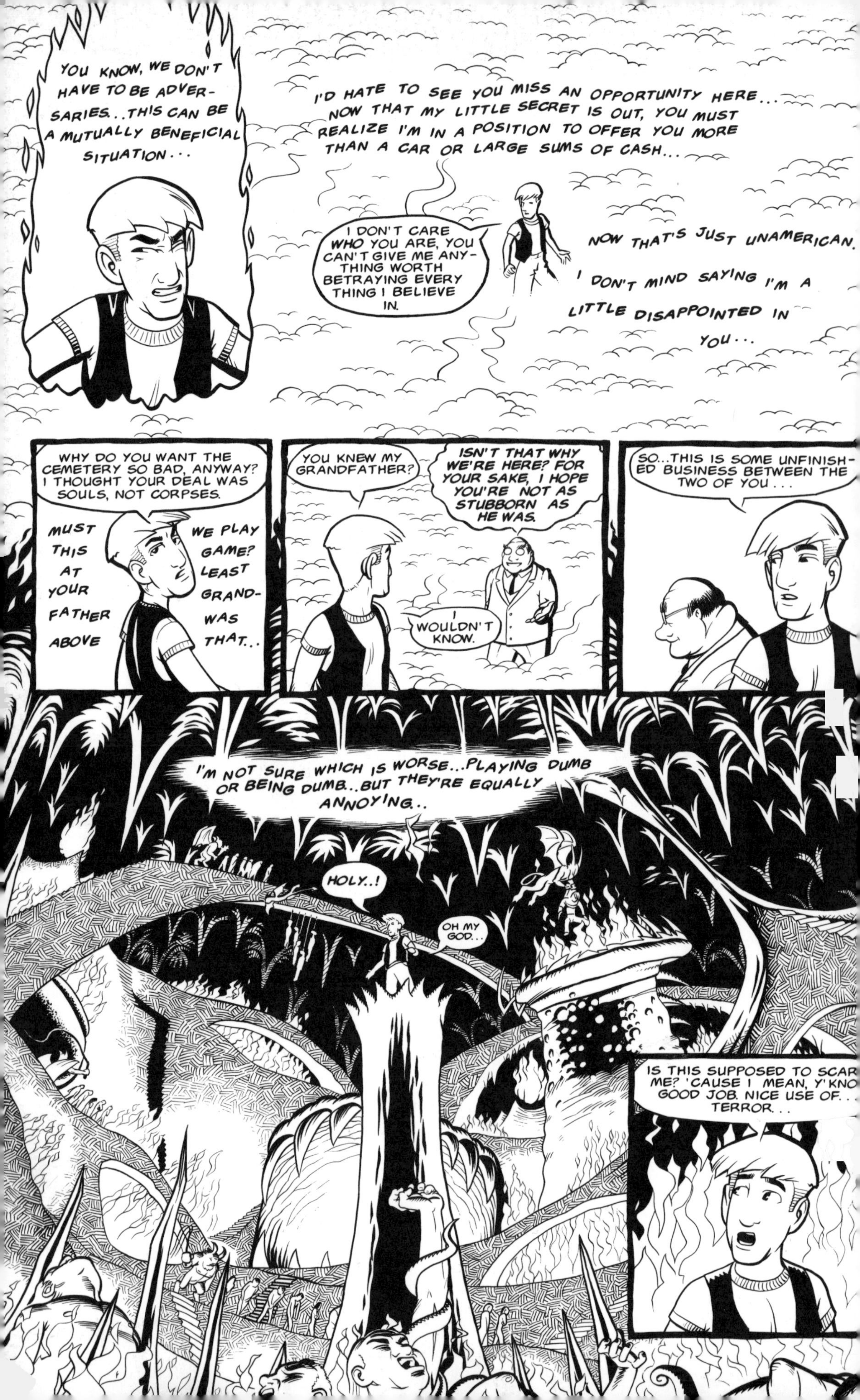

YOU KNOW, WE DON'T HAVE TO BE ADVERSARIES...THIS CAN BE A MUTUALLY BENEFICIAL SITUATION...
I'D HATE TO SEE YOU MISS AN OPPORTUNITY HERE... NOW THAT MY LITTLE SECRET IS OUT, YOU MUST REALIZE I'M IN A POSITION TO OFFER YOU MORE THAN A CAR OR LARGE SUMS OF CASH...
I DON'T CARE WHO YOU ARE, YOU CAN'T GIVE ME ANYTHING WORTH BETRAYING EVERY THING I BELIEVE IN.
NOW THAT'S JUST UNAMERICAN.
I DON'T MIND SAYING I'M A LITTLE DISAPPOINTED IN YOU...
WHY DO YOU WANT THE CEMETERY SO BAD, ANYWAY? I THOUGHT YOUR DEAL WAS SOULS, NOT CORPSES.
MUST WE PLAY THIS GAME? AT LEAST YOUR GRANDFATHER WAS ABOVE THAT...
YOU KNEW MY GRANDFATHER?
ISN'T THAT WHY WE'RE HERE? FOR YOUR SAKE, I HOPE YOU'RE NOT AS STUBBORN AS HE WAS.
I WOULDN'T KNOW.
SO...THIS IS SOME UNFINISHED BUSINESS BETWEEN THE TWO OF YOU...
I'M NOT SURE WHICH IS WORSE...PLAYING DUMB OR BEING DUMB...BUT THEY'RE EQUALLY ANNOYING..
HOLY..!
OH MY GOD...
IS THIS SUPPOSED TO SCAR ME? 'CAUSE I MEAN, Y'KNO GOOD JOB. NICE USE OF... TERROR...

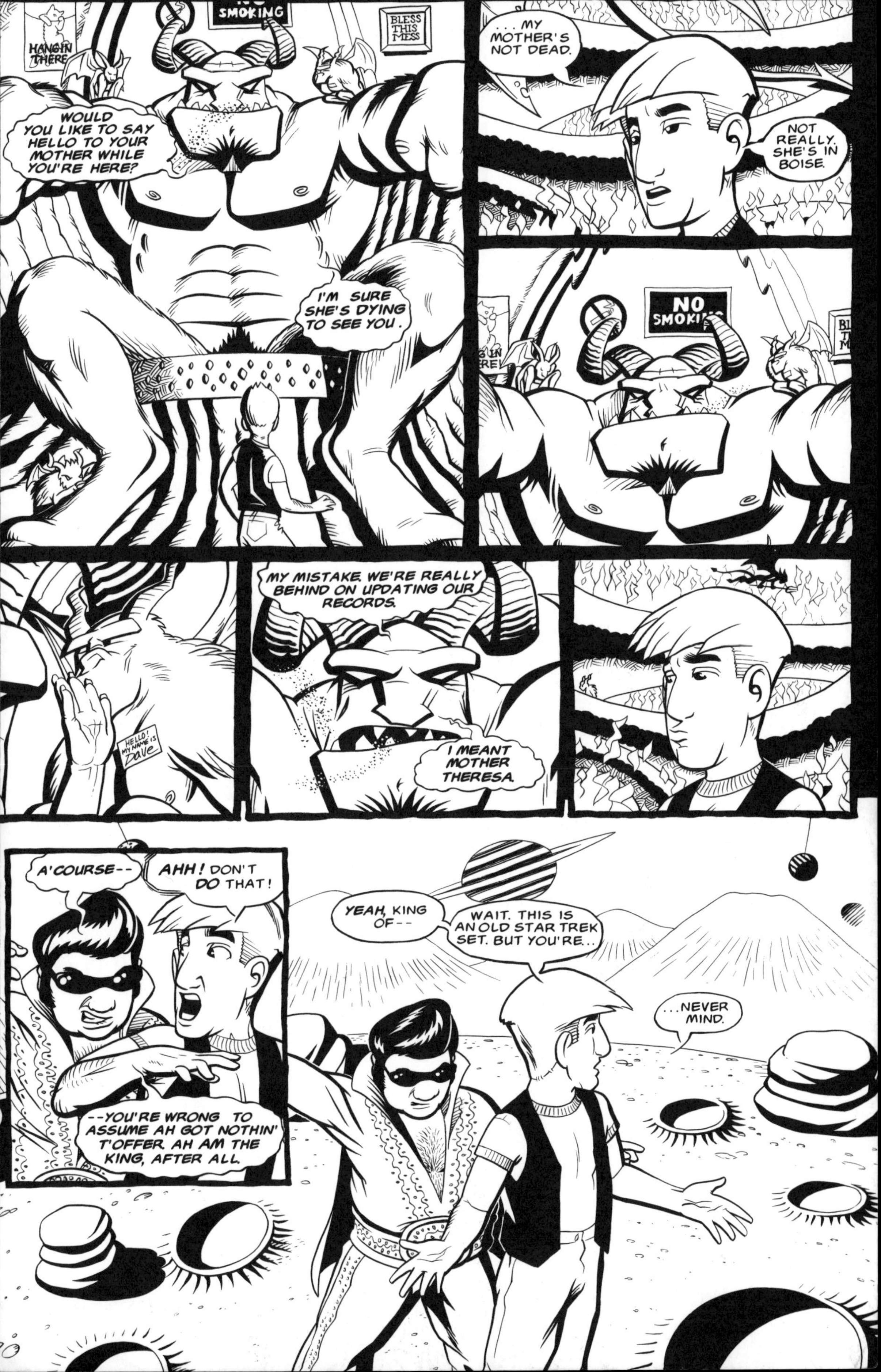
NO SMOKING
HANG IN THERE
BLESS THIS MESS
WOULD YOU LIKE TO SAY HELLO TO YOUR MOTHER WHILE YOU'RE HERE?
I'M SURE SHE'S DYING TO SEE YOU.
. . . MY MOTHER'S NOT DEAD.
NOT REALLY. SHE'S IN BOISE.
NO SMOKING
HELLO! MY NAME IS Dave
MY MISTAKE. WE'RE REALLY BEHIND ON UPDATING OUR RECORDS.
I MEANT MOTHER THERESA.
A'COURSE--
AHH! DON'T DO THAT!
--YOU'RE WRONG TO ASSUME AH GOT NOTHIN' T'OFFER. AH AM THE KING, AFTER ALL.
YEAH, KING OF--
WAIT. THIS IS AN OLD STAR TREK SET. BUT YOU'RE...
...NEVER MIND.

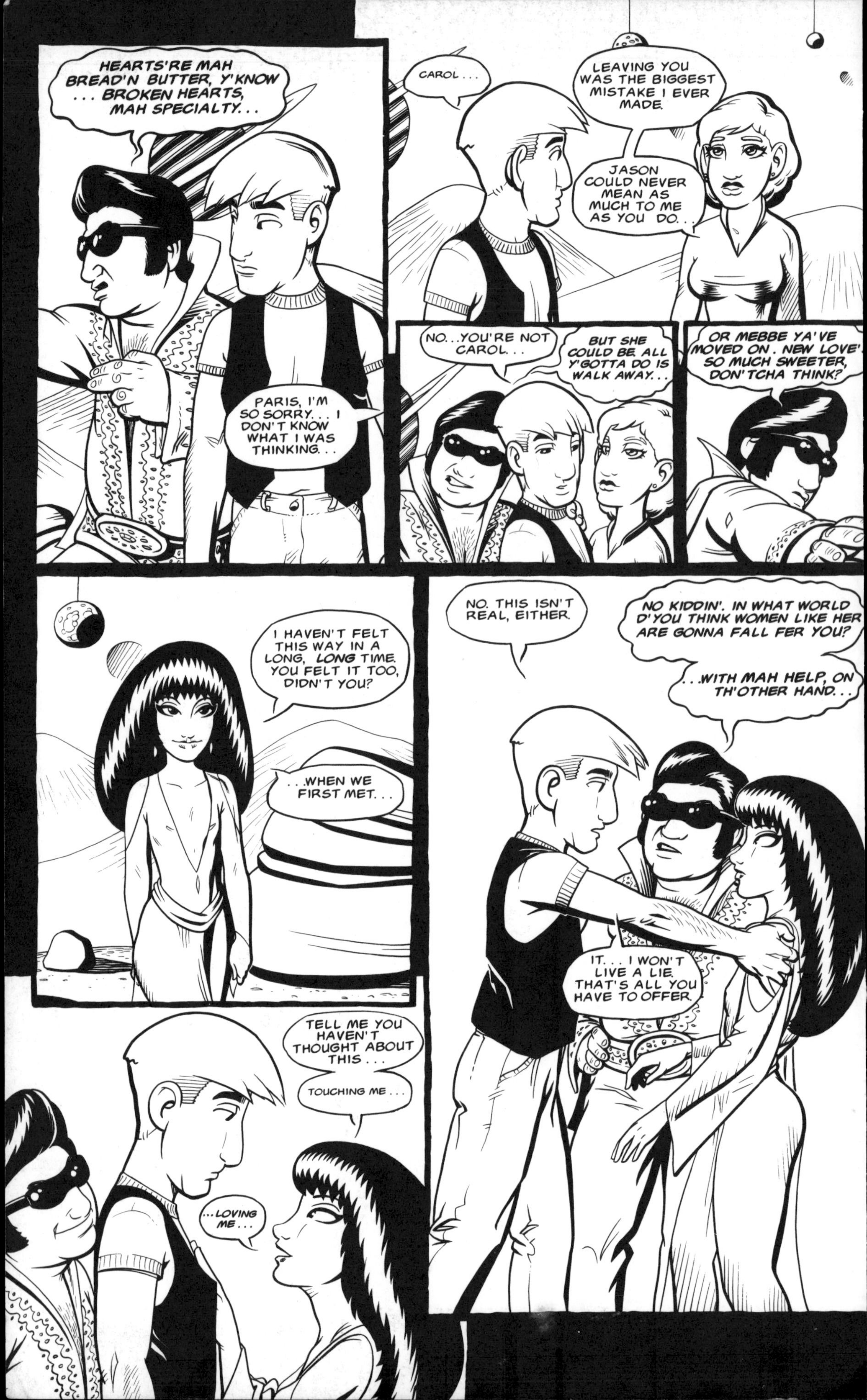
HEARTS'RE MAH BREAD'N BUTTER, Y'KNOW . . . BROKEN HEARTS, MAH SPECIALTY. . .
PARIS, I'M SO SORRY. . . I DON'T KNOW WHAT I WAS THINKING. . .
CAROL . . .
LEAVING YOU WAS THE BIGGEST MISTAKE I EVER MADE.
JASON COULD NEVER MEAN AS MUCH TO ME AS YOU DO. . .
NO. . .YOU'RE NOT CAROL. . .
BUT SHE COULD BE. ALL Y'GOTTA DO IS WALK AWAY. . .
OR MEBBE YA'VE MOVED ON. NEW LOVE'S SO MUCH SWEETER, DON'TCHA THINK?
I HAVEN'T FELT THIS WAY IN A LONG, LONG TIME. YOU FELT IT TOO, DIDN'T YOU?
. . .WHEN WE FIRST MET. . .
TELL ME YOU HAVEN'T THOUGHT ABOUT THIS . . .
TOUCHING ME . . .
. . .LOVING ME . . .
NO. THIS ISN'T REAL, EITHER.
NO KIDDIN'. IN WHAT WORLD D'YOU THINK WOMEN LIKE HER ARE GONNA FALL FER YOU?
. . .WITH MAH HELP, ON TH'OTHER HAND. . .
IT. . . I WON'T LIVE A LIE. THAT'S ALL YOU HAVE TO OFFER.

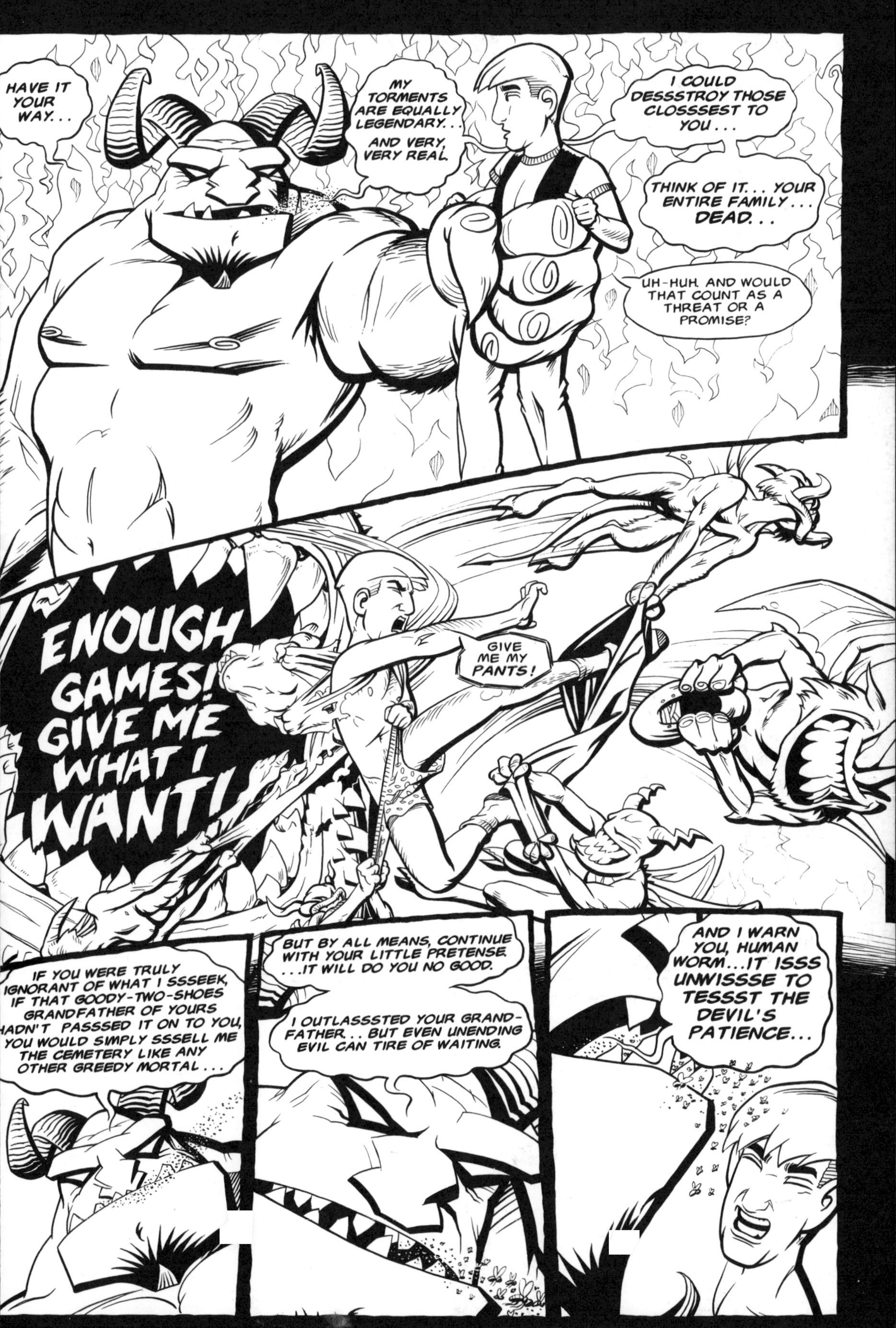
HAVE IT YOUR WAY...
MY TORMENTS ARE EQUALLY LEGENDARY... AND VERY, VERY REAL.
I COULD DESSSTROY THOSE CLOSSSEST TO YOU...
THINK OF IT... YOUR ENTIRE FAMILY... DEAD...
UH-HUH. AND WOULD THAT COUNT AS A THREAT OR A PROMISE?
ENOUGH GAMES! GIVE ME WHAT I WANT!
GIVE ME MY PANTS!
IF YOU WERE TRULY IGNORANT OF WHAT I SSSEEK, IF THAT GOODY-TWO-SHOES GRANDFATHER OF YOURS HADN'T PASSSED IT ON TO YOU, YOU WOULD SIMPLY SSSELL ME THE CEMETERY LIKE ANY OTHER GREEDY MORTAL...
BUT BY ALL MEANS, CONTINUE WITH YOUR LITTLE PRETENSE. ...IT WILL DO YOU NO GOOD.
I OUTLASSSTED YOUR GRAND-FATHER... BUT EVEN UNENDING EVIL CAN TIRE OF WAITING.
AND I WARN YOU, HUMAN WORM...IT ISSS UNWISSSE TO TESSST THE DEVIL'S PATIENCE...

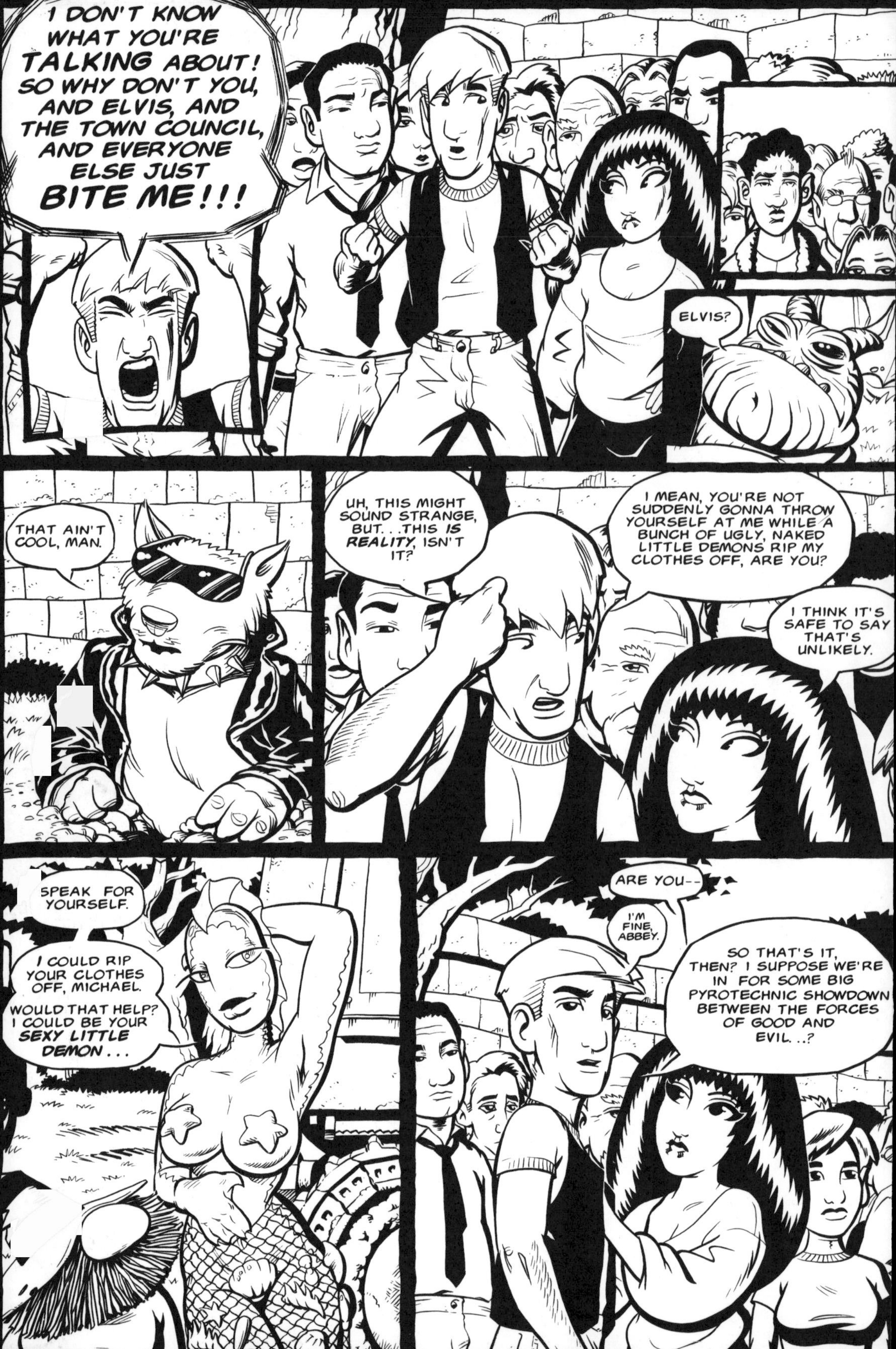
I DON'T KNOW WHAT YOU'RE TALKING ABOUT! SO WHY DON'T YOU, AND ELVIS, AND THE TOWN COUNCIL, AND EVERYONE ELSE JUST BITE ME!!!
ELVIS?
THAT AIN'T COOL, MAN.
UH, THIS MIGHT SOUND STRANGE, BUT...THIS IS REALITY, ISN'T IT?
I MEAN, YOU'RE NOT SUDDENLY GONNA THROW YOURSELF AT ME WHILE A BUNCH OF UGLY, NAKED LITTLE DEMONS RIP MY CLOTHES OFF, ARE YOU?
I THINK IT'S SAFE TO SAY THAT'S UNLIKELY.
SPEAK FOR YOURSELF.
I COULD RIP YOUR CLOTHES OFF, MICHAEL.
WOULD THAT HELP? I COULD BE YOUR SEXY LITTLE DEMON...
ARE YOU--
I'M FINE, ABBEY.
SO THAT'S IT, THEN? I SUPPOSE WE'RE IN FOR SOME BIG PYROTECHNIC SHOWDOWN BETWEEN THE FORCES OF GOOD AND EVIL...?

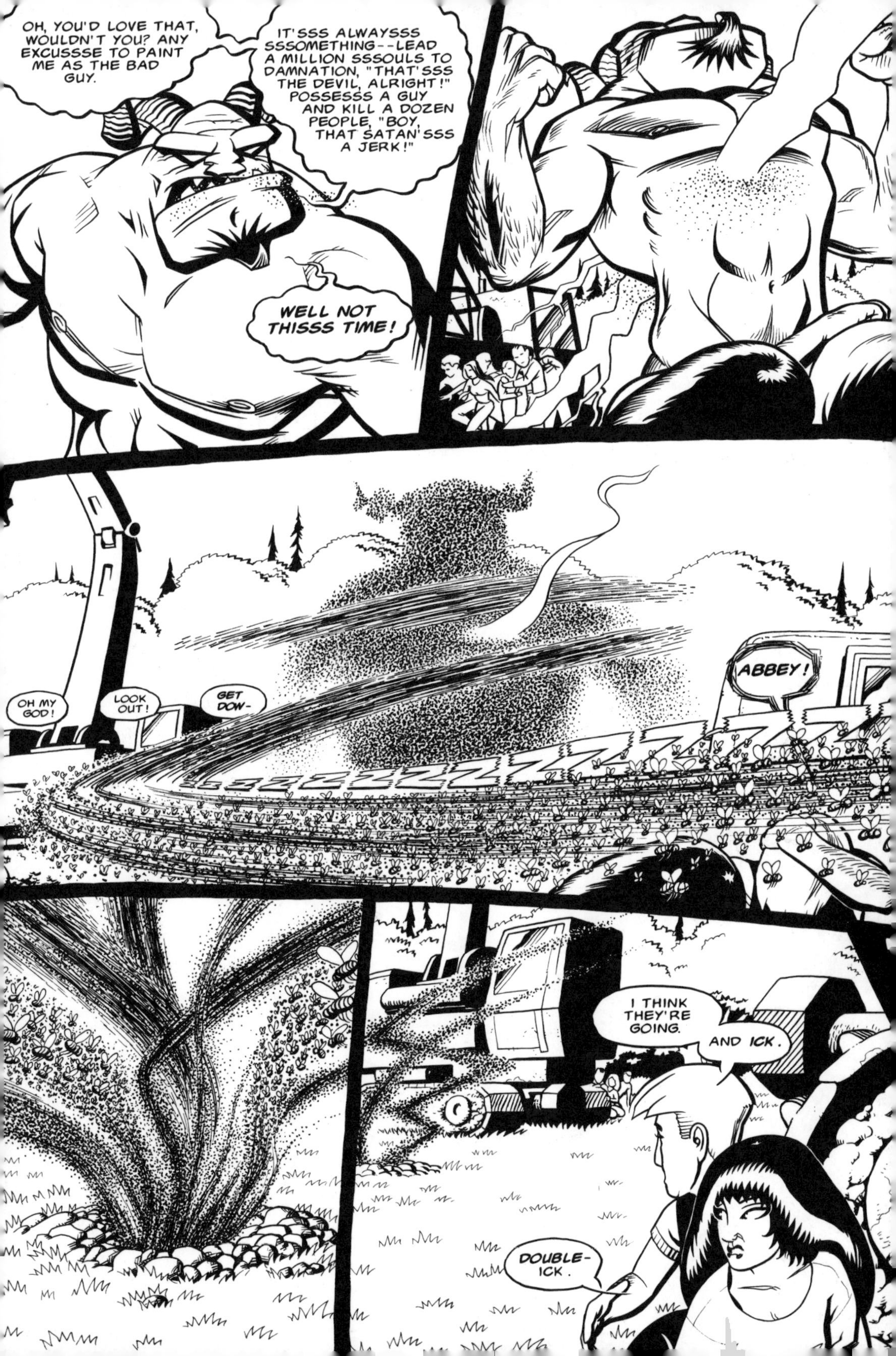
OH, YOU'D LOVE THAT, WOULDN'T YOU? ANY EXCUSSSE TO PAINT ME AS THE BAD GUY.
IT'SSS ALWAYSSS SSSOMETHING--LEAD A MILLION SSSOULS TO DAMNATION, "THAT'SSS THE DEVIL, ALRIGHT!" POSSESSS A GUY AND KILL A DOZEN PEOPLE, "BOY, THAT SATAN'SSS A JERK!"
WELL NOT THISSS TIME!
OH MY GOD!
LOOK OUT!
GET DOW-
ABBEY!
I THINK THEY'RE GOING.
AND ICK.
DOUBLE-ICK.

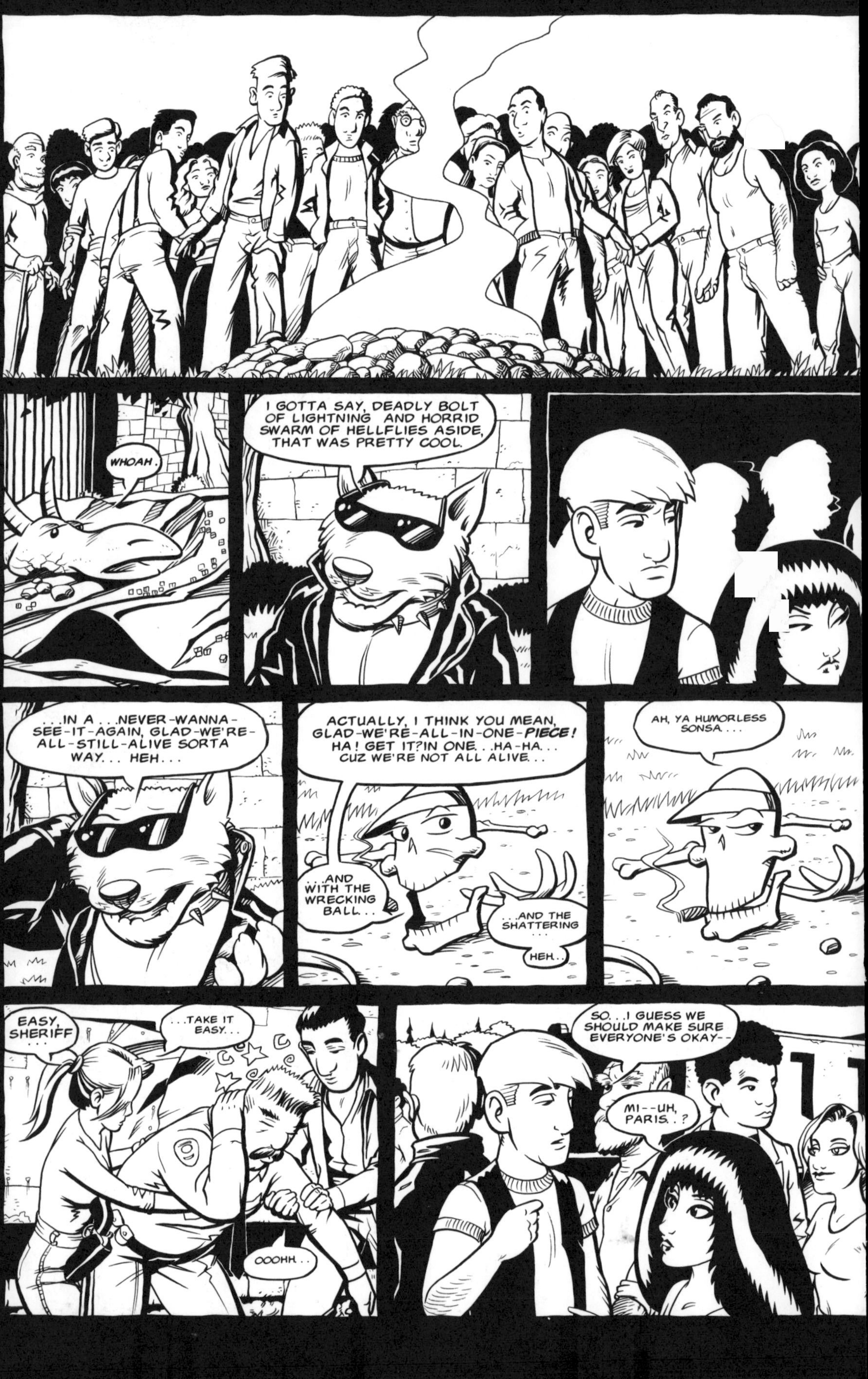
WHOAH.
I GOTTA SAY, DEADLY BOLT OF LIGHTNING AND HORRID SWARM OF HELLFLIES ASIDE, THAT WAS PRETTY COOL.
...IN A...NEVER-WANNA-SEE-IT-AGAIN, GLAD-WE'RE-ALL-STILL-ALIVE SORTA WAY... HEH...
ACTUALLY, I THINK YOU MEAN, GLAD-WE'RE-ALL-IN-ONE-*PIECE!* HA! GET IT?IN ONE...HA-HA... CUZ WE'RE NOT ALL ALIVE...
...AND WITH THE WRECKING BALL...
...AND THE SHATTERING...
HEH...
AH, YA HUMORLESS SONSA...
EASY, SHERIFF...
...TAKE IT EASY...
OOOHH...
SO...I GUESS WE SHOULD MAKE SURE EVERYONE'S OKAY--
MI--UH, PARIS..?

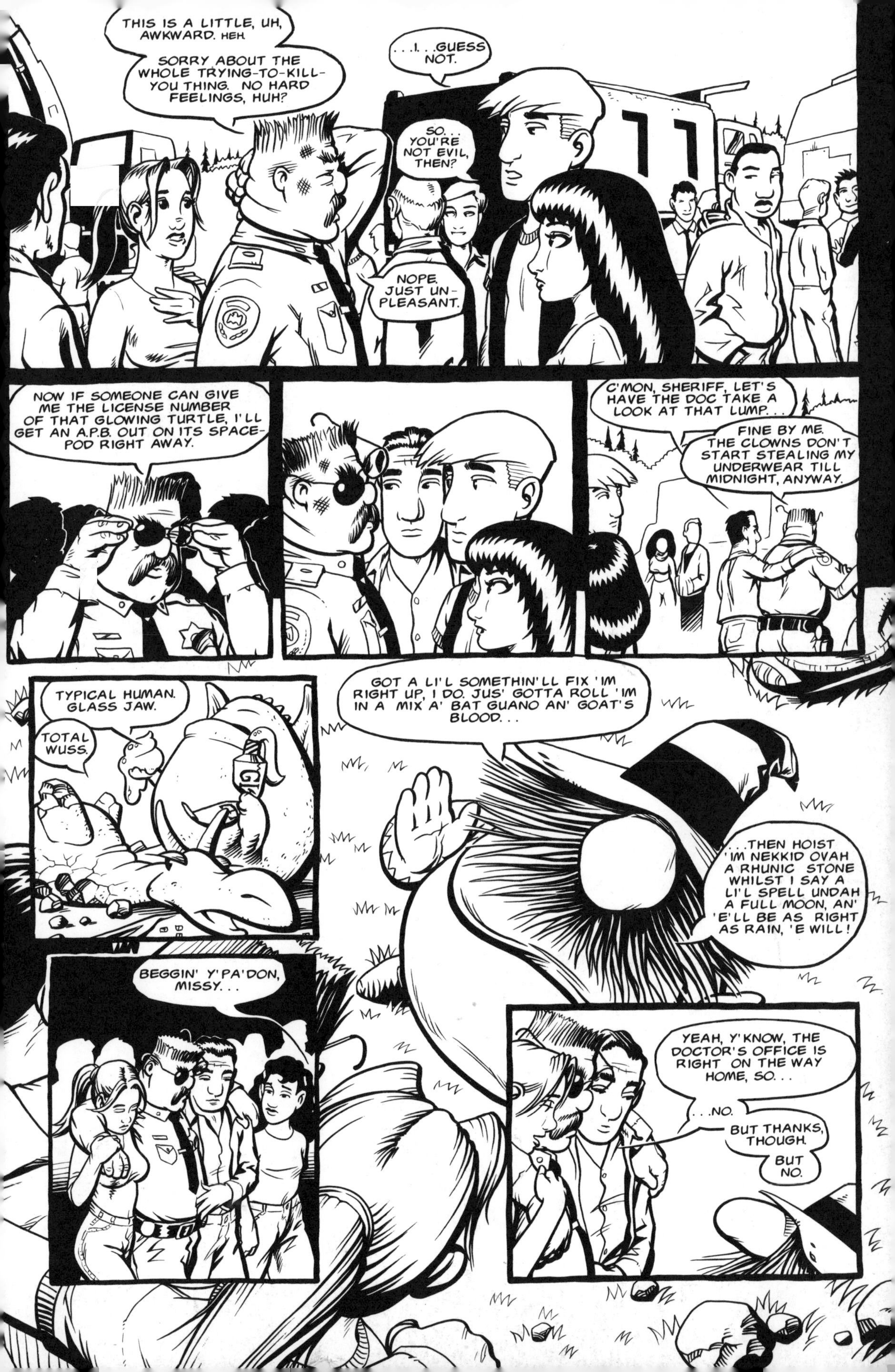
THIS IS A LITTLE, UH, AWKWARD. HEH.
SORRY ABOUT THE WHOLE TRYING-TO-KILL-YOU THING. NO HARD FEELINGS, HUH?
. . .I. . .GUESS NOT.
SO. . . YOU'RE NOT EVIL, THEN?
NOPE. JUST UN-PLEASANT.
NOW IF SOMEONE CAN GIVE ME THE LICENSE NUMBER OF THAT GLOWING TURTLE, I'LL GET AN A.P.B. OUT ON ITS SPACE-POD RIGHT AWAY.
C'MON, SHERIFF, LET'S HAVE THE DOC TAKE A LOOK AT THAT LUMP. . .
FINE BY ME. THE CLOWNS DON'T START STEALING MY UNDERWEAR TILL MIDNIGHT, ANYWAY.
TYPICAL HUMAN. GLASS JAW.
TOTAL WUSS.
GOT A LI'L SOMETHIN'LL FIX 'IM RIGHT UP, I DO. JUS' GOTTA ROLL 'IM IN A MIX A' BAT GUANO AN' GOAT'S BLOOD. . .
. . THEN HOIST 'IM NEKKID OVAH A RHUNIC STONE WHILST I SAY A LI'L SPELL UNDAH A FULL MOON, AN' 'E'LL BE AS RIGHT AS RAIN, 'E WILL!
BEGGIN' Y'PA'DON, MISSY. . .
YEAH, Y'KNOW, THE DOCTOR'S OFFICE IS RIGHT ON THE WAY HOME, SO. . .
. . .NO.
BUT THANKS, THOUGH.
BUT NO.

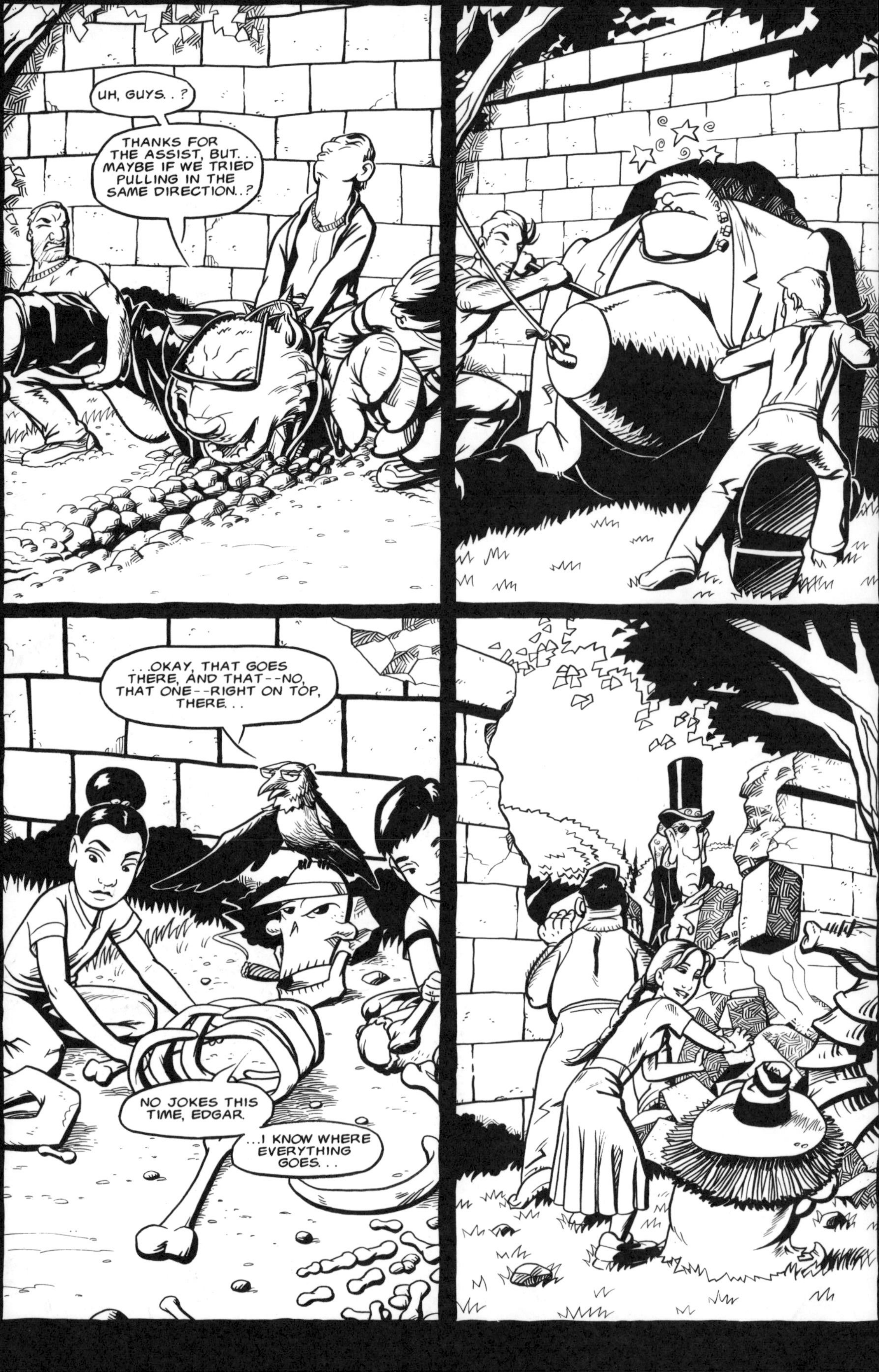
UH, GUYS. . ?
THANKS FOR THE ASSIST, BUT. . . MAYBE IF WE TRIED PULLING IN THE SAME DIRECTION. .?
. . .OKAY, THAT GOES THERE, AND THAT--NO, THAT ONE--RIGHT ON TOP, THERE. . .
NO JOKES THIS TIME, EDGAR.
. . .I KNOW WHERE EVERYTHING GOES. . .

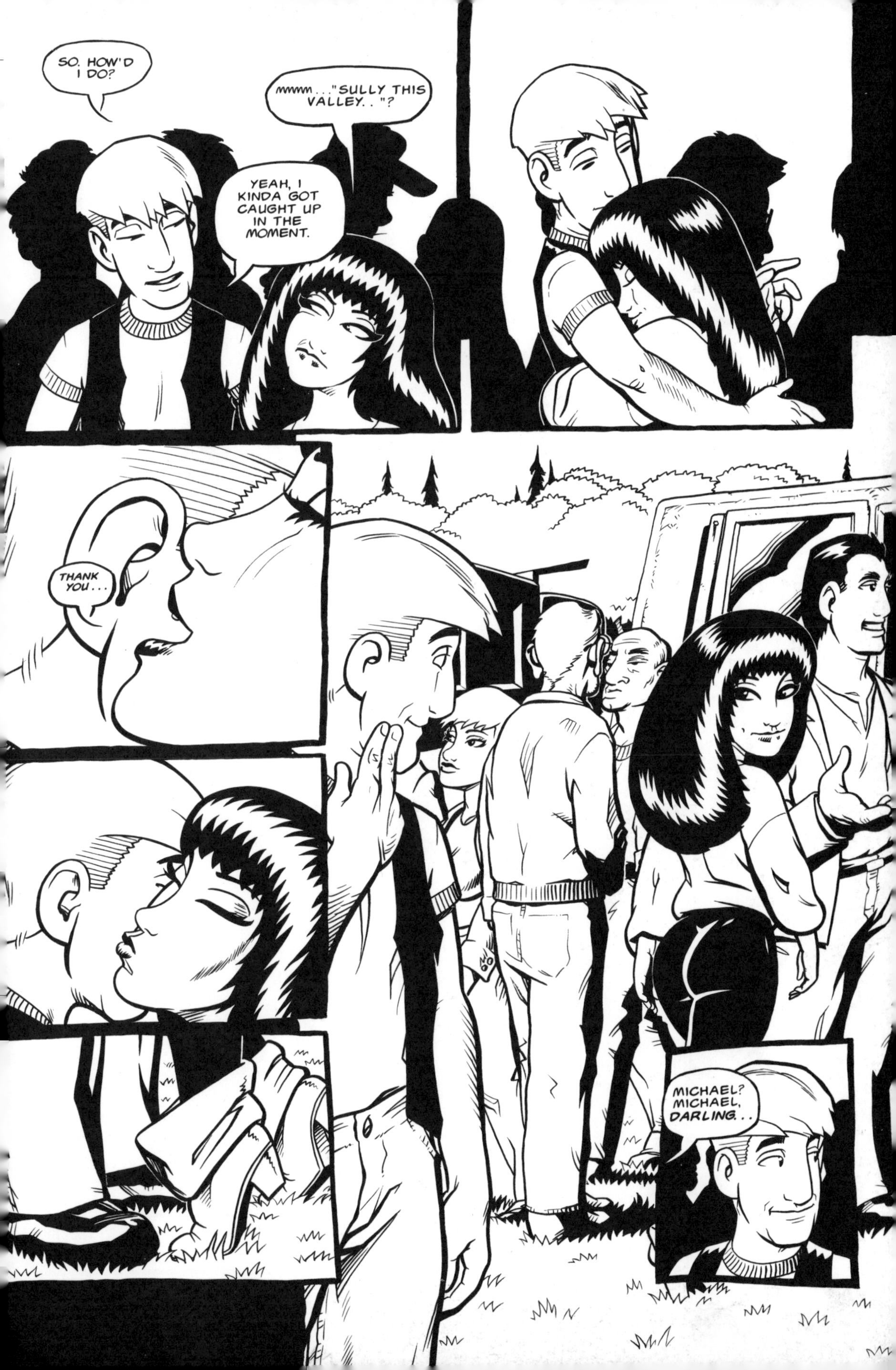
SO. HOW'D I DO?
MMM..."SULLY THIS VALLEY.."?
YEAH, I KINDA GOT CAUGHT UP IN THE MOMENT.
THANK YOU...
MICHAEL? MICHAEL, *DARLING*...

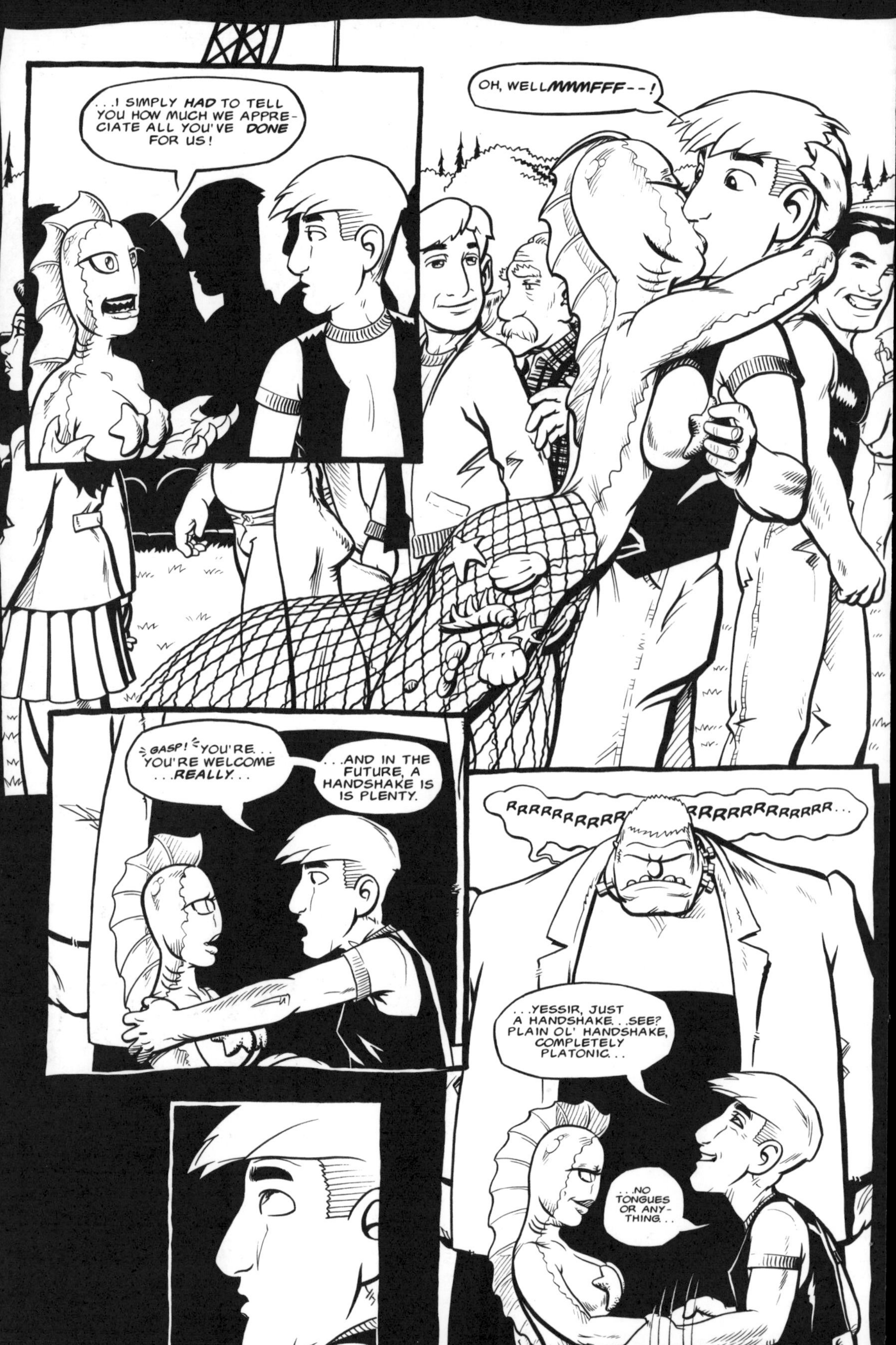

...I SIMPLY HAD TO TELL YOU HOW MUCH WE APPRECIATE ALL YOU'VE DONE FOR US!
OH, WELLMMMFFF--!
GASP! YOU'RE... YOU'RE WELCOME ...REALLY...
...AND IN THE FUTURE, A HANDSHAKE IS IS PLENTY.
RRRRRRRRRRRRRRRRRRRRRRRRRRRR...
...YESSIR, JUST A HANDSHAKE...SEE? PLAIN OL' HANDSHAKE, COMPLETELY PLATONIC...
...NO TONGUES OR ANYTHING...

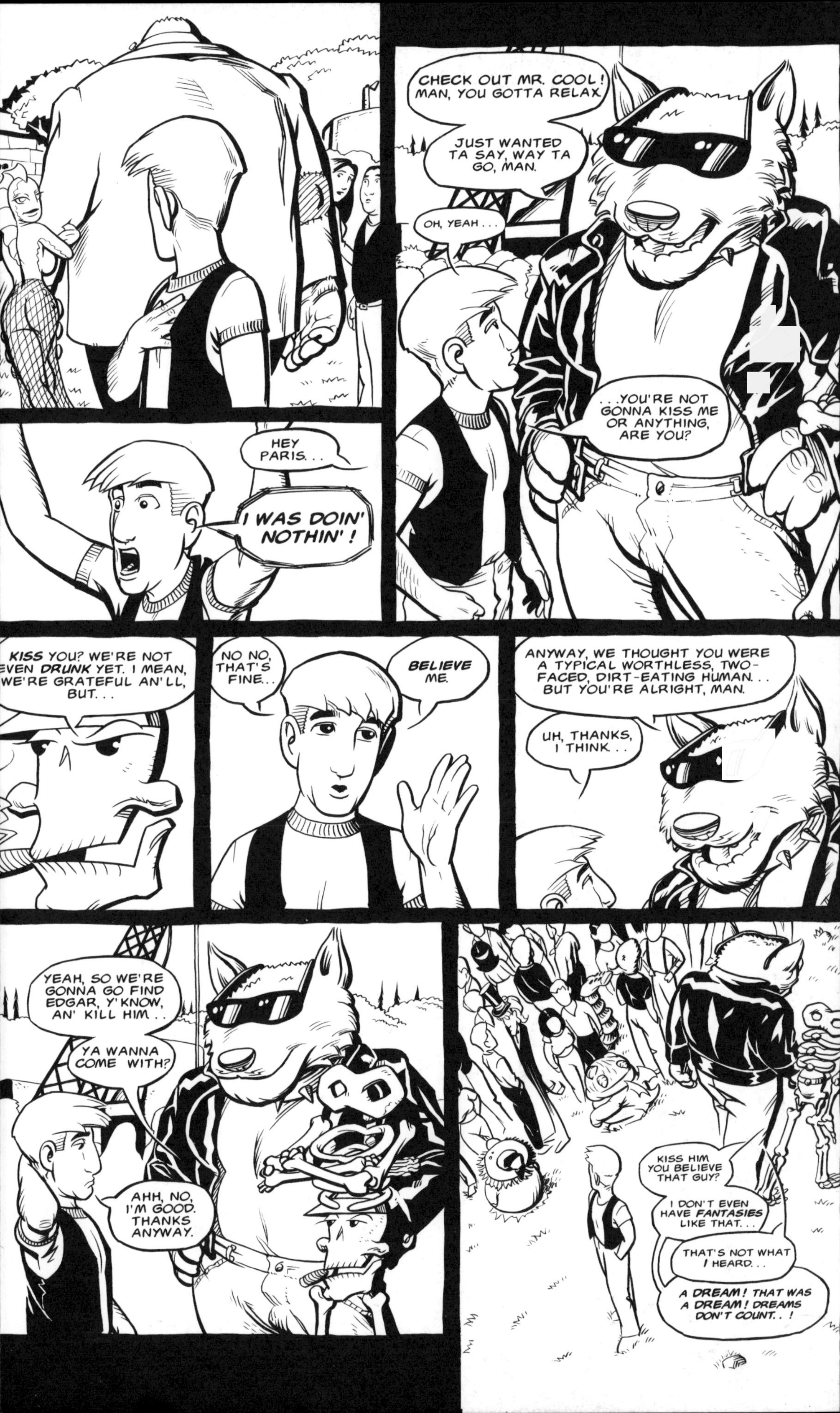
CHECK OUT MR. COOL! MAN, YOU GOTTA RELAX.
JUST WANTED TA SAY, WAY TA GO, MAN.
OH, YEAH...
...YOU'RE NOT GONNA KISS ME OR ANYTHING, ARE YOU?
HEY PARIS...
I WAS DOIN' NOTHIN'!
KISS YOU? WE'RE NOT EVEN DRUNK YET. I MEAN, WE'RE GRATEFUL AN'LL, BUT...
NO NO, THAT'S FINE...
BELIEVE ME.
ANYWAY, WE THOUGHT YOU WERE A TYPICAL WORTHLESS, TWO-FACED, DIRT-EATING HUMAN... BUT YOU'RE ALRIGHT, MAN.
UH, THANKS, I THINK...
YEAH, SO WE'RE GONNA GO FIND EDGAR, Y'KNOW, AN' KILL HIM...
YA WANNA COME WITH?
AHH, NO, I'M GOOD. THANKS ANYWAY.
KISS HIM YOU BELIEVE THAT GUY?
I DON'T EVEN HAVE FANTASIES LIKE THAT...
THAT'S NOT WHAT I HEARD...
A DREAM! THAT WAS A DREAM! DREAMS DON'T COUNT..!

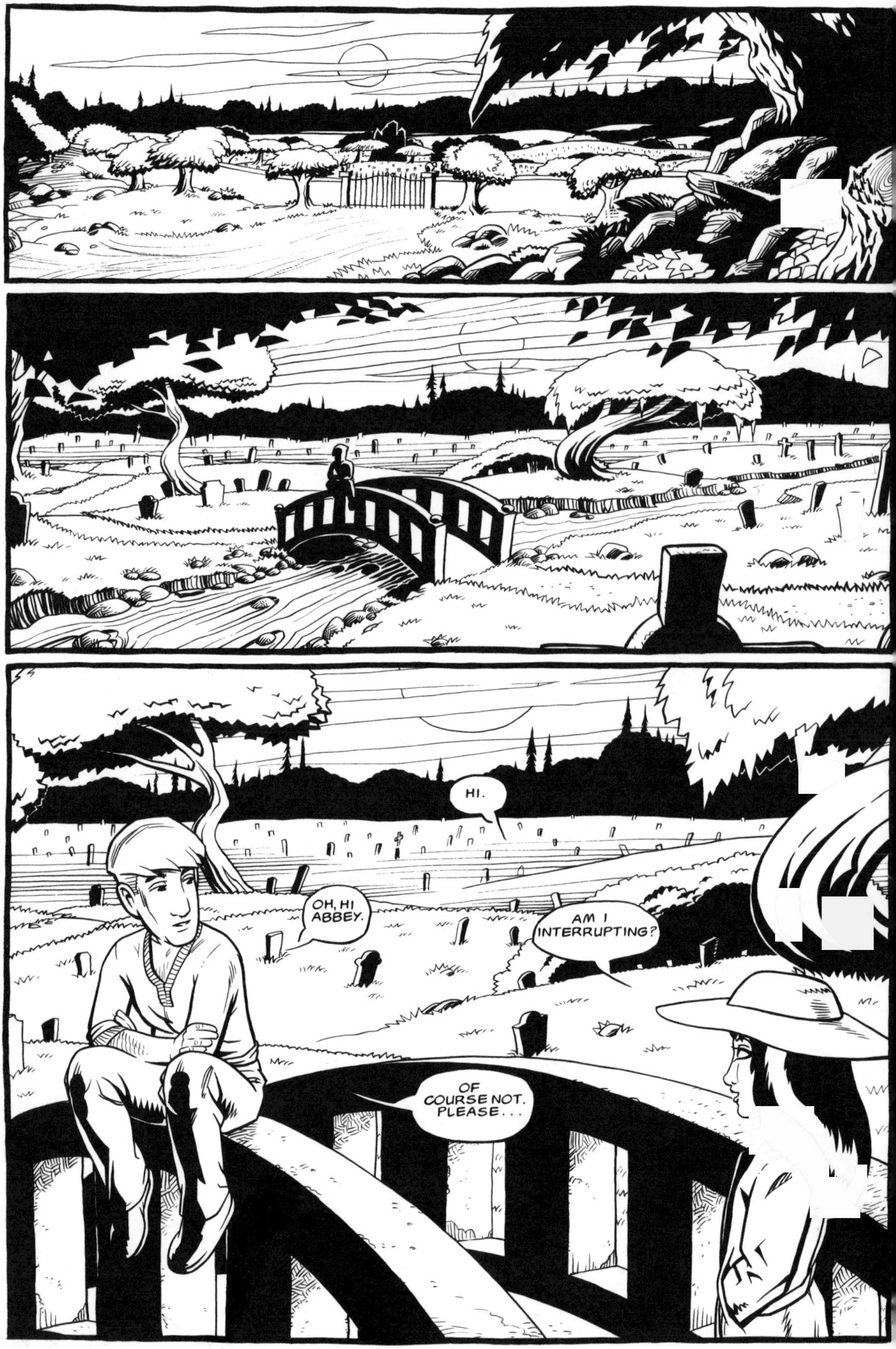
HI.
OH, HI ABBEY.
AM I INTERRUPTING?
OF COURSE NOT. PLEASE...

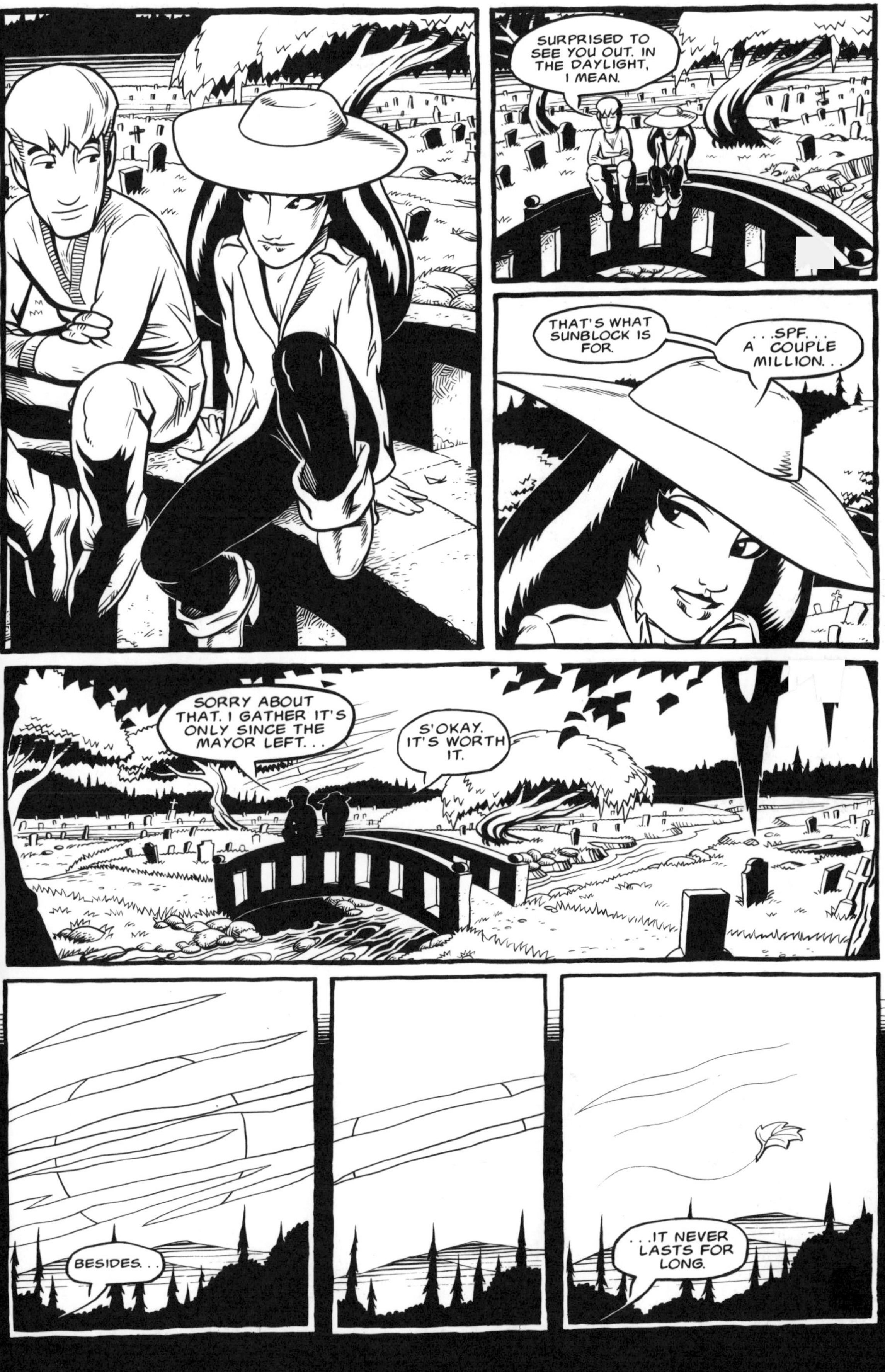
SURPRISED TO SEE YOU OUT. IN THE DAYLIGHT, I MEAN.
THAT'S WHAT SUNBLOCK IS FOR.
. . .SPF. . . A COUPLE MILLION. . .
SORRY ABOUT THAT. I GATHER IT'S ONLY SINCE THE MAYOR LEFT. . .
S'OKAY. IT'S WORTH IT.
BESIDES. . .
. . .IT NEVER LASTS FOR LONG.

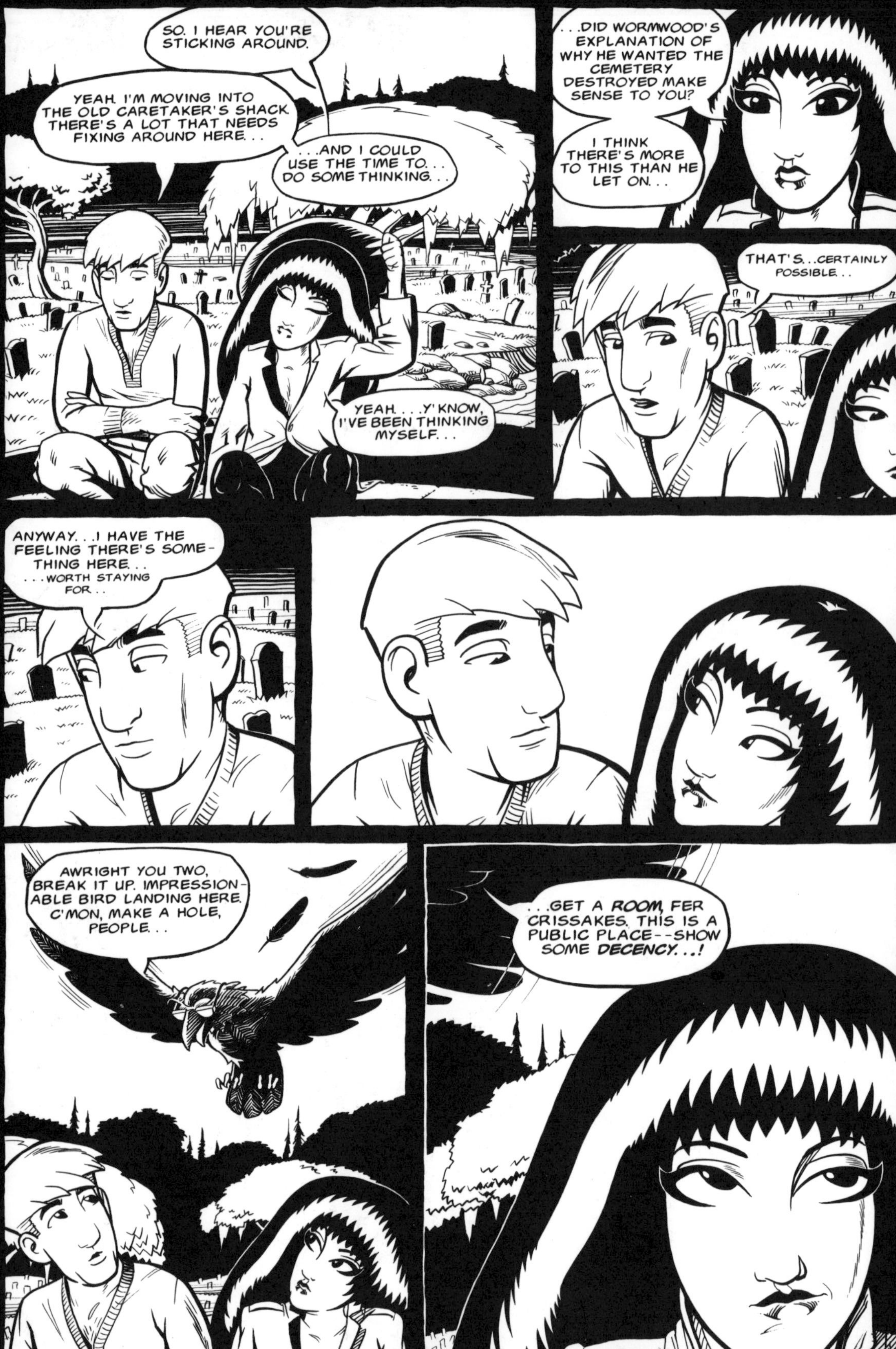
SO. I HEAR YOU'RE STICKING AROUND.
YEAH. I'M MOVING INTO THE OLD CARETAKER'S SHACK. THERE'S A LOT THAT NEEDS FIXING AROUND HERE...
...AND I COULD USE THE TIME TO... DO SOME THINKING...
YEAH.... Y'KNOW, I'VE BEEN THINKING MYSELF...
...DID WORMWOOD'S EXPLANATION OF WHY HE WANTED THE CEMETERY DESTROYED MAKE SENSE TO YOU?
I THINK THERE'S MORE TO THIS THAN HE LET ON...
THAT'S...CERTAINLY POSSIBLE...
ANYWAY...I HAVE THE FEELING THERE'S SOME-THING HERE... ...WORTH STAYING FOR...
AWRIGHT YOU TWO, BREAK IT UP. IMPRESSION-ABLE BIRD LANDING HERE. C'MON, MAKE A HOLE, PEOPLE...
...GET A ROOM, FER CRISSAKES. THIS IS A PUBLIC PLACE--SHOW SOME DECENCY...!

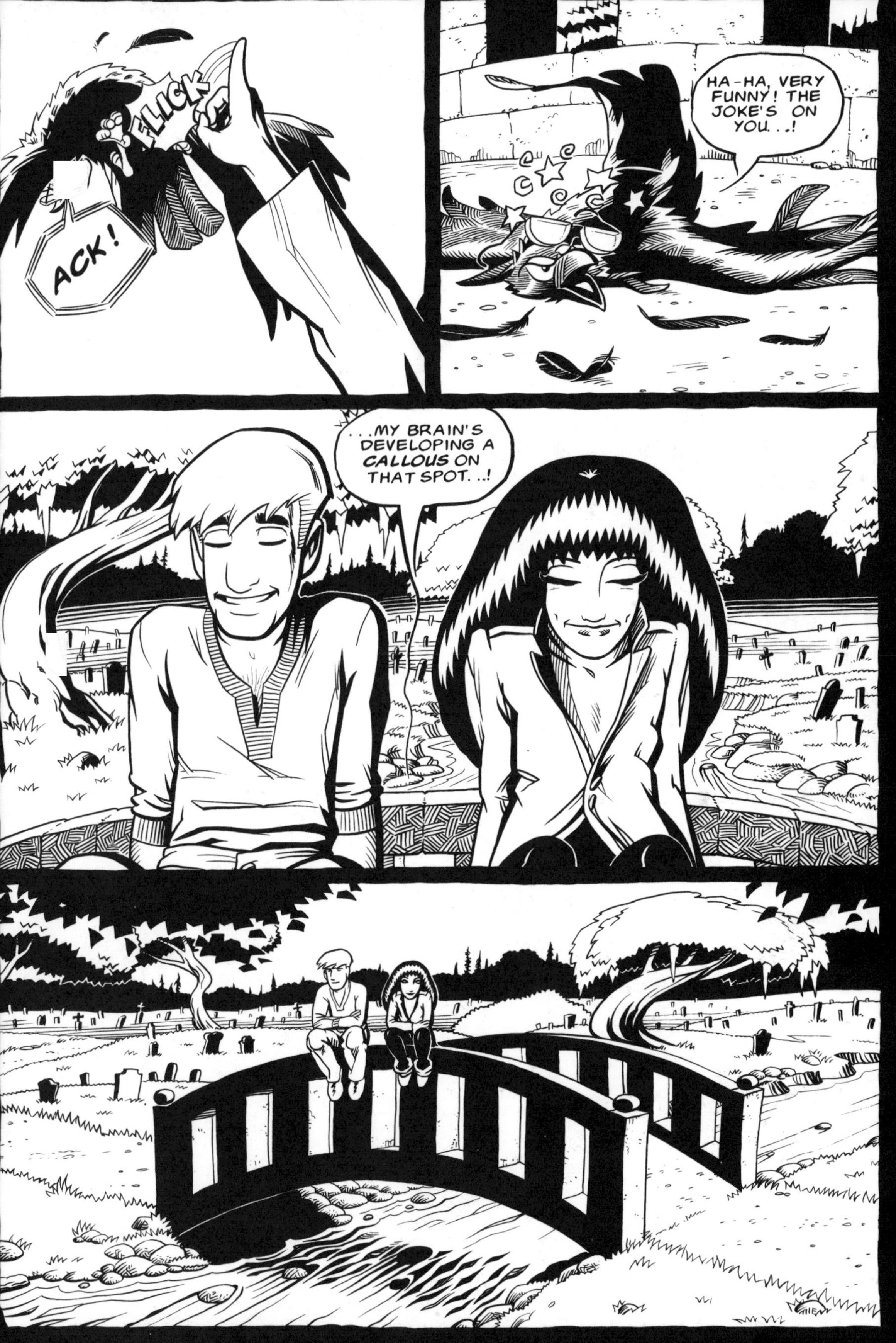
FLICK
ACK!
HA-HA, VERY FUNNY! THE JOKE'S ON YOU...!
...MY BRAIN'S DEVELOPING A *CALLOUS* ON THAT SPOT...!

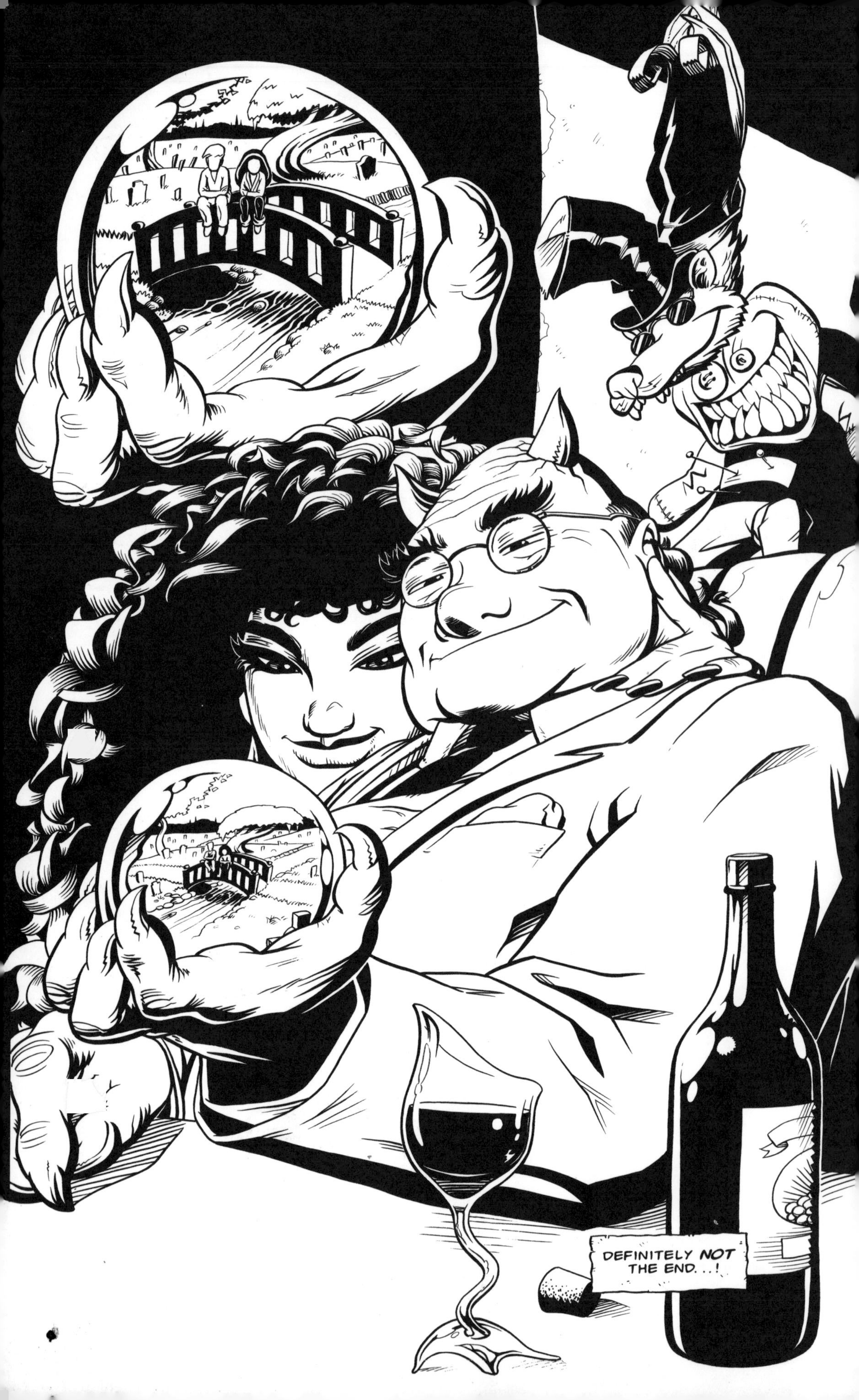
DEFINITELY NOT THE END...!

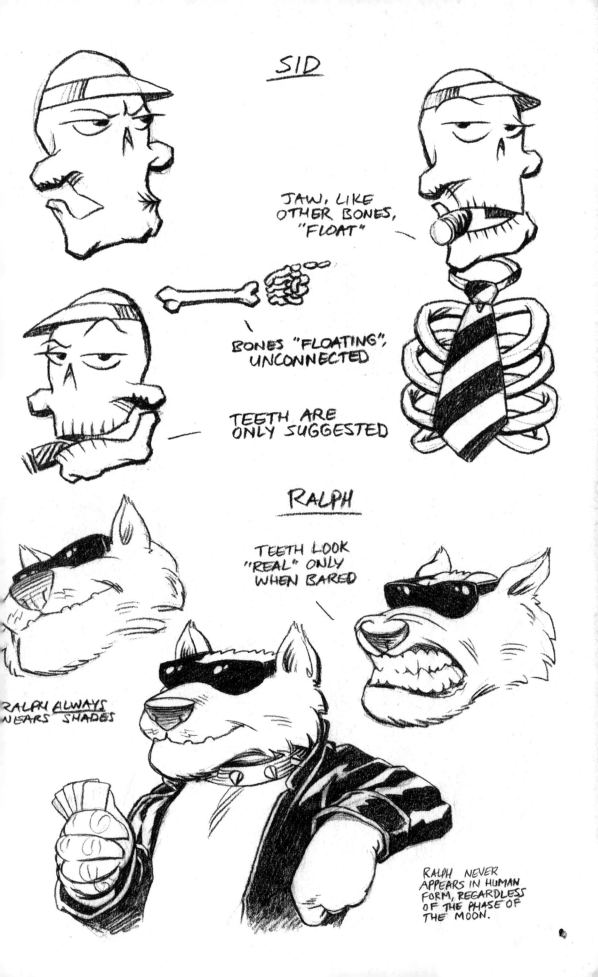

SID

JAW, LIKE
OTHER BONES,
"FLOAT"

BONES "FLOATING",
UNCONNECTED

TEETH ARE
ONLY SUGGESTED

RALPH

TEETH LOOK
"REAL" ONLY
WHEN BARED

RALPH ALWAYS
WEARS SHADES

RALPH NEVER
APPEARS IN HUMAN
FORM, REGARDLESS
OF THE PHASE OF
THE MOON.

EDGAR

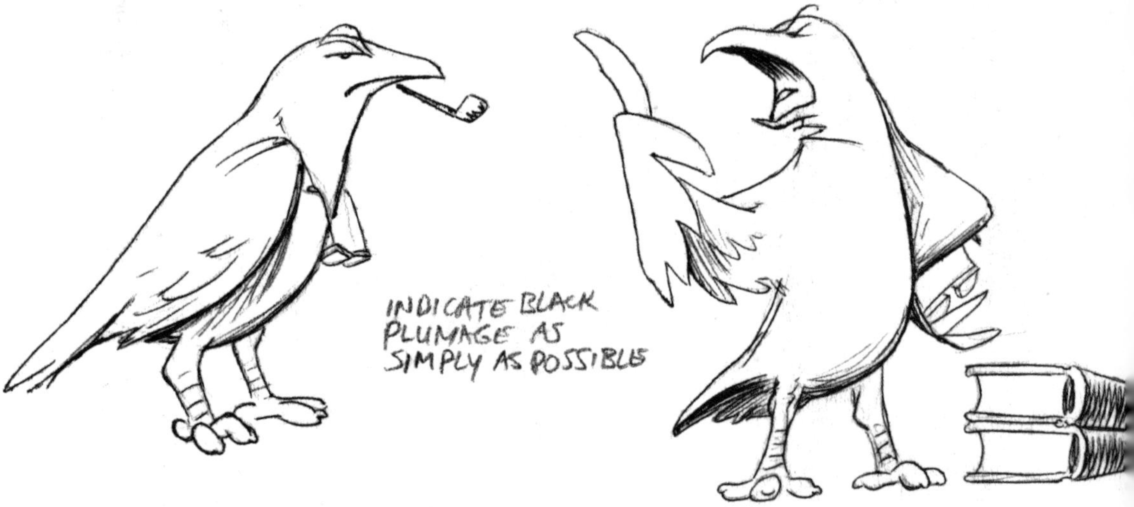
INDICATE BLACK PLUMAGE AS SIMPLY AS POSSIBLE

EDGAR THINKS THE PIPE & GLASSES MAKE HIM LOOK INTELLECTUAL

EDGAR'S INTELLECTUAL CONCEIT MASKS A DARK, GUILTY SECRET

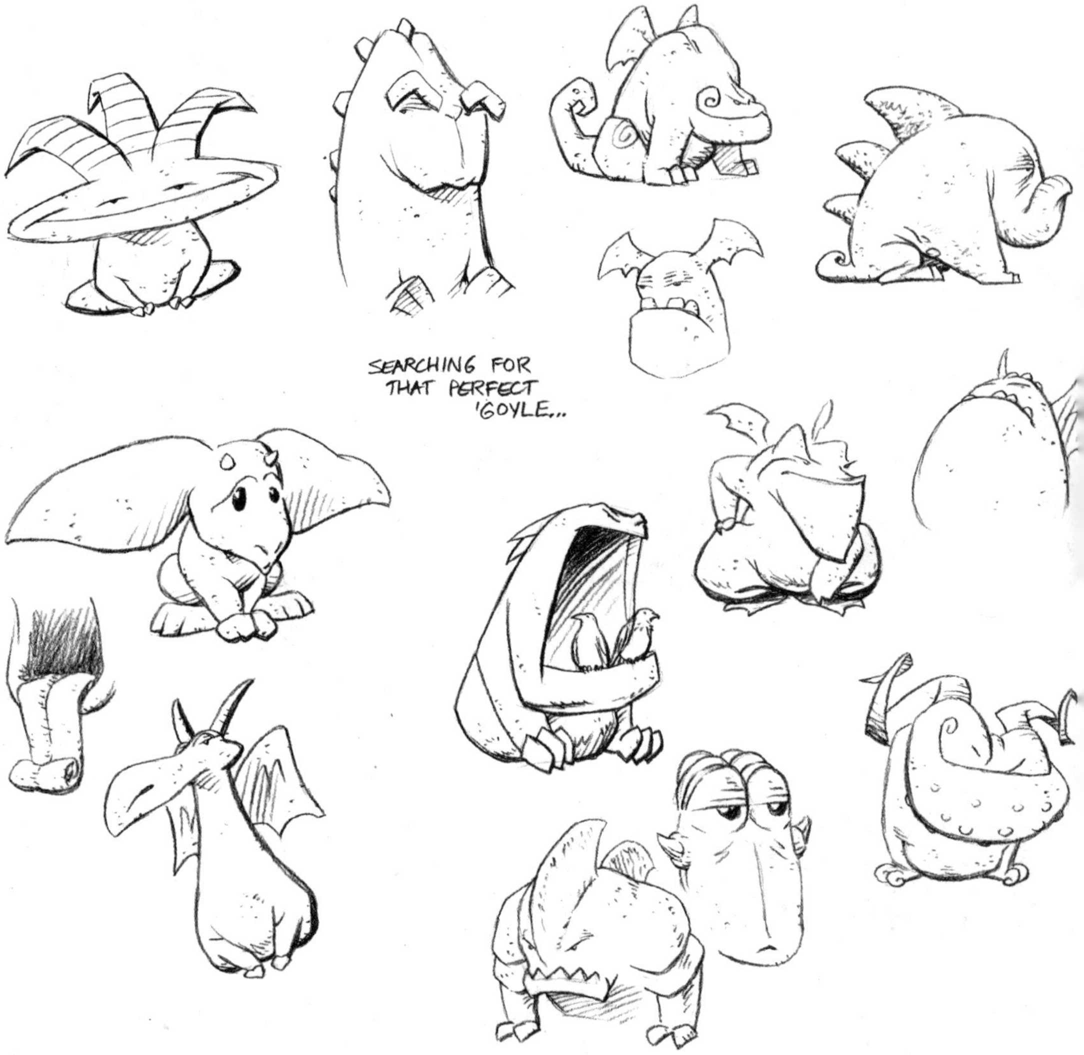
SEARCHING FOR THAT PERFECT 'GOYLE...

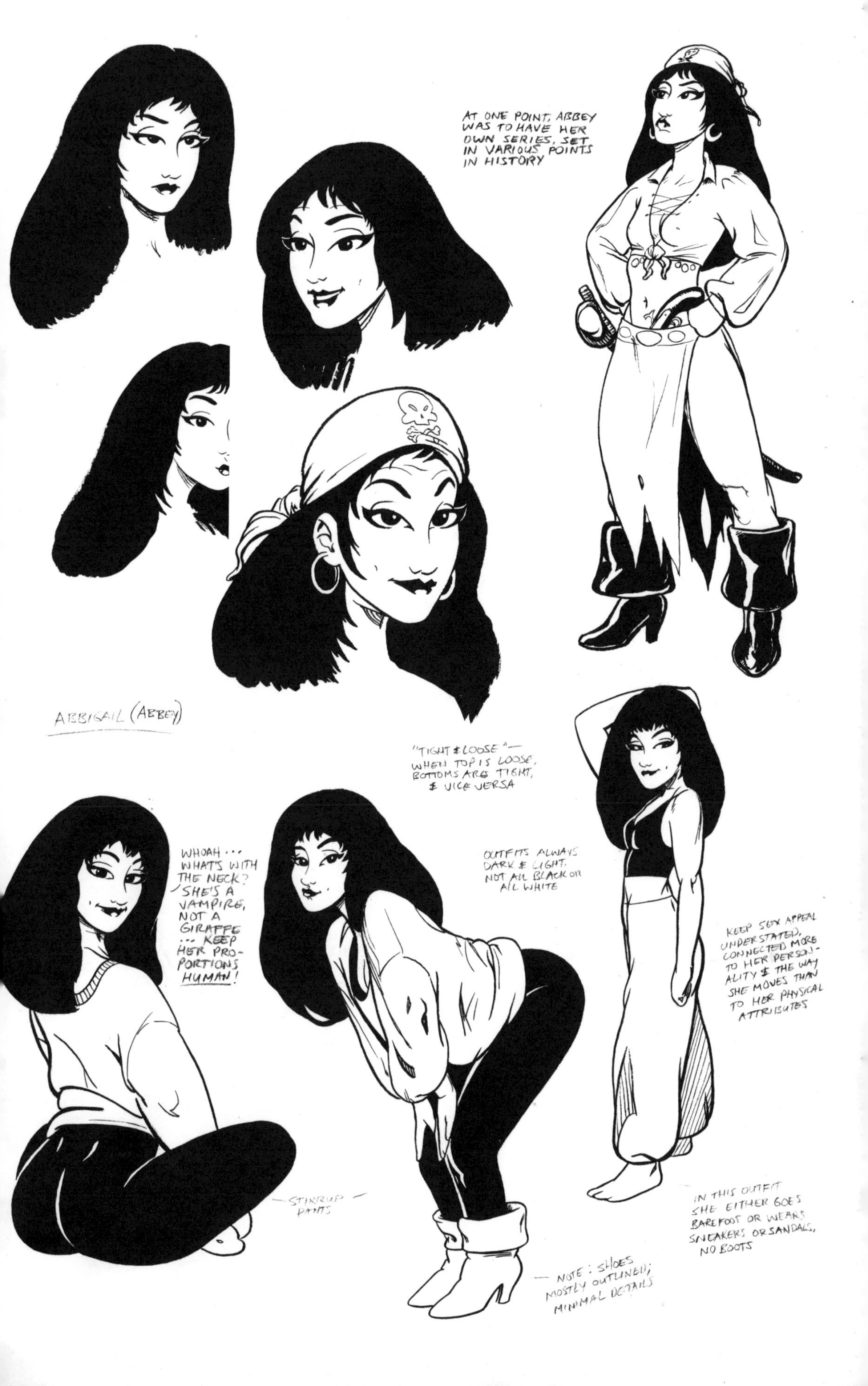
AT ONE POINT, ABBEY WAS TO HAVE HER OWN SERIES, SET IN VARIOUS POINTS IN HISTORY
ABBIGAIL (ABBEY)
"TIGHT & LOOSE"— WHEN TOP IS LOOSE, BOTTOMS ARE TIGHT, & VICE VERSA
WHOAH... WHAT'S WITH THE NECK? SHE'S A VAMPIRE, NOT A GIRAFFE ... KEEP HER PRO-PORTIONS HUMAN!
OUTFITS ALWAYS DARK & LIGHT. NOT ALL BLACK OR ALL WHITE
KEEP SEX APPEAL UNDERSTATED, CONNECTED MORE TO HER PERSON-ALITY & THE WAY SHE MOVES THAN TO HER PHYSICAL ATTRIBUTES
— STIRRUP — PANTS
IN THIS OUTFIT SHE EITHER GOES BAREFOOT OR WEARS SNEAKERS OR SANDALS, NO BOOTS
— NOTE: SHOES MOSTLY OUTLINED; MINIMAL DETAILS

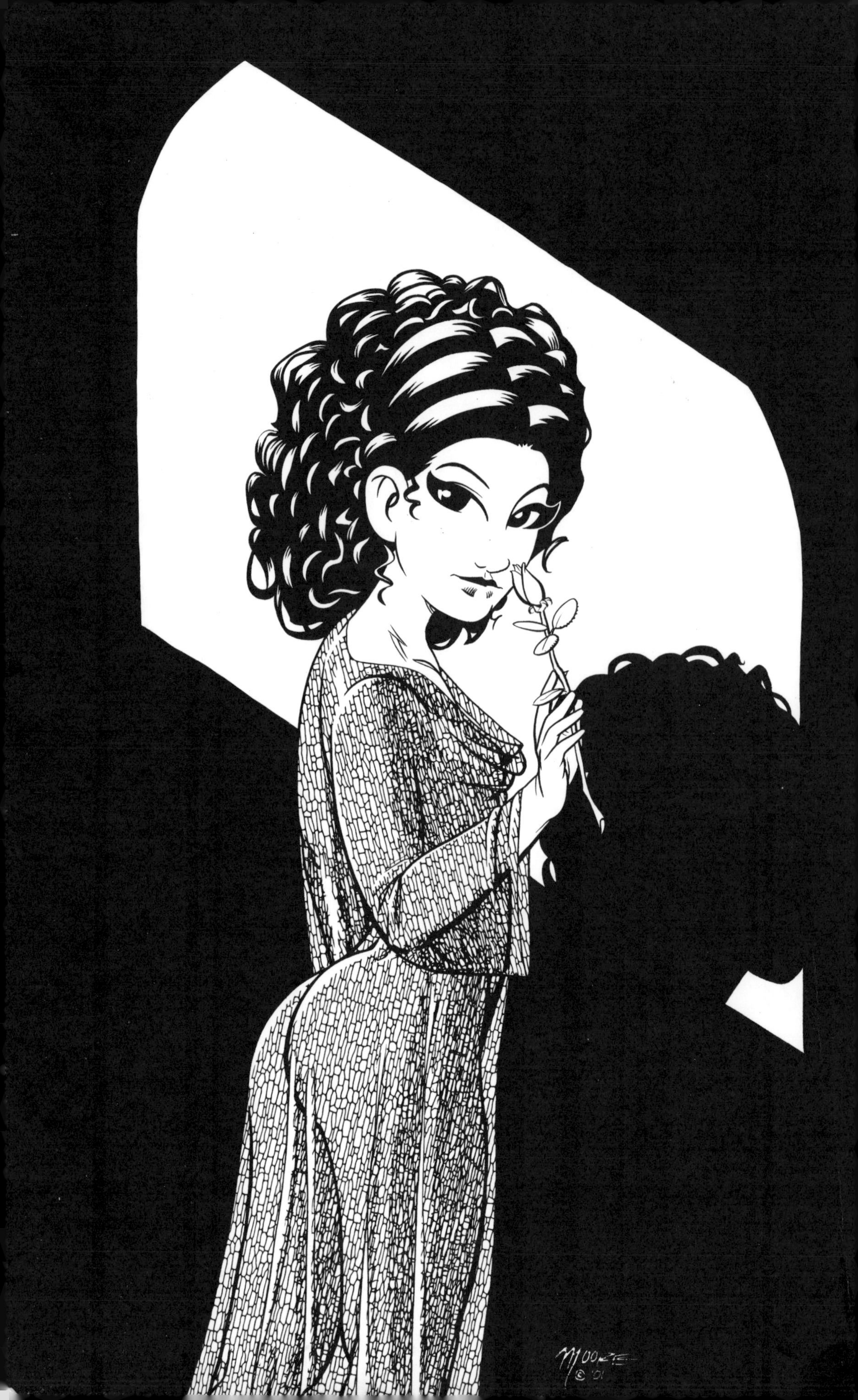
MOORE
© '01